EVALUATION & DEVELOPMENT

World Bank Series on Evaluation and Development
Robert Picciotto, Series Editor

Evaluation and Development:
The Institutional Dimension
edited by Robert Picciotto and Eduardo Wiesner

Involuntary Resettlement:
Comparative Perspectives
edited by Robert Picciotto, Warren van Wicklin, and Edward Rice

Evaluation and Poverty Reduction
edited by Osvaldo N. Feinstein and Robert Picciotto

Making Development Work:
Development Learning in a World of Poverty and Wealth
edited by Nagy Hanna and Robert Picciotto

Managing a Global Resource:
Challenges of Forest Conservation and Development
edited by Uma Lele

Evaluation and Development:
The Partnership Dimension
edited by Andres Liebenthal, Osvaldo N. Feinstein, and Gregory K. Ingram

EVALUATION & DEVELOPMENT

THE PARTNERSHIP DIMENSION

WORLD BANK SERIES ON
EVALUATION AND DEVELOPMENT

VOLUME 6

Andres Liebenthal
Osvaldo N. Feinstein
Gregory K. Ingram

With a foreword by Robert Picciotto

Routledge
Taylor & Francis Group
LONDON AND NEW YORK

First published 2004 by Transaction Publishers

Published 2017 by Routledge
2 Park Square, Milton Park, Abingdon, Oxon OX14 4RN
605 Third Avenue, New York, NY 10017

Routledge is an imprint of the Taylor and Francis Group, an informa business

Library of Congress Catalog Number: 2003061801

Library of Congress Cataloging-in-Publication Data

Evaluation & development: the partnership dimension / edited by Andres Liebenthal, Osvaldo Feinstein, Gregory K. Ingram.
p. cm.—(World Bank series on evaluation and development; v. 6)
Includes bibliographical references and index.
ISBN 0-7658-0171-X (cloth : alk. paper)—ISBN 0-7658-0974-5 (pbk : alk. paper)
1. Developing countries—Economic policy. 2. Public-private sector cooperation—Developing countries—Evaluation. 3. Developing countries—Economic policy—Citizen participation. 4. Public-private sector cooperation—Developing countries—Case studies. I. Title: Evaluation and development. II. Liebenthal, Andres, 1947- III. Feinstein, Osvaldo Néstor. IV. Ingram, Gregory K. V. Series.

HC59.7.E875 2004
338.9'009172'4—dc22 2003061801

ISBN 13: 978-0-7658-0171-5 (hbk)
ISBN 13: 978-0-7658-0974-2 (pbk)

Contents

Acknowledgments

This book is based on presentations made at the Fourth World Bank Conference on Evaluation and Development: The Partnership Dimension, held on July 23–24, 2001, in Washington, D.C.

The Operations Evaluation Department (OED) of the World Bank organized the conference. Enver Kamal made a distinguished contribution as the conference administrator. This publication has benefited from the support of Caroline McEuen, Elizabeth Campbell-Page, and Rachel Weaving.

Foreword

This volume contains work presented at the Fourth World Bank Conference on Evaluation and Development. Its subject—partnership—has emerged as a key characteristic of effective development assistance, along with a comprehensive and long-term development vision, ownership of good governance and policies, and a results orientation. Accordingly, the World Bank has adjusted its corporate priorities and business processes to facilitate interaction with other development actors.

Relationships among government, private corporations, and civil society have been changing under the combined pressure of technical progress, global integration, and rising popular expectations. In the public mind, globalization is often associated with increased inequity, social disruption, and confrontation among various interest groups. However, the same forces have led to creative and rewarding experiments in devolution, deregulation, and de-layering of bureaucracies. Hybrid institutions have multiplied, seeking to combine the public goods characteristics of government action, the innovative management techniques of the private sector, and the moral energy of the voluntary sector. New divisions of labor among development actors have been introduced, and informal networks of bewildering diversity are filling some of the institutional gaps that have resulted from a more integrated global economy.

Equally, new and very diverse forms of partnership have helped to define and try out new forms of cooperation and mediation among the public, private, and voluntary sectors. Against this background, the World Bank itself has been changing its priorities and operating approaches. As long as the Bank saw its role as largely that of a project lending organization working through the public sector, the need for partnership with the private sector and civil society was limited. Today, the Bank is equally concerned with economic growth, social equity, and environmental sustainability as means to alleviate poverty, and uses a rising share of its resources to support policy reform and institutional development. It has delegated authority to its offices in developing countries to foster more collaborative decision making on its programs, and increasingly it has designed collaborative arrangements with other assistance agencies within the Comprehensive Development Framework.

While the World Bank has continued to work with and through governments, it has also reached out to the private sector and to civil society organizations—and in many cases it now depends on them for its effectiveness in alleviating poverty.

The Bank's experience with public-private-civil society partnerships in developed countries is already quite well documented. The study of industrial alliances has become a staple in business schools. Moreover, the new institutional economics contributes valuable analytical concepts for assessing partnerships. In development work, partnership has been consecrated as a critical linchpin of effective cooperation. But relatively little is known about the costs and benefits, and the risks and rewards, of different types of partnerships, or about how best to conduct partnerships for different purposes. This is why the chapters that follow may have operational relevance both for development practitioners and for policy analysts.

Robert Picciotto
former director-general, Operations Evaluation
The World Bank

Overview

Gregory K. Ingram

The chapters in this volume cover many aspects of development partnerships and their evaluation. This overview highlights the key points made, along with a few omissions. It discusses the typical goals of partnerships in the field of social and economic development, outlines some of the challenges in evaluating partnerships, and summarizes lessons offered by the authors for making partnerships succeed.

Growth and Diversification of Partnerships

Partnership has become much more important in development work in recent years. Awareness of the limitations of government activity is growing, and partnerships among state, private business, and civil society organizations are increasingly used to deliver the goods and services required for balanced, broadly based growth and poverty reduction.

Aid activities have shifted from a project focus to a more strategic and holistic focus on programs, sectors, and policies. With this new orientation, partnerships are often essential to deal with the added complexity and the larger number of agencies, groups, and stakeholders involved. Another factor encouraging assistance agencies to seek partnerships has been their broad move away from imposing conditions and toward a concern with development effectiveness. The focus on results calls for less hierarchical relationships between providers and recipients of aid, and a move from "You do as I say" to "We do what we agreed." There is a greater recognition that everybody's view is needed and that everyone brings something to the relationship. Aid relations are still not equal, but they are less unequal than before.

We still have much to learn about when, where, and how best to use partnerships, and, in particular, partnerships that involve less traditional combinations of actors. Consider the several possible combinations of five main actors in the aid arena—governments, donors, international financial institu-

---

Gregory K. Ingram is director-general, Operations Evaluation, The World Bank.

tions (IFIs), nongovernmental organizations (NGOs) and civil society, and private sector partners—as outlined in the matrix shown in Figure 1.1. We have a good deal of experience with partnerships and relationships along the diagonal of this matrix (marked XX)—for example, through treaties among countries; consultative groups of donors, development agencies, and committees of IFIs; or business partnerships among private sector companies. With the newer forms of partnerships involving the off-diagonal relationships (marked OO), and particularly relationships involving NGOs/civil society and the private sector, we have less experience. Several of the chapters in this volume discuss such new-style partnerships, such as global partnerships for public policy, country-focused aid partnerships organized according to the principles of the Comprehensive Development Framework, private sector partnerships for knowledge creation, and partnerships for community development involving business, NGOs, and government.

Figure 1
Main Actors in Development Partnerships

	Government	Donors	IFIs	NGO/civil soc.	Private sector
Government	XX	OO	OO	OO	OO
Donors		XX	OO	OO	OO
IFIs			XX	OO	OO
NGO/civil soc.				XX	OO
Private sector					XX

Foundations of Partnership

What do we expect partnership to achieve? What are its advantages? Partnerships are so diverse that generalizations are not always possible or helpful. Even so, four main reasons for undertaking development partnerships seem to emerge. When done well, partnerships achieve the following:

- Help to ensure that things are done right, improving the efficiency of resource use.
- Help ensure the right things are done. That is, the decisions made by partnerships, reflecting local knowledge and local ties in the recipient country or community, are more likely to fit real needs, and hence to yield lasting benefits, than decisions made by government agencies or aid sources alone.
- Constitute a means for capacity building and institutional development.
- Provide accountability for actions promised and for resources used.

Doing Things Right

Arguments about why and when to partner have most often been based on traditional concepts of efficiency. Partnership makes sense when it offers more and better results, better information, better skills and capacity, and/or better risk management than the parties could achieve on their own.

Many of the studies focus on the benefits of partnerships between institutions of government and civil society; as Elliot Stern points out, "we know from several pieces of evaluation research that partnerships involving beneficiaries, local agencies, and groups can dramatically reduce the costs of implementation." Stern cites Europe's partnerships for regional policy as examples of what well-functioning partnerships can achieve: "better-planned action, better project selection, faster decision making, and greater support for eventual outcomes." Margaret Catley-Carlson and several other authors allude to similar findings for partnerships in developing countries. Other benefits that Stern cites include effective knowledge transfer, greater cross-national cooperation, the creation of new networks and capacity, and penetration of new markets.

Private firms, as Laurence Prusak points out, use partnerships with competitors to learn or reduce risk—they use those with complementors and customers to help develop products, those with suppliers to improve efficiency and integration, and those with companies in different industries from their own to help create new markets.

Risk is also an important consideration, although rather little discussed in this book. Good risk management (or risk reduction) contributes strongly to the technical bases of efficiency based on knowledge, to the process arguments of efficiency based on reduced transaction costs, and to the political bases of efficiency based on legitimacy, access, and support.

The efficiency argument for partnerships suggests that the benefits accrue to the partners—that is, the benefits are largely private goods. But benefits can in fact accrue much more broadly if they reduce transaction costs for suppliers and improve the availability of goods and services to consumers. Also, since partnerships facilitate cooperation among groups that have different scopes of activity, they can link people who are interested in local benefits with people interested in regional benefits, with people interested in national benefits, and with people interested in global benefits. Possibilities of this kind suggest that partnership outcomes can also have public-good dimensions.

Doing the Right Things

The need for local "ownership" of development interventions has been a well-accepted mantra in the development community for at least a decade. Various forms of partnership are espoused as a way to obtain such ownership, recognizing that development initiatives that are imposed from the outside are likely to be neglected if not outright rejected. Stuart Salter of the Canadian Agency for International Development notes, "It is our experience that projects that do not have the engagement of a local entity fail, almost by definition . . . the successful projects begin with the engagement and support of local civil society."

Consensual decision making typically yields better, more relevant choices of projects, programs, or policies. As a result, solutions and interventions are tailored to the problems as perceived by those affected, and the resulting benefits are more likely to be sustained. Akalu Tumebo describes how reliance on partnership helped ActionAid Ethiopia (AAE), a national branch of an international NGO, to better focus its work on needs. In the mid-1990s, AAE scaled up its operations by changing its strategy from one of independent activity to one of working through partnerships with community-based organizations, governmental organizations, and other NGOs. Partnership enhanced AAE's understanding of the different dimensions of poverty and suitable means to address them, and strengthened its ability to work with target groups.

Often there has appeared to be a tradeoff between efficiency and the consensual working arrangements that are an essential feature of partnership. But Anastassios Bougas, commenting on the implementation of European regional policies in the 1990s, notes that, "In practice it appears that the benefit obtained through partnership—a better fit of the priorities and greater ownership of the program goals—outweighs any detrimental effects of the more protracted decision-making process."

Partnership as a Means to Institutional Development

Douglass North and several other authors focus on the contributions of development partnership to institution building. North views development partnership as an instrument to build the institutional capacity that is needed to improve economic performance. To achieve good economic performance requires a political and institutional framework that provides the right incentives. And, given the historical association between prosperity and democracy, North perceives the task for aid partnership as "not just to build up improvements in health, education, and the judiciary but also to build the human capacity needed for a consensual polity."

Several of the practitioners of partnerships take a similar view, among them Frank Cookingham of the international NGO, World Vision, who believes that "a primary outcome of a partnership for development should be sustainable processes of change." Vuyo Mahlati and Mandivamba Rukuni review the outcomes of several southern African community partnerships whose central goal was building the capacity of communities to articulate their own needs and run their own affairs.

Transfer of knowledge and skills from one partner to another is an important means for institutional development. As Robert Picciotto notes, "Where one or more of the participants do not enjoy the organization and skills available to other participants, capacity building is a prerequisite of true partnership."

Accountability

A fourth goal of development partnerships is to promote accountability, whether this is the mutual accountability of one partner to another or accountability to the population that the partnership is intended to serve. In practice, achieving accountability may be the most difficult challenge of pa

Chapters by Jorge Braga de Macedo and Maria Barrados address issues raised by today's trend toward partnerships for delivering public services. Involving nongovernmental entities in governing—in policy formulation, planning, design, or decision making about how and to whom government services are delivered—raises concerns about accountability, transparency, and how best to identify and protect the public interest. Braga suggests that the creation of partnerships with components from both above and below the government level reinforces accountability for the use of public resources and for delivering public goods and services. His experience also suggests that in partnerships for delivering public services, nonprofit business associations can play a valuable role as intermediaries in the fight against corruption. Barrados describes Canada's experience with a framework for safeguarding accountability and public trust; she emphasizes that public-private-voluntary sector partnerships for providing public services and programs can increase efficiency and quality, but that arrangements need to be carefully designed and monitored to ensure there is credible reporting, that accountability mechanisms are effective, that there is adequate transparency, and that the public interest is protected. She presents a framework for evaluating such public service partnerships.

Another Argument for Partnership

One can also make a powerful argument for partnership based on trade theory and the gains from trade, though that topic is barely mentioned in this volume. For example, partnership can allow cooperating entities to specialize in their core competency or to specialize in their comparative advantage. These two arguments sound similar, but they actually differ. Core competencies typically change little over time, while comparative advantage is context dependent. In a trade regime, trade with one partner can differ from trade with another partner because comparative advantage depends on the relative characteristics of trading partners. Comparative advantage indicates one reason why partnerships can be complex. Entities and organizations will have different relationships with different partners that are context specific.

Evaluating Partnerships

Elliot Stern draws on aspects of organizational theory concerned with trust, hierarchy, and the relations of partnerships to their wider environment. His hypothesis might be termed organizational Darwinism: observing that organizations exist in stressful environments, he argues that certain organizational forms are reinforced in such environments and that new organizational forms can emerge. The implication is that approaches to the analysis of organizations and to the conduct of partnerships need to differ across countries and regions. He notes that today's imperatives—"to pursue holistic development policy objectives, to integrate administration, to improve implementation and sustainability by increasing participation and consent, and to improve knowledge management"—give rise to a new organizational ecology that raises new questions for evaluators, centering on the justification and rationale of partnerships. For example:

- "In what ways do the goals being pursued require partnership working? What are the goals and what is the scope of specific partnerships?
- How inclusive are partnerships?
- Who was involved in the planning and initial definition of partnership tasks?
- How important is knowledge transfer in a particular partnership?"

Robert Klitgaard distinguishes among needs for evaluations of partnerships, at three levels (benefits and costs for a specific partner, benefits and costs for the partnership as a whole, and evaluating the environments in which partnerships of various kinds emerge and function well or badly); evaluations for partnerships, to help them develop and succeed; and evaluations through partnerships, which must be managed in a way that preserves dissenting perspectives.

Several authors focus on issues in the evaluation of aid partnerships. Certainly evaluation plays an essential role in accountability for the use of aid resources. Both Jean-Claude Faure and Stuart Salter emphasize the need for effective monitoring and evaluation systems that recognize the leading role of the recipient country but also meet the legitimate requirements of the donor country with regard to its governing body and constituencies. Here Faure reminds us that the key to all successful partnerships is shared values, and that to nurture shared values donors and recipients must "move to a shared process, setting targets and using strategic indicators to measure progress and to judge success and failure."

Kwesi Botchwey describes the characteristics of effective aid partnerships, emphasizing the key role of national ownership. Evaluating experience thus far with the Comprehensive Development Framework, he finds "still a substantial gap between the partnership rhetoric and the reality on the ground. The mood in recipient countries is one of 'pragmatic engagement'—a euphemism for resignation—with many countries simply going through the motions to get development assistance. . . . Countries that are in receipt of aid need to be more proactive, and donors need to allow more space and time for national debate."

Faure notes that involving all stakeholders in joint evaluations makes it much easier to integrate evaluation results and a proper understanding of risks into partnership endeavors. Similarly, Cookingham emphasizes that evaluation must benefit practitioners. In community development partnerships, he argues, the development program evaluator should see his role more as a facilitator than as an expert. "I believe the purpose of facilitation in community development evaluation is to encourage and guide deeper understanding [by the community itself] of whatever is being evaluated, and to enhance development and evaluation knowledge and skills."

Approaches and Methods

To evaluate the success of partnerships, a variety of techniques is available, including program evaluation, objective-based evaluation, and results-based evaluation. But there are some real challenges. It is easier to evaluate a partnership if it has clear goals, specific performance indicators, a monitoring and evaluation system, and measurable outputs and outcomes. Many partnerships lack these features. Many are relatively high-level and of broad scope, with long-term impacts and multiple constituents, and involve people with a range of different values and different views of what constitutes credible evidence. These characteristics weaken the evidence chain and often make evaluation difficult. That said, the authors in this book make a range of useful proposals for sharpening evaluation approaches and methods.

Klitgaard suggests that to make progress on evaluating partnerships in a world of imperfect data, one should focus on cases that are broadly acknowledged to be outrageous successes and outrageous failures, and for sharing the results with one another and with the partners to derive generalizations of practical use. Such an undertaking, he suggests, might be an early priority for the International Development Evaluation Association.

Margaret Catley-Carlson suggests that since organizations use partnerships because they believe partnerships will yield benefits of their own, evaluators should "use separate criteria to address *project* success (whether or not the project activity was performed, and its outcome) and *partnership* success (whether the partnership was sustained and whether it produced what it was supposed to produce)." Evaluators should distinguish between the incentives of the different partners to achieve efficiency as well as sustainability and equity. She emphasizes the importance of matching the evaluative criteria to the goals that the partners agreed on at the outset, to make sure that the partnership is evaluated according to what it was trying to accomplish. She and several other authors also note that because better decisions are reached by incorporating a broad range of views, evaluations should measure the extent to which the partners' decision processes take heed of disparate viewpoints.

Sandra Libunao proposes that the effectiveness of a business–NGO engagement or partnership should be assessed in three areas: progress toward goals, success of the negotiation process between the parties, and the accountability of each party to its stakeholders. She argues that efficiency should be gauged by asking, "Could the same results have been achieved at less cost or better results achieved for the same cost?" Since some authors suggest that partnership increases transaction costs, while some suggest it should do the opposite, it might be helpful if evaluators could develop a cost/benefit tool to help would-be partners assess the anticipated increase in these costs, versus the expected gain in terms of development impact, from partnership.

Nicoletta Stame focuses her chapter on community development partnerships. She explains that evaluators have traditionally understood development projects as investments in physical infrastructure, but that much local development is actually based on enhancements in social capital. Development founded on social capital is typically regarded as spontaneous growth, and not evaluated. Looking at different types of policies for creating or enhancing social capital in Italy, Stame derives pointers for evaluating the value added by community-based partnerships.

Diana Stone's chapter focuses on methods for evaluating research partnerships. Not just the quality of research but also the effectiveness or influence of that research is critical. She points out that techniques for evaluating the application of knowledge can range from assessing whether or not research is relevant for policy to judging the extent to which that research has in practice helped to alleviate problems of poverty.

Picciotto argues that, "In the end, partnerships should be judged by their results." A partnership is justified only if the benefits exceed the costs and the net benefits are fairly shared by the parties. In turn, he explains, this implies that the partnership is "relevant, efficacious, and efficient from the perspective of the participants:

- Relevance means that there is a bedrock of shared values and that the participants 'own' the objectives of the partnership.
- Efficacy means that the design and operation of the partnership is appropriate and likely to lead to achievement of the joint objectives.

- An efficient partnership is one that uses joint resources with economy and achieves substantial results at limited cost. Replicability and sustainability are the acid tests of efficiency."

Making Partnerships Work

Drawing on both theory and practice, this volume offers many lessons for making partnerships work.

Robert Axelrod draws on game theory for his advice for would-be partners: be careful to select a partner with a good chance for a favorable payoff (which for development agencies these days means client countries with good policy regimes); set up a partnership with clear objectives and arrangements for prompt feedback; respond quickly to defections; restore cooperation; respond mildly; be contrite; start small; be willing to walk out if necessary; and have information standards and validation of actions.

These points sound rather like a "tough love" regime from a twelve-step program of some kind. They may be telling us as much about successful human relations in general as about effective strategies for partnership, yet several of them are also stressed by the individual partnership practitioners in the case studies. Repeatedly across countries and sectors, the practitioners emphasize the contribution made by simple principles of successful business interaction: perceptions of mutual benefit; building trust, awareness, and transparency with the partner; articulating and communicating learning objectives; mechanisms for conflict resolution; and managing partners holistically as well as individually. And Prusak notes that, on the basis of extensive empirical research, "increasingly, the critical component of partnering is seen to be relationship management."

North argues that since the success of partnerships depends greatly on incentives, we need to understand partnerships not simply as tools but as political processes. If partnerships are to improve economic performance they must lower transaction costs, while being sensitive to local conditions and traditions—including the time horizons of politicians—and working within the limitations imposed by local institutional structures.

Stern emphasizes that trust is typically a key ingredient of successful partnership—as stressed, too, by most of the practitioners. As to how trust is created, he distinguishes pessimists and optimists: the pessimists feel that it takes a long time for trust to be created, and that it is likely to be inherited; the optimists feel that trust can be quickly acquired and can be fostered. The degree of trust has many implications for how partnerships are set up and how they function: where trust is low, partnerships are likely to be more hierarchical, and relations tend to be disciplined by rules or by past practices. There is much that is worth testing empirically in these hypotheses.

As to the prerequisites for success, Picciotto's findings from evaluation, Stern's from a review of empirical research, and Margaret Catley-Carlson's from direct experience, yield similar messages:

- *Goals* must be adequately defined and fully owned by the partners. It is difficult to realize a shared vision if no shared vision exists.
- Partnership must focus on the *ultimate objective.* If it focuses only on the intermediate steps, it will fail.
- *Understanding each other's motives.* All partners need to understand what the separate members of the partnership hope to achieve.
- *Understanding each other's roles.* All partners need to understand the obligations of each partner, and the rationale behind those obligations.
- *Differentiated roles* minimize confusion and overlap.
- *Internal backing* is important. The partners must secure full consensus for the goals of the partnership within their organizations.
- Each partner must maintain *accountability to its constituents.*
- The partners must reach out and engage in *broad-based participation* in support of partnership goals.
- The partners must demonstrate intellectual conviction through *concrete, up-front actions.*
- It may be best to superimpose a *light collaboration infrastructure* that permits the partners to retain their own working methods.
- *Capacity development* must be built into the partnership to ensure that the weaker members can participate fully and exercise influence.
- Partners *learn from each other* and should adjust to each other's interests.

The authors of the case studies make clear that partnerships fail as often as they succeed. Everything that can go wrong when you do things yourself can go wrong in a partnership, and on top of this, partnerships add their own problems. Partnerships may increase risk as well as offer opportunities to reduce it.

Lastly, we do not just have to worry about the failure of partnerships. We should also worry about sinister success. For example, private sector partners can and do get together to restrict trade, fix prices, and produce monopoly outcomes; much regulation of partnerships in the private sector is designed explicitly to prevent such outcomes. Relationships between the private sector and government also produce corruption, regulatory capture, and other types of pathologies. Similarly, NGOs and the private sector can partner to produce fraud, false legitimization, and lobbying for narrow interests.

Conclusion

In several respects, having more information from evaluation should help potential partners make better choices about whether and when to partner and about how to conduct partnerships. Here the learning, feedback, and dissemination aspects of evaluation are crucial.

Partnerships may be an area in which the evaluation profession can make more progress on learning than on accountability. This is because attribution is likely to be a serious problem. To some people, being unable to attribute success or failure could turn out to be a weakness of partnerships; to others, it could be a strength. If a partnership is difficult to evaluate, one could claim that the partnership was a success—or at least that one's own contribution was a success—and it may be very difficult for others to refute this.

To conclude, partnerships offer hope in many situations, but their more rigorous evaluation requires all the efforts we can muster. Certainly partnering agencies and their goals, governance arrangements, and operating environments are diverse. Yet the overall message of the studies seems to be both that context matters and that generalizations are possible. This suggests that work on typologies is likely to have a high payoff. Stern's suggestion of comparative studies as a preferred way to evaluate partnerships appears to be a very promising approach.

Part 1

Foundations of Partnerships and Their Evaluation

1

Partnership as a Means to Improve Economic Performance

Douglass C. North

This chapter considers partnership from the standpoint of economic development in history. It first discusses the factors that underlie good economic performance, and then addresses the conditions necessary to put those factors in place. Partnership is seen as the collaborative effort by which we can create the conditions to improve performance.

Defining good economic performance should be a straightforward matter. Unfortunately, the economic and development theory that has evolved is inadequate in this regard. It takes as its model a world of laissez-faire and free markets. Yet, no successful political or economic market evolves naturally. A successful market must be structured, and if mies around the world, we find that if they do not work well, it is because they deliver high payoffs for doing things that are not productive or creative.

Economists have tended to underplay the role that politics plays in economic performance. In reality, it is economics that is secondary to politics. The first requirement for better economic performance is a polity that establishes a set of economic rules that encourages the development of appropriate incentives.

Encouraging Incentives

A polity that encourages the right incentives can be authoritarian or consensual. It must support or provide (1) an institutional matrix that produces a set of organizations and establishes a set of rights and privileges; (2) stable exchange relationships in political and economic markets; (3) an underlying

---

Douglass C. North is Bartlett Burnap Senior Fellow, Hoover Institution; Department of Economics, Washington University.

structure that credibly commits the state to a set of political rules, and enforcement that protects organizations and exchange relationships; and (4) conformity as a result of some mixture of norm internalization and coercive enforcement. Only when this framework is in place can the necessary economic rules be established.

Among the conditions necessary for performance improvement is an effective price system—that is, a set of property rights that reduces the costs of transacting. Transaction costs in their simplest form are the costs of measuring and enforcing agreements. Where it is possible to measure exactly what is being exchanged, it is also possible to devise rules that can define whether or not exchange agreements are being observed. Where measurement is imprecise, however, the integrity of the relationship cannot be confirmed. This makes it messy and difficult to make exchanges, and enables corruption.

There are four main kinds of transaction costs. Their mitigation can be addressed through institutions.

The first cost is that of measurement. Goods and services have multiple dimensions that are valuable, and we must be able to measure all of them if we are to eliminate subterfuge and corruption. To make this possible, we need to establish a uniform system of weights and measures. We must also be able to measure exactly what is being exchanged. Measurement is becoming much more difficult as more complex kinds of things are exchanged—as, for example, in the capital markets and over the Internet.

The second cost is incurred in protecting individual property rights. A working judicial system is necessary to protect these rights. This is something we have long talked about, and which is absent in many developing countries.

The third cost has to do with enforcing agreements. As in the case of protecting property rights, mitigating this cost requires an effective judicial system; it also requires the creation of additional institutions to monitor agreements and punish defectors.

Integrating Dispersed Knowledge

The fourth transaction cost is the cost of integrating the knowledge that is dispersed throughout society. This cost can be mitigated—though only to some extent, given the complexity of modern society—through the establishment of a price system. This fourth transaction cost is often the most significant obstacle to moving from understanding performance in rich countries to understanding what must be done in poor countries. Consequently, it is at the heart of the problems with which we are concerned.

The dispersal of knowledge is a function of the specialization and division of labor that underlie economic growth. To support continuing growth, however, that dispersed knowledge should be brought together for the benefit of the broader society. Such integration can involve high transaction costs if the different parties do not trust each other or do not know how to measure the qualities and characteristics of each other's work.

An effective price system can go a long way toward integrating dispersed knowledge, but there will always be externalities and information costs that are asymmetric among the different players. Nonetheless, a poor country trying to become wealthier must coordinate its economic performance, which implies integration of the disparate parts of its economy.

For us to help realize coordinated economic performance, we must also understand what kinds of transaction costs exist in a specific market. No two markets are the same, and radical alterations in information costs and technology continue to evolve. Thus, we must continually modify and revise our institutional frameworks. Recent World Bank projects in water and telecommunications have shown how difficult it is to create a framework within which players from different backgrounds, each with their own polities, technologies, and institutional arrangements, can be encouraged to do things the way we would want them to. Telecommunications, which has changed from being a natural monopoly to a rapidly evolving, competitive industry, strongly demonstrates that even a framework that works well will need to be modified over time.

A framework that does not work well brings its own problems. Paths that discourage incentives to produce and create tend to persist, once established; the institutional framework that engenders such paths can create entrenched interests that resist change.

Finding the Right Institutional Framework

How do we overcome these problems? Let us start with the political markets, the most crucial markets of all.

The formal rules are easy. The characteristics of a polity that encourages the right sort of incentives constitute a formal institutional matrix. But while they are a step in the right direction, formal rules are not sufficient: informal norms are needed that get people to play the game in ways that will make the formal rules effective, and they must be supported by enforcement mechanisms.

When Latin America became independent in the early nineteenth century, many of the newly independent countries adopted the U.S. Constitution, or something like it, believing that the rules that worked for the United States would also work for them. This proved not to be the case. The informal norms and enforcement characteristics of the U.S. market were radically different from those of Latin America. The original colonies of the United States bequeathed a heritage of self-assembly and self-government, but colonial rule in Latin America left no such foundation.

In countries that have no heritage of self-government, self-government cannot be created overnight, but authoritarian rule can provide a short-term solution. The examples of Singapore and the Republic of Korea show how it can be easier to put essential economic rules in place within the context of an authoritarian polity, but the long-term validity of this approach is less clear. Indonesia, for example, enjoyed a high rate of growth under an authoritarian regime, but now is disintegrating.

In the long run, a consensual polity may be the only way to go. But democracy is a difficult form of government, and it takes time to build the necessary human capital to support a successful consensual system. The task for aid, therefore, is a delicate and difficult one. With the assistance of NGOs and through partnerships between donors and recipients, we need to build up improvements in various sectors of the receiving society, such as health, education, and the judiciary, that not only raise the performance of those sectors but which also develop the human capital essential to a consensual polity.

Capitalizing on Local Conditions

What we need to bring to our partnerships with developing countries, therefore, is an understanding of the constraints and limitations imposed by the institutional structure of those countries. At what margins can cooperation and the dissemination of information and knowledge make partnership work effectively?

Crucially, we must not allow ourselves to become chained to the formal institutions that have worked in developed countries. China, for example, has none of the conditions that we think of as making for successful economic growth. It has no clearly specified property rights and it has a judicial system that is essentially arbitrary, but it has nonetheless achieved high rates of growth. It has been able to do this because it has provided informally a set of incentives that have been effective surrogates for the kind of formal institutions found in developed economies. (China's most difficult problems lie ahead, since it must transform this system into one that will work in the future.)

Economists do not believe in culture. We tend to think that everybody is alike. But the lesson of China surely is that we should learn to see the heritage and the cultural background of the country as a benefit, and that we should seek to capitalize on this benefit to create the most effective development strategy possible.

Partnership is an incremental process. Results cannot be achieved overnight, but suggest this to a politician and the answer is always the same: "I am not going to be around in 20 or 50 years. I need things that are going to work in the short run." Our time horizon is much longer than that of the politician, but the reality is that we must work within the politician's time horizon. We must modify our advice accordingly. The results we are seeking are not possible in the short term, but by changing the game over time we can realize them incrementally.

A final challenge for partnerships is that of making knowledge transferable and communicable. Much of that knowledge is tacit rather than overt, and it is important that we find ways of codifying it to make it accessible to other people. If we can do this, we can use that knowledge in different cultures to help solve the many development problems we face.

2

Theoretical Foundations of Partnership

Robert Axelrod[1]

This chapter describes the theoretical foundations of a development partnership between an aid donor and a recipient. The framework offered is deliberately very simple, to best highlight certain important principles. Rather than furnish a full rendition of the complexities of partnerships for economic development, I seek to provide insight into some fundamental issues.

Because a donor and a recipient may have divergent as well as complementary interests, a partnership between the two can be analyzed in terms of a mixed-motive game between two players. The model used here is the iterated Prisoner's Dilemma game, which can suggest some of the implications of selecting a partner, setting up a partnership, choosing a modus operandi, building trust, achieving selectivity, and performing monitoring and evaluation. We begin, however, by seeking to define what constitutes a partnership in development.

How Partnerships Differ from Other Kinds of Relationships

A working definition of partnership is a collaborative relationship between entities to work toward shared objectives through a mutually agreed division of labor. We can expand on this to further distinguish partnerships from other forms of aid relationships.

A partnership is not a gift. A partnership aims to take advantage of what the recipient, as well as the donor, can bring to the relationship. This can include local expertise, on-site workers, and a better understanding of priorities, needs, and constraints. Crucially, a partnership seeks also to establish joint ownership of the relationship and to build the capacity of the recipient government to undertake sustainable development.

Robert Axelrod is Arthur W. Bromage Distinguished University Professor of Political Science and Public Policy, Gerald R. Ford School of Public Policy, University of Michigan.

A partnership is not a relationship based on one-sided conditionality—that is, on the imposition by the donor of conditions that would coerce the recipient to do things it does not want to do, in order to obtain resources.[2] Some researchers question whether strict conditionality has been effective under any circumstances in promoting development (Gilbert, Powell, and Vines 2000). Partnership recognizes that both sides must be involved in defining the terms of the relationship.

A partnership is not a principal–agent relationship between a donor and a recipient. The donor in a partnership cannot prescribe the terms of the relationship in the way that an employer can specify terms of employment when hiring a worker.[3]

A partnership is not simply a team activity. On a sports team, everyone has the same interest in winning, and either everyone wins or everyone loses. In contrast, while the members of a partnership for economic development will have strong interests in common, they are also likely to have some divergent interests.

Finally, although the formal terms of a partnership may be expressed in a contract valid under international law, the donor and recipient usually will have no thought of using the courts to resolve conflicts between them. Instead, like nations bound by treaties, partners rely mainly on each other's need to maintain a good reputation to secure future agreements.

A Partnership as a Prisoner's Dilemma

It is helpful to use game theory to understand the theoretical foundations of a partnership.[4] In game theory, a relationship is defined by (1) identifying the players, (2) specifying the choices they have, and (3) spelling out the consequences of those choices in terms of the payoffs to the players. Analyzing the strategies available to the players reveals what is needed to foster mutually beneficial outcomes.

As an analogy to a partnership for economic development, the game is constructed as follows:[5]

The players are the donor and the recipient. The donor might be an international financial institution, such as the World Bank; a nongovernmental organization (NGO); a foundation; a group of countries, such as the Organization for Economic Co-operation and Development (OECD); a single country; or even a coalition of diverse contributors. The recipient in a partnership is often the government of a single country, but also might be a group of countries, a ministry in charge of some sector of a single country, or a local organization.

The choices available to the players in reality can be complex, but for highlighting the theoretical aspects of a partnership, they can be reduced to just two: cooperate or defect. By choosing to cooperate, the player elects to perform the agreed-upon terms of the partnership promptly and fully. By choosing to defect, the player opts to fulfill its obligations less than completely, or more slowly than agreed upon.

The consequences depend on the choices made. The basis of a partnership is that there is mutual gain to be had by working together: if both partners cooperate, both do well. However, there is typically a temptation to defect. A donor, for example, might be tempted to avoid some of its commitments in a desire to increase the amount of tied aid or to reduce costs—presumably after being credited for "flag raising"—or it may in practice exhibit a reluctance to support leadership by the recipient government.[6] The recipient might in turn be tempted to divert some of its limited resources away from the partnership toward other needs. In general, each side would typically prefer that the other fulfill its commitments, while itself having the freedom to select which of its commitments to honor. Should both sides defect, however, neither will do well because neither will benefit from the partnership. These, and the consequences of other permutations of the players' decisions, are shown in the matrix in Box 2.1.

Box 2.1
Partnership as a Prisoner's Dilemma

		Donor	
		Cooperate	*Defect*
Recipient	*Cooperate*	***R*=3, *R*=3**	*S*=0, *T*=5
	Defect	*T*=5, *S*=0	*P*=1, *P*=1

The first number in each cell is the payoff to the recipient, and the second number is the payoff to the donor. *R* is the reward for mutual cooperation, *T* is the temptation to defect, S is the sucker's payoff, and *P* is the punishment for mutual defection.

The numbers are meant to be suggestive only; what matters is their rank. It should be noted also that the payoffs need be neither symmetric nor comparable-all that is necessary is that the payoffs for each player separately fulfill the conditions of the Prisoner's Dilemma; that is, that $T > R > P > S$ (and technically also $R > (T + S)/2$). This is likely to be true in almost any development partnership.

The payoff matrix is a fundamental tool for understanding the theoretical foundations of partnerships. The ranking of the payoffs in a partnership relationship, from best to worst, is as follows: the temptation payoff for defecting when the other partner cooperates; the reward for mutual cooperation; the punishment for mutual defection; and the sucker's payoff for cooperating when the other partner defects.[7] This is the ranking of the classic Prisoner's Dilemma. The dilemma is that each side has an incentive to defect, no matter what the other side does—but if both defect, then both do worse than had they cooperated.[8]

If the Prisoner's Dilemma is played only once, there is no getting around the problem that each side has an incentive to defect, no matter what the other side does. This would imply that the benefits of mutual cooperation are unattainable. If the game is played repeatedly, however, the strategic possibilities are much richer. Fortunately, in a development partnership the relationship is not based on a single choice but on an ongoing interaction between the donor and recipient (Branson and Hanna 2000). Thus, the iterated Prisoner's Dilemma provides the most useful model for this discussion.

Many strategies are possible in the iterated Prisoner's Dilemma because each player's choice is contingent on what has previously happened in the relationship. Cooperation theory is the study of what strategy a sophisticated player should use, and what conditions will sustain mutual cooperation. To study these questions, I organized two round-robin computer tournaments in the late 1970s at which I invited a group of experts and amateurs to submit a computer program that embodied their favorite strategy (Axelrod 1984). A single strategy, the Tit for Tat strategy, got the highest overall score in both of these tournaments.

Using Tit for Tat, the player cooperates on the first move and subsequently does whatever the other side did on the previous move. The strategy's robust success was founded on its being nice, provocable, and forgiving. Niceness means not being the first to defect. Provocability means retaliation when the other side defects, thereby discouraging the other side from persisting in defection. Cooperating again as soon as the other player does is the hallmark of forgiveness. Through such behavior, Tit for Tat helps to restore and sustain mutual cooperation.

An interesting aspect of the Tit for Tat strategy is that, because a Tit for Tat player cannot defect more often than the other player, it cannot outscore the other player. This curious fact highlights the single most important lesson of game theory in general, and the iterated Prisoner's Dilemma in particular: most human interactions are not zero-sum games in which one side's loss is the other side's gain.

Perhaps the biggest surprise from the tournaments, however, was the complementary point that to maintain stable cooperation in an iterated Prisoner's Dilemma it is necessary to be provocable. In fact, the sooner one responds to a defection by the other side, the easier it is to restore mutual cooperation by establishing that defection does not pay. Other variants of the nice, provocable, and forgiving strategy, such as Tit for Two Tats, which needs two defections to be provoked, confirm the importance of reciprocity. Where Tit for Tat holds the advantage over other forms of reciprocating strategy is that it is easy for the other player to recognize. Once recognized, it is clear that the best way to respond to a Tit for Tat player is to cooperate.

A further fundamental theoretical result is that the potential for mutual cooperation depends on "the shadow of the future." This is measured by w, the rate at which the payoff of the next move is discounted relative to the present one. Cooperation based on Tit for Tat is stable if and only if w is at least as great as the larger of $(T - R)/(T - P)$ and $(T - R)/(R - S)$ (Axelrod 1984). As long as the shadow of the future is large enough, if one player uses Tit for Tat the other player can do no better than use Tit for Tat as well, thus establishing mutual cooperation on a stable basis.

An unavoidable feature of partnership is the possibility of misimplementation or misunderstanding. With misimplementation, a player intends to do one thing but actually does another; for example, a leader may decide to cooperate, but the rest of the organization may not properly implement the leader's choice. Misunderstanding occurs when a player does one thing, but the other player perceives it as something else. A single error of either description would throw a game between two Tit for Tat players into an infinite cycle of provocation and retaliation (Molander 1985). A measure of generosity needs therefore to be incorporated into simple Tit for Tat. For example, a player might be generous at the 10 percent level, meaning that 10 percent of the time that the player would otherwise defect, it cooperates instead. If a player realizes that it is responsible for the trouble through its own misimplementation, it could furthermore avoid responding to the other player's retaliatory defection. This is called contrition. Deductive theory and computer simulation demonstrate that a generous Tit for Tat strategy is effective at dealing with either type of error. Adding contrition further minimizes the disruptive effects of misimplementation (Wu and Axelrod 1995).

I now turn to the implications of the theoretical framework.

Implications for Selecting a Partner

The principle of selectivity is usually taken to mean that program aid should be reserved for countries that have efficient pro-development policies (Hopkins et al. 2000). Cooperation theory based on the iterated Prisoner's Dilemma suggests a related, but somewhat different, set of considerations for choosing a partner:

- The more favorable the payoff structure, the easier it will be to achieve and sustain mutual cooperation. This implies that a potential donor or recipient should consider more than just the potential gains from mutual cooperation; the magnitude of the temptation to defect should also be considered.
- The stronger the shadow of the future, the easier it will be to achieve and sustain mutual cooperation. A good partner is therefore one that has a long enough time horizon to suggest that it would not exploit the relationship for immediate gain.
- A partner needs the organizational and managerial capacity to fulfill its responsibilities. It should not be overextended with other commitments.
- The potential for follow-on projects enhances the attractiveness of a partner. A follow-on project, especially one that may be larger than the project under consideration, can make success in the original project an investment in a continuing relationship.
- Selecting a partner that has a good reputation for cooperation has two benefits: it rewards the past good behavior of that partner, and it increases the chances that the current partnership will succeed.

Implications for Setting up the Partnership

Once a donor and a recipient have agreed to set up a partnership, the terms of the agreement need to be worked out. Theoretical and empirical research suggests there are three aspects of an ongoing relationship that facilitate cooperation based upon reciprocity: (1) clarity of obligations, (2) promptness of feedback, and (3) institutionalization of reciprocity. When setting up a partnership, the participants should take care that these three conditions will be met throughout the partnership.

Clarity of obligations is needed so that a cooperative choice can be distinguished from a defection. If partners are unable to agree on whether or not a given action is consistent with their obligations, they are likely to get involved in mutual recriminations. Unfortunately, clarity of obligations competes with flexibility of implementation. Until a bond of trust has developed between the two sides, it may be better to err on the side of clarity of obligations rather than flexibility of implementation when setting up a partnership.

Promptness of feedback implies that each side should be able to monitor the behavior of the other, so that emergent problems can be addressed before they become major grievances. Prompt feedback can strengthen the shadow of the future by enabling timely response to a perceived problem. The obligations of the two sides should thus be set such that their fulfillment (or nonfulfillment) is quickly observable.

Institutionalization of reciprocity can help by specifying in advance the available forms of review and redress should either side have a complaint against the other. Maxwell and Riddell (1998) suggest that aid administration generally needs an agreement akin to those that govern trade under the World Trade Organization. In the absence of formal agreements, however, even informal norms can help prevent problems spinning out of control (Axelrod and Keohane 1985).

Implications for a Modus Operandi

The partners in a relationship need a modus operandi to guide their behavior in the relationship. Mutual cooperation is the ideal, but what should one partner do if the other fails to fulfill its commitments in a timely manner? Theory and simulations show that the sooner one acts on a provocation, the smaller the response needed to be effective (Axelrod 1984). Failure to respond promptly to defection risks sending the wrong signal: the longer defections go unchallenged, the more likely it is that the defecting player will conclude that defection pays—and the more strongly this pattern is established, the harder it is to break it.

The importance of provocability is increased when others that are or may become partners with either of the participants are observing the relationship. Reputation is important, to the extent even that it can give a recipient leverage over a donor. For example, if a recipient is provoked, it may withhold part of its contribution to the partnership, and it can also threaten to criticize the donor in forums that are important to the donor's reputation and self-image (Fox 2000).

Provocability is also important for the donor. If, for example, a lending organization earns a reputation for failing to hold its partners to their commitments, it may become difficult for that lender to hold future partners accountable. This is the reason why the Grameen Bank, for example, is so insistent on prompt repayment of micro-credit loans, absent an external shock beyond the foresight or control of the recipient (Bornstein 1996).[9]

The complement of provocability is forgiveness when an erring partner returns to cooperation. In a partnership for economic development, for instance, a recipient government may lack the capacity to implement its decisions. Donors, too, occasionally make promises that they are unable to keep. Given that cultural differences between the donor and recipient can contribute to misunderstanding, it is important that both partners remain aware that a perceived defection might be due to misimplementation or misperception. It can consequently be worthwhile avoiding a response to some defections or moderating the response to others—with the understanding, of course, that too much generosity invites exploitation. Contrition can also help defuse a potential conflict, should the other side's defection be a response to one's own unintended defection.

Implications for Building Trust

Trust is crucial for establishing cooperation based on mutual obligation.[10] Building trust takes time, and as a result takes place mostly in the context of repeated projects rather than within a single project. This suggests the importance of comparing the time that a particular project will take with the time the relationship is expected to last. An example is the relationship between Conservation International and Starbucks (Purcell 2000). In the first partnership project, Starbucks signed a three-year contract, committing $150,000 to the promotion of shade-grown coffee. Conservation International at the end of this period publicly praised Starbucks for helping farmers and for improving the natural environment. With this endorsement and with shade-grown coffee becoming accepted by its customers, Starbucks signed a new three-year contract with Conservation International, this time with a commitment of $600,000.

Theoretically, playing the same game over a longer period has the advantage of returning more reliable feedback but also has the disadvantage of slow feedback. For building trust, however, partners need the strong shadow of the future that comes with a long time horizon. As confirmed by theoretical work, starting with small stakes and raising them as a relationship develops can help partners avoid having to take "leaps of faith" (Roberts and Sherratt 1998).

Implications for Selectivity

Donors clearly need to avoid spreading their resources too thinly. Cooperation theory suggests some guidelines for how they might select their partners; specifically, it presents some strategic considerations to assist selection, based on how reciprocity can work at the project level: The donor should express willingness to withhold new support for a project, or to refuse to entertain new proposals, for a recipient who fails to fulfill the obligations of a joint project. This has the advantage of helping to establish the understanding that cooperation needs to be mutual.[11] Put another way, to overcome a recipient's temptation to exploit the relationship, the donor needs to be provocable on the long time scale as well as on the short time scale.

To avoid retreating altogether from a country in need, a donor can be selective about the sector in which it engages, rather than the country. Thus, if a project in one sector has not worked well, the donor may switch to a project in another sector of the same country. This can be an effective strategy, but only if the decision makers in the two sectors are not the same.[12]

Implications for Monitoring and Evaluation

Monitoring is the continuous assessment of project implementation; evaluation is the periodic assessment of the project. In the aid community, the evaluation process is intended to serve two functions: institutional credibility and organizational learning. For institutional credibility, the acid test is performance on the ground. For this reason, accountability for results has become a fundamental imperative of development assistance (Picciotto 2002). For organizational learning, the goal is not only to improve individual programs but also to make the results available to the global evaluation community.

From the point of view of cooperation theory, monitoring and evaluation can play an active role in sustaining the conditions needed for mutual cooperation. For stable cooperation in an iterated Prisoner's Dilemma, each player needs to know in a timely fashion whether or not the other is fulfilling mutually agreed commitments. In particular, it is essential for provocability and forgiveness to know when the other side has defected; and for contrition, it is essential to know when one's own side has defected, intentionally or otherwise.

Determining if the partners are doing what they promise is different from the traditional role of evaluating of how well the partnership is achieving its goals. Periodic evaluation can be joined with continuous monitoring to reassure the partners when mutual cooperation is being achieved, and to warn them when it is not.

Theoretically, the stability of cooperation relies on both partners having timely information about the actions of the other. In practice, the donor is more likely to monitor and evaluate the recipient than the other way round: Whereas the behavior and performance of low-income developing countries is measured and assessed in ever-increasing detail within the international community, the behavior and performance of the donor "partners" receives only cursory attention except at the aggregate level, which is of little operational usefulness to individual recipients (Helleiner 2000).

Independent evaluation of donor performance, such as practiced by the Operations Evaluation Department of the World Bank, is designed to fill this gap. The Bank's recently established Inspection Panel, which investigates claims by local stakeholders that the Bank may have failed to adhere to its own operational policies, design procedures, appraisal, or implementation of ongoing or new operations, also helps to redress the imbalance (Fox 2000).

The unique position of the World Bank allows it to play an important role in economic development activities even when it is not a direct participant. The Bank's multinational character, size, and experience allow it to play an increasingly active role as catalyst in identifying and promoting promising activities (see, for example, Gilbert, Powell, and Vines 2000). Cooperation theory suggests that even after a partnership is set up there are valuable services that could be performed by a credible outside organization such as the World Bank. Among these potential services are:

- promotion of accounting standards to allow timely feedback on the performance of partners;
- certification that partners are being responsible in fulfilling their obligations; and
- sponsorship of institutional mechanisms for redress if one side of a partnership has a complaint about the other side.

Conclusion

A partnership for economic development includes divergent interests as well as shared objectives. Analyzing a partnership as an iterated Prisoner's Dilemma reveals the theoretical conditions needed to sustain mutual cooperation. These conditions lead to practical conclusions on how to promote the effectiveness of such partnerships. They concern selecting a partner, setting up a partnership, choosing a modus operandi, building trust, achieving selectivity, and performing monitoring and evaluation.

Notes

1. I thank Kathryn Dominguez, Jude Hayes, James Levinsohn, Andres Liebenthal, and Diane Kaplan Vinokur for their help, but the opinions expressed are solely those of the author. I also thank Todd Sandler and Uma Lele, the discussants at the conference, for their useful criticisms. For financial assistance I thank the Intel Corporation and The University of Michigan College of LS&A Enrichment Fund.
2. A partnership is consistent, however, with conditionality that functions as a process over time, with mutual accountability (Branson and Hanna 2000).
3. The principal–agent framework is useful for the examination of issues that arise from information asymmetries. For example, in partnerships for economic development the recipient often knows more than the donor about what is happening at the local level.
4. Game theory provides methods for analyzing a wide range of strategic problems. Because the Prisoner's Dilemma occurs in many contexts, it is one of most thoroughly studied games. A good introduction to game theory is Dixit and Skeath (1999). A more advanced game theory text is Fudenberg and Tirole (1992). For reviews on the theoretical and empirical literature on the Prisoner's Dilemma, see Axelrod and Dion (1988) and Hoffmann (2000).
5. Game theory has previously been used to model other aspects of development aid. For example, conditionality has been modeled as a principal–agent game (Squire 2000), and the enforcement of debt service has been modeled as a game with a choice to default (Anderson, Gilbert, and Powell 1991).
6. These concerns were voiced in the workshop "Making Partnerships Work on the Ground" (Swedish Ministry of Foreign Affairs 1999).
7. Different games have different payoff structures. For example, in the Assurance Game, mutual cooperation has a higher payoff than unilateral defection, with the result that there is no temptation to defect—the only issue is for the players to assure each other that they will act rationally.
8. The original story involves two prisoners who are being interrogated by the police. Each is given an incentive to confess to help convict the other, but if both confess, the police do not need the testimony of either.

9. Another reason for adjusting the terms of the partnership would be if the premises underlying the project were revealed to be inaccurate. Suppose, for example, the partnership was designed to supply water from wells. If the wells do not give the expected yield, then the partners should renegotiate their commitments, perhaps switching to laying pipes. The new agreement would redefine what counts as cooperation or defection in the partnership.
10. This point is confirmed by a study of seventeen joint ventures in the United Kingdom and Malaysia (Butler and Gill 1999).
11. Numerous simulation studies show that ability and willingness to leave an unsatisfactory relationship actually foster cooperation in the long run. For a review, see Axelrod (2000).
12. To the degree that aid is fungible across sectors, the effectiveness of this approach is reduced. See Devarajan and Swaroop (2000).

References

Note: The word *processed* describes informally reproduced works that may not be available through libraries.

Anderson, R. W., C. L. Gilbert, and A. Powell. 1991. "Securitizing Development Finance: The Role of Partial Guarantees and Commodity Contingency." In T. Privolos and R. C. Duncan, eds., *Commodity Risk Management and Finance.* New York: Oxford University Press.

Axelrod, Robert. 1984. *The Evolution of Cooperation.* New York: Basic Books.

_____. 2000. "On Six Advances in Cooperation Theory." *Analyse & Kritik* 22: 130–51.

Axelrod, Robert, and Douglas Dion. 1988. "The Further Evolution of Cooperation." *Science* 242: 1385–90.

Axelrod, Robert, and Robert Keohane. 1985. "Achieving Cooperation under Anarchy." *World Politics* 38: 226–54.

Bornstein, David. 1996. *The Price of a Dream.* New York: Simon and Schuster.

Branson, William, and Nagy Hanna. 2000. "Ownership and Conditionality." OED Working Paper No. 8, World Bank, Washington, D.C. Available at *www.worldbank.org/html/oed*

Butler, Richard, and Jas Gill. 1999. "The Dynamics of Trust in Partnership Formation and Operation: Project Summary." Processed. Bradford, U.K.: University of Bradford Management Centre.

Devarajan, Shantayanan, and Vinya Swaroop. 2000. "The Implications of Foreign Aid Fungibility for Development Assistance." In Christopher L. Gilbert and David Vines, eds., *The World Bank: Structure and Policies.* New York: Cambridge University Press.

Dixit, Avinash, and Susan Skeath. 1999. *Games of Strategy.* New York: Norton.

Fox, Jonathan A. 2000. "The World Bank Inspection Panel: Lessons from the First Five Years." *Global Governance* 3: 279–318.

Fudenberg, Drew, and Jean Tirole. 1992. *Game Theory.* Cambridge, Mass.: MIT Press.

Gilbert, Christopher L., Andrew Powell, and David Vines. 2000. "Positioning the World Bank." In Christopher L. Gilbert and David Vines, eds., *The World Bank: Structure and Policies.* New York: Cambridge University Press.

Helleiner, Gerry. 2000. "Towards Balance in Aid Relationships: Donor Performance Monitoring in Low-Income Developing Countries." *Cooperation South* (UNDP) 2: 21–35. Available at *www.ecdc.net.cn/events/co_south200002/4.htm*

Hoffmann, Robert. 2000. "Twenty Years On: The Evolution of Cooperation Revisited." *Journal of Artificial Societies and Social Simulation* 3(2). Available at *www.soc.surrey.ac.uk/JASSS/3/3/forum/1.html*

Hopkins, Raul, Andrew Powell, Amlan Roy, and Christopher L. Gilbert. 2000. "The World Bank, Conditionality and the Comprehensive Development Framework." In Christopher L. Gilbert and David Vines, eds., *The World Bank: Structure and Policies.* New York: Cambridge University Press.

Maxwell, Simon, and Roger Riddell. 1998. "Conditionality or Contract: Perspectives on Partnership for Development." *Journal of International Development* 10: 257–68.

Molander, Per. 1985. "The Optimal Level of Generosity in a Selfish, Uncertain Environment." *Journal of Conflict Resolution* 29: 611–18.

Picciotto, Robert. 2002. "Evaluation in the World Bank: Antecedents, Methods, and Instruments." In Jan-Eric Furubo, Ray C. Rist, and Rolf Sandahl, eds., *International Atlas of Evaluation.* Piscataway, N.J.: Transaction.

Purcell, Randall. 2000. *Good Practices and Regional Programs.* Washington, D.C.: World Bank.

Roberts, Gilbert, and Thomas N. Sherratt. 1998. "Development of Cooperative Relationships through Increasing Investment." *Nature* 394: 175–79.

Squire, Lyn. 2000. "Why the World Bank Should Be Involved in Development Research." In Christopher L. Gilbert and David Vines, eds., *The World Bank: Structure and Policies.* New York: Cambridge University Press.

Swedish Ministry of Foreign Affairs. 1999. *Making Partnerships Work on the Ground.* Stockholm, Sweden: Ministry of Foreign Affairs.

Wu, Jianzhong, and Robert Axelrod. 1995. "How to Cope with Noise in the Iterated Prisoner's Dilemma." *Journal of Conflict Resolution* 39: 183–89.

3

Foundations of Partnerships: A Practitioner's Perspective

Margaret Catley-Carlson

The purpose of this chapter is to offer observations from practice on the essential elements of a successful partnership, followed by thoughts on the criteria needed to evaluate partnerships.

Defining "Partnership"

Particularly in today's politically correct environment, the word "partnership" is overused with respect to contractual relationships. Partnerships should in fact be rigorously differentiated from contractual relationships: the essence of a true partnership is that each partner brings something to the enterprise and there is a clear agreed understanding of what that contribution should be. Contractual relationships can be effective in getting things done, but they are not the same as partnerships.

When evaluating the results of a partnership activity, we also need to differentiate between the results themselves and the way in which they were achieved. It is possible to achieve good results without meeting the criteria of partnership. For example, all the children in a country may be immunized, but if foreign interests perform the immunizations while the department of health does nothing, the partnership should be seen as failing. Such a situation can yield results that have no long-term effectiveness.

Evaluations should use separate criteria to address *project* success (whether or not the project activity was performed, and its outcome) and *partnership* success (whether the partnership was sustained and whether it produced what it was supposed to produce).

Margaret Catley-Carlson is chair, Global Water Partnership.

Why Partnership?

Organizations form partnerships when they need a more dynamic approach or a more diverse set of inputs than they can achieve alone. This point should be specifically addressed during partnership evaluation: the evaluative criteria should describe why a partnership arrangement was chosen over unilateral implementation.

Experience has made clear that international development needs much more than just government-to-government relationships or government-to-donor relationships. Awareness of the limitations of government activity is growing; it is clear that the nation state is neither small enough to do important work at the community and individual levels nor large enough to contend with the forces that govern monetary and economic flows and the flow of international trade. Concerns about national competitiveness in a global market have constrained government activity by depressing spending power as governments seek to maintain competitive taxes and manageable debt ratios; the combined efforts of the International Monetary Fund and the World Bank in stabilization arrangements have been to move governments out of activities. Similarly, the crisis of welfare and the failure of state-led development models have made governments in the North pull back from some activities.

For government and nongovernmental agencies alike, however, the essential reason to engage in partnership is that success is outside the purview of those who are seeking to make the change. As an example, take the problem of maternal mortality. To prevent the death of a mother due to delivery complications, three things have to happen. First, somebody—a traditional birth attendant, friend, or regional health official—must signal the existence of a potential delivery difficulty (and must have the incentive to do so). Second, somebody must be willing to spend money to get the mother to medical care. Third, transport must be available to bring the woman to where that care is available. Only the first of these three conditions is under the control of the health system; neither of the latter two is under the control of those who normally would work on maternal mortality. Tackling a problem like maternal mortality thus means creating partnerships at the community level to bring together everyone who can have an impact in the problem area. All partners must be willing to engage, and the partnership must be able to adapt to changing circumstances and new working methods.

Pro-partnership Adjustments in Working Methods

Before addressing the problems of Gilgit in northeastern Pakistan, Shoab-Sultan Khan of the Aga Khan Rural Development Foundation said that he would first spend three years talking to villagers in the region about their living conditions and development priorities. In stark contrast, the modus operandi for most rural development projects requires the donor agency to quickly specify how many wells will be dug or where and how roads will be built. I cite this example to illustrate how dramatically working methods can differ. It is essential that partners adapt to new working methods. This is true for organizations as well as for individuals. If an aid agency, for example, is hidebound by regulations, the potential of the partnership may be limited, whether or not people within the agency are willing to change.

This point suggests that evaluative criteria should consider the extent to which possible clashes in working methods were considered at the time of project design and commencement.

Outreach and Policy

Partnerships undoubtedly contribute to better outreach, with many partnerships becoming not only innovative but also involving all sorts of different players. For example, for many years the lead combatants against tobacco were health officials—the doctors who were working one-to-one with patients and agitating for stronger public health measures. Leading the attack today, particularly in North America and Europe, are lawyers, who through litigation have significantly changed corporate behavior. Health officials have achieved more by putting health information in the hands of lawyers than they did by advising governments. This new partnership, whose different members have very different motives, is actually winning some battles in the tobacco war.

On policy development, awareness is growing that much more than the official view is needed on many issues. For example, at the UN conference in Cairo on gender issues, in the official building there were 3,000 government delegates, 80 percent of whom were men; meanwhile in the sports stadium were 5,000 NGOs, 80 percent of whose representatives were women. The views coming out of those two assemblies were quite different, but both were essential ingredients in the policymaking process.

This point suggests that the evaluative criteria for policy processes must assess how far the partnership incorporates disparate viewpoints and contradictory elements.

Private Sector Partnerships

Partnerships with the private sector can be particularly constructive in improving public sector efficiency, for example in delivering municipal water services. However, for this kind of arrangement to work requires a great deal of transparency in the contractual relationships. Hence, the civil sector should probably be involved in monitoring, and for equity reasons, communities or NGOs should participate to extend water delivery to the most disadvantaged communities. In addition to how well the contractual elements of the partnership are carried forward, the project itself must ultimately be evaluated in terms of who gets water and how efficiently it is delivered.

Because of conflicting interests, public–private partnerships can be difficult to set up. For example, to an NGO the perfect contraceptive would be inexpensive and long lasting; to the manufacturer, making an inexpensive, long-lasting contraceptive would be commercial suicide. Therefore, evaluative criteria in the assessment of public–private partnerships must take account of the different types of associations involved. The criteria must distinguish between the incentives of the different partners to achieve efficiency as well as sustainability and equity.

Where regulatory effectiveness is an issue, an evaluation may need to assess the transparency of regulations.

Nongovernmental Organizations

NGOs can provide partners when the private sector is not interested and governments are unable to act. Where governments cannot collect and distribute used dental chairs, for example, NGOs can. NGOs can also bring in people who previously have been left out of power structures, including women, ethnic minorities, special interest groups, and, above all, the poor.

In such cases, the evaluative criteria must address the extent to which each partner brings in new capacity. To be able to assess the contributions of each partner to the activity, the evaluation may also need to explore the incentives behind the participation of each. The incentives of a profit-making private sector firm will differ from those of a community-based women's group, for example.

The evaluative criteria must include an assessment of how far the incentives of each partner were aligned during project design.

Assembling Partnerships

A true partnership is shaped in the definitional phase of the issue it addresses. The would-be partners must be in broad agreement on the problem diagnosis and on the type of remedies sought before they can work effectively together. For example, a government might define excessive population growth as a problem of fertility, where an NGO might see it as a function of the low status of women.

Most partnerships ignore the public persuasion phase and disregard the fact that without supporting cultural norms, science and policy change do not influence society. There is a dangerous but common presumption that just because the partners are convinced their goal is valid, the partnership will work. Far too little time is spent evaluating how the partnership and its activities can contribute to reaching the goal. If there is no analysis of what needs to change so that change can occur, the partners will not succeed. For example, in Tamale, Ghana, people did not pay their water bills, and the government did not deliver water. The fundamental question was not simply which design to use for a new water system, but how to change the behaviors of the people and the government. Two basic issues had to be addressed: What had to happen for the system to produce water? And, what had to happen to make people pay their water bills? Until these two questions were resolved, the partnership could not achieve sustainable and equitable water supply services.

Thus, evaluative criteria should examine the extent to which the working methods and means chosen by partners contribute to the accomplishment of project goals.

Some Partnerships that Have Worked

The HIV/AIDS Alliance. The Alliance funneled bilateral donor money to communities in developing countries. Big bilateral donors knew that they could not reach communities on their own, and the solution was to create an intermediary that took on the relationship with the groups on the ground. This partnership worked because there was a good understanding on all sides of where the accountability was and what the expectations were.

River blindness (onchocerciasis). This was a partnership with a light administrative structure. Merck was either unable to supply the drug Ivormectin on the ground or was discouraged from so doing by litigation concerns. A partnership structure involving government committees and local distributors was created to distribute the drug.

The Bangladesh Population Program. In this innovative partnership led by the World Bank, the goal is to bring primary health care and family planning to individual households, using young women as providers. Some of the donors use a common administration. The project has a single organizer, a single methodology, and a single output, but permits all donors to keep their own program guidelines, budgets, and formalities. Although the program has been successful, its monitoring and administrative arrangements have been horrendously complex.

The Child Health Survival Partnership. This may be the most famous of the major health partnerships. Given the institutional rivalries that existed between the World Health Organization and the United Nations Children's Fund, a partnership led by one would have been unacceptable to the other. Instead, the World Bank took the lead in a Task Force on Child Survival that also brought in the United Nations Development Program and the Rockefeller Foundation. Every three months, the partners jointly assessed what they were doing individually and therefore collectively to meet the goal of immunizing all of the world's children. Developing countries were brought in as they signaled an interest in joining the partnership. The partnership was characterized by a few light administrative arrangements and by the freedom of each member to pursue the shared goals of the partnership.

The lessons of these programs emphasize that evaluative criteria should allow for separate elements to be assessed separately. A project can succeed in some measures while being less successful in others.

The Global Water Partnership

I chair the Global Water Partnership (GWP), a near-virtual organization dedicated to creating partnerships that, through Integrated Water Resource Management (IWRM), will change the way the world manages water. The concept is subtle. Worldwide, there is a wealth of experience in action and investment, and a multitude of policies and approaches to water resource management. This experience and knowledge is held variously by practitioners, policymakers, theorists, experts, and users of water, none of whom singly can possibly be aware of all the possibilities for managing water.

GWP uses regional, part-time, and voluntary structures to encourage regional and national organizations to implement the IWRM concept. It also seeks to link the various national dialogues on water policy.

IWRM has four major thrusts: to establish partnerships and mobilize political will; build strategic partnerships for action; promote good practice; and develop and promote regional actions. To support these thrusts, the Global Water Partnership does the following:

- Works with partners to advance the debate on the most important issues and to build on other regional and national debates;
- Supports debates on issues of regional priority, with the goal of achieving a more cross-sectoral approach;
- Provides a discussion platform to advance the debate on controversial issues and acts as a neutral player by organizing roundtables or workshops; and
- Provides input, such as expert submissions, to help achieve informed debate.

Several lessons have emerged:

- Partnership must focus on the ultimate goal; if it focuses only on the intermediate steps, it will fail.
- Partnership should start at the planning stage; it is difficult to realize a vision if no shared vision exists.
- All partners must understand what each of them hopes to achieve. For the purposes of evaluation, the expectations of each partner should be

set down at the beginning. The appraisal process must track these as the project develops.

- There is no standard model for partnership.
- Checklists can be useful.
- It is difficult to change the internal mechanisms of governments, NGOs, and universities. It may be best to superimpose a light collaboration infrastructure that permits the partners to retain their own working methods.
- All parties must understand the obligations of each partner and the rationale behind those obligations.
- Partnerships are not opportunities to convert others.
- Partnerships usually do not enrich the participants, though they can be used to generate funds to pursue the shared goal.
- To the extent possible, each partner should take credit where credit is due. Be sensitive, however, to cultural differences that may give rise to misunderstandings.

Overlapping efforts within the partnership are easy to find because they will result in institutional frictions. Gaps are much more difficult to discover. Part of the surveillance process should thus be a consistent and constant effort to find out where the partnership is weak. The evaluative criteria must take account of what each member brings to the partnership, how conflicts will be resolved, and how the partnership can be made more effective.

Conclusion

A world of new partnership opportunities awaits us. The first policy-based partnerships are just emerging, pulling people together to make sense of complex issues, such as those surrounding genetically modified food and intellectual property management. These new issues cannot solved by regulatory or government agencies alone.

The kinds of labor and environmental issues that anti-globalization protesters are raising must be put on the table with trade and capital issues, and these will need to be addressed by new policy partnerships. New and innovative private sector initiatives, such as ISO 9000 and 9001 certification, triple-bottom-line reporting, and sustainability and environmental reporting must be expanded and replicated.

Governments may have to accept that they are in the second row in the new types of policy partnerships that will develop. This will be a hard and painful adjustment. But problem-solving partnerships are going to change how we deal with the problems we face. Partnerships are, to coin a phrase, a triple E-D: *e*ssential for *d*evelopment, *e*xcruciatingly *d*ifficult, and much *e*asier said than *d*one.

4

Evaluating Partnerships

Elliot Stern

The intent of this chapter is to illustrate the potential of a theory-based approach to partnership evaluation. I shall draw on ideas that come from various bodies of theory, especially organization theory, and from practice-based evaluation studies. I shall not seek to define partnerships or to distinguish among different forms of partnership. Rather, I shall take an inclusive view of the many kinds of sustained inter-organizational arrangements that try to achieve some more or less agreed-upon goal. I do this because I regard the underlying issues as similar across many variants of what are commonly called partnerships.

Issues in Partnership Design

What Partnerships Are Asked to Do

The basis for many contemporary policies is holistic, multifaceted, and complex and the theories that underlie those policies require that the problem-space be conceived of in broad terms. For example, public health policies increasingly address behavioral, environmental, and social issues as well as medical issues (Gwatkin 2000; Evans and Stoddart 1994). Similarly, traditional ideas of schooling are giving way to theories of learning and pedagogy that are embedded in social relations and communities of practice (Lave and Wenger 1991).

"Development" itself has become a contemporary metaphor for system-wide change that seeks to improve performance and to address deep-seated social, institutional, and socioeconomic problems. Development now confronts existing patterns of culture and norms as well as of behavior, and requires that a broad cross-section of stakeholders shift, learn, and develop capacity—if not simultaneously, at least in step with each other.

Elliot Stern is head of Evaluation Studies, The Tavistock Institute, London; president, European Evaluation Society, 2002–03

The Need for Administrative Integration

The broad scope of much contemporary development work requires that diverse actors integrate their actions, typically in relation to a specific geographical territory or domain. The boundaries of public administrations are often ill adjusted to their responsibilities. In part this is the result of historical accidents and more recently the unintended consequence of wholesale reorganization of public sectors through marketization, privatization, and decentralization. Administrations are often specialist rather than generalist, occupying a narrower "niche" than hitherto. Ensuring coherence and integration on the ground requires the different agencies at least to be aware of each other's actions and intentions, and to interrelate their plans, policies, and budgets. This need for integration on the ground demands the concomitant development of inter-administrative partnerships. Furthermore, many public policy tasks require the participation of the private sector and civil society as well.

Consent and Ownership

Development initiatives, as the Comprehensive Development Framework recognizes, are sustainable only when the intended beneficiaries are allowed to shape and take responsibility for them; imposing them from the outside rarely works. They require participation and consent, especially by citizens, intended beneficiaries, and the various expressions of civil society and the "third" sector, including nongovernmental organizations and community-based organizations. A sense of ownership is a precondition of development.

We know from several pieces of evaluative research that partnerships involving beneficiaries, local agencies, and groups can dramatically reduce the costs of implementation (Tavistock Institute 1999a). Successful partnerships can achieve this in various ways—for example, by drawing on local knowledge when developing plans and allocating resources; by advising administrators on better ways to implement plans; by evaluating implementation processes and products; and by taking up the services and resources realized through implementation. Conversely, if a development initiative is seen as irrelevant or imposed, it may end up being underused, neglected, or even vandalized.

The Need to Manage Knowledge

The need to combine different bodies of skill and know-how in order to plan and deliver complex policies means that good knowledge management—knowledge production and knowledge sharing, including the sharing of "organizational memory" (Cibbora and Lanzarra 1994)—is critical. In trans-European vocational training programs, partnerships often act as vehicles for knowledge transfer (Tavistock Institute 1996), suggesting that the need to share knowledge and to draw on dispersed bodies of knowledge and specialization is a factor underpinning the spread of partnerships. The need to produce new knowledge, or to collate knowledge that will enable us to apply what we already know to a specific local or sectoral context, is also driving the decentralization and differentiation of policy contexts.

Evaluation Questions Regarding Partnership Design

Together, these imperatives—to pursue holistic development policy objectives, to integrate administration, to improve implementation and sustainability by increasing participation and consent, and to improve knowledge management—constitute a new organizational ecology (Hannan and Freeman 1977). Ecological approaches to organization suggest that the environments in which organizations operate are more or less likely to offer them opportunities, resources, and supports. The new ecology requires constant renegotiation of organizational boundaries and offers less support to single players or vertically integrated "suppliers"; it can be expected to support the emergence of new organizational populations.

These imperatives also raise a number of evaluation questions, mainly at the design stage, regarding the justification and rationale of partnerships:

- In what ways do the goals being pursued require partnership working? Is the partnership intended to combine complementary expertise, know-how, and resources? Is it intended to implement an innovative response and a new conceptualization of problems and their solutions?
- How inclusive are partnerships? Do they involve all those who will need to learn, adapt, and cooperate in planning, implementation, and delivery? Does the partnership reach those territories and domains where it is expected to have impact?
- How much of a barrier to effective implementation are existing agency or administrative boundaries? What is the scope of the partnership (does it stop at information exchange and consultation, or are programs and budgets modified and shared)?
- Who was involved in the planning and initial definition of partnership tasks? Did this involve potential beneficiaries? And if so, what was their role? Are they informants, priority setters, resource allocators involved in overseeing program management or evaluating progress and outcomes?
- How important is knowledge transfer in a particular partnership? Are there large discrepancies between the partners in know-how and expertise and, if so, how are they being addressed? Is the partnership mainly to transfer knowledge or to produce new knowledge? Are there plans to invest in the partnership's own organizational memory?

Successful Partnerships

There is a high level of agreement among practitioners and theoreticians across various domains—including international development partnerships—on what an ideal partnership should be. Most sources (see, for example, Maxwell and Conway 2002; Picciotto 1998; and Alter and Hage 1993) emphasize that partnerships should be committed to the following:

- a shared vision and shared purposes;
- interdependence and a clear division of labor;
- trust building and capacity development;
- equitable distribution of costs and benefits;
- equality and empowerment of weaker partners; and
- mutual adjustment and learning.

These ideals are consistent with what we find in empirical studies of partnerships. For example, the Tavistock Institute's evaluation of the European Union Structural Fund partnerships (Tavistock Institute 1999a) confirmed that:

- differentiated roles minimize confusion and overlap;
- effective partnerships are characterized by high trust, exemplified by conflict resolution and perceptions of mutual benefit;
- partners in such partnerships learn from each other and adjust to each other's interests; and
- partners in effective partnerships share a vision across the partnership about what they are trying to achieve.

There is also strong evidence on what a well-functioning partnership can achieve. For example, examination of the EU Structural Fund partnerships indicates the achievement of better planned action, better project selection, faster decision making, and greater support for eventual outcomes. Studies of trans-European vocational training partnerships identify as benefits effective knowledge transfer, greater cross-national cooperation, the creation of new networks and capacity development, and penetration of new markets (Tavistock Institute 1996). And an analysis of national programs in the United Kingdom to address the needs of the long-term unemployed (Tavistock Institute 1999b) found that partnerships, when they work well, influence positively employers' recruitment policies toward the unemployed, encourage local ownership of local and regional schemes, and increase the range of training and of jobs offered to those reentering the labor market.

Opening the Partnership "Black Box"

Partnerships do not always work, however. Common problems include the lack of a shared vision, low trust, an uneven balance of influence among partners, and the absence of agreement among the partners that costs and benefits are fairly distributed. As evaluators of partnerships, we need to understand the dynamics underpinning a working partnership—we must open up the black box if we are to explain success and failure and learn for the future. To do this, we should focus on three interlinked bodies of theory concerned with trust, hierarchy, and the relatedness of partnerships to their wider environment.

Partnerships and Trust

Trust is widely acknowledged to be at the heart of a working partnership. It can be framed as arising from predictable behavior among parties, or more positively as confidence about the intentions of others (Gambetta 1988). There are two main theoretical debates about trust, both of which place optimists and pessimists in opposition.

The first debate is between those who see trust accumulating slowly and those who see it accumulating faster. To the pessimists, trust is more likely to be inherited than acquired (Putnam 1993). Optimists, in contrast, believe that trust can be learned through dialogue and practical participation and activity. Many successful partnerships in the European Structural Fund stand on the shoulders of previous partnerships; many successful business alliances bring together companies that have previously worked together.

This distinction is described by Evans (1996) as one of "constructability" and "endowment." I take the view that these are alternative mechanisms rather than alternative explanations of trust creation, however. From an evaluation viewpoint, we need to look at both the inheritance and the acquisition of trust, and recognize that acquisition is more demanding when there is little inheritance on which to build. That is, the measurement of success must take account of the starting position.

The second debate about trust is more serious. There are three camps. Out-and-out pessimists follow the dominant economists' view of human behavior as innately selfish, characterized by free-riding and rent seeking (Olsen 1965) and by the belief that, given the chance, partners will always cheat. In this Hobbesian world, only hierarchical power can ensure order. Circumspect pessimists believe that, while difficult, it is possible to overcome distrust through routine interactions that positively demonstrate reliability and cumulatively provide incentives and reinforce cooperation—achieving what Zucker (1986) calls "process-based" trust. In the third camp are the optimists, who believe in altruism and community, and that cooperative behavior can become the norm. Adler (2001) argues that "modern trust" is a coordinating mechanism that is normative and value-based, and that "a propensity for altruism . . . coexists and competes with a propensity for egoism."

My own reading of these debates is that they are clearly interrelated. In situations of low trust it is indeed difficult to take an optimistic view of human nature. At the same time, if we look at international development partnerships (and many other partnerships that are not simply about market competition) we see much evidence of altruism and cooperative behavior.

These debates on trust point to several important evaluation questions:

- What is the starting level of trust? Are partners inheriting trust or must they create it? What mechanisms are in place to support and develop trust?
- What is the balance of self-interest versus community or altruistic behavior? Are the expectations of partners geared to reciprocity within each transaction or activity round?
- What systems are in place to monitor the evolution of trust? How does trust evolve over time and in relation to different issues?
- What effect does trust have on knowledge management and knowledge transfer among partners?

By including questions about trust in the evaluation of partnership arrangements, we can provide data that can help advance the wider debate about trust in partnerships and other inter-organizational configurations.

Partnerships and Hierarchy

Theories about hierarchy in partnerships are related to theories of trust. A core assumption of pessimists is that hierarchies are necessary to manage the self-interested, the free-riders, and the rent seekers. Karl Weick (1995) suggests that "tight control of core values and beliefs allows for local adaptation in decentralized systems." Optimists, in their turn, see hierarchy as a means of setting fair parameters, facilitating joint working, and articulating common values; Adler (2001) refers to "reflective trust" based on open and equitable exchange that is shaped by hierarchy to ensure fairness and equity, and by competition to ensure innovation.

Empirical studies and evaluations of partnerships support these views. Evaluations of partnership in the EU Structural Funds found that the hierarchical role of European Commission officials within partnerships was often seen to have positive value (Tavistock Institute 1999a), mainly because of the officials' enforcement of regulations and their ability to protect the weaker members of a partnership.

Debates about hierarchy in partnerships also focus attention on how inequalities of power are handled, and on how risks and potential benefits are shared. Most partnerships have unequal partners, and there is a danger where commitment is weak of the risks of partnership being disproportionately imposed on those least able to shoulder them. Studies of the so-called delivery partnerships for unemployed young people in the United Kingdom for example, have found that weaker partners often drop out, perceiving the risks as too high (Tavistock Institute 1999b). In cases such as this, the practice, common in the United Kingdom and elsewhere in Europe, is to use a two-tier hierarchy of a strategic level and an operational or delivery level, to help accommodate partners who lack the resources to commit to extensive partnership activities.

The debate about hierarchy raises several questions for partnership evaluation:

- What are the governance arrangements within the partnership? How are the modus operandi agreed and set? What is done to help the partnership work?
- What are the power relationships? How do the powerful and the less powerful interrelate? How far do the more powerful set most of the partnership objectives?
- Are the risks and rewards equitably shared? Does the distribution of risks take account of the different abilities of partners to carry them?

Partnerships in Their Environment

The third body of theory considers partnership from an inter-organizational and organizational environment (or "open systems") perspective. As Emery and Trist (1965) argued over thirty-five years ago, organizations operate in environments of various degrees of uncertainty, and inter-organizational linkages are seen as a way to manage that uncertainty. This line of thinking is consistent with contemporary ideas of strategic collaboration between firms. In the face of global competition, for example, the automobile industry has pioneered ways of streamlining production through joint ventures and supply chains of linked organizations (Lamming 1993); Johnston and Lawrence (1991) discuss similar partnerships in other industries. According to Lamming, these kinds of supply chains "may require . . . collaborators to view the relationship as a 'quasi-firm' with its own organizational structure and goals, communication mechanisms and culture." Lamming also identifies a tendency toward "equality in partnership: the sharing of responsibility and benefit as a result of increased confidence and cooperation."

Following an "open-systems" perspective partnerships need to represent in their composition, inclusiveness, and dynamic a wider system. To work, they must reproduce this environment within partnership arrangements. There is a subtle balance to be struck here between replication and transformation. Within a context such as this, partners need to construct shared meanings, understandings, vision, and even language if they are to work together. At the same time, however, they must remain open to and in touch with broader networks and constituencies. There is a real danger that a partner can become so committed to the partnership, often adopting the partnership's special language and goals, that it loses touch with and legitimacy in its own hinterland. The consequence is loss of reach, and an inability of the partner to carry, into both the partnership and its own headquarters, its original constituency.

The same can happen with international NGOs. For example, local or regional NGOs in a decentralized structure may begin to adapt to local circumstances and priorities and begin to diverge from the head office perspective. The head office may be driven by its own corporate plan or by the priorities of its main donors. The local/regional office may be more responsive to local/beneficiary priorities. The consequence of partnerships not managing this balance between constructing distinctive understandings and visions and remaining in touch with their natural hinterland is loss of "reach." There is a reduced ability to carry with them a wider constituency whether among administrations in multilaterals or bilaterals or in civil society—or even in their own headquarters.

The same is true for those who participate in partnerships at the level of their own organization. To work, partnership nearly always requires internal change within the participating organizations. To work in a partnership, an organization must devolve authority on to those who represent it within the partnership. A simple demonstration of failure to devolve in this manner was recently encountered in a number of employment and regeneration partnerships in the United Kingdom (Tavistock Institute 1999b). Some of the participating partners had decentralized and de-layered, and as a result their representatives around the table could commit their organizations. Others had not adapted in the same way.

Evaluators need to address certain questions deriving from the environmental, open systems, and inter-organizational understanding of partnerships:

- What characterizes the environment within which a partnership operates? Is it relatively stable or highly uncertain? Does the strength of inter-organizational links match the environment concerned?
- Does the partnership add value? Does it constrain the independence of partners more than it enhances their capabilities?
- Is there tension between partnership commitment and legitimacy within the broader organization or system from which partners come? Are partners able to carry their own natural constituencies? If not, are there implications for partnership reach?
- Do the partner organizations face demands for internal change as a result of partnership working? Are there differences in the degree to

which partners have adapted to such demands? Do these create difficulties for partnership working?

Designing Evaluation Frameworks for Partnerships

Highlighting the dynamics and issues likely to be faced in partnerships, and posing evaluation questions, are important first steps in designing evaluation frameworks for partnerships. However, the way that such perspectives are implemented will vary considerably with the purpose of the evaluation (see, for example, Arvidsson 1986; Stern, Cullen, and Kelleher 1992; Stern 1993; and Chelimsky 1997). There are four main evaluation purposes: evaluation as design, as development, as management, and as explanation. Each purpose will be salient in some settings, but may be irrelevant in others.

Evaluation as Design

Evaluation at the design stage is very much an appraisal or ex ante exercise. It allows us to do the following:

- contextualize what we know, because general principles and rules need to be understood in specific settings;
- explicate assumptions, especially about the justification for partnerships, because those who create partnerships are often not clear about their rationale and goals;
- identify mechanisms and pathways, because it is at the design stage that one should begin to identify how program activities are expected to lead to desired results; and
- set reasonable goals, because these will provide a benchmark against which future progress can be judged, both in terms of implementation and of results.

Evaluation as Development

Evaluation itself can be seen as a developmental activity contributing to better implementation and capacity building among program participants or partners. Formative evaluation will often pursue such developmental purposes, allowing mid-term corrections in the course of program implementation. The intent here is to give partners enough feedback to allow them to learn, and if necessary, to modify their initial plans. Evaluation as development allows us to achieve the following:

- exchange knowledge, because evaluation offers the opportunity for structured exchange of knowledge in the course of program implementation;
- enhance capacity at both partner and partnership levels, because evaluation experience shows that program failures are often the result of capacity problems rather than low commitment by partners;

- develop trust and consensus, because evaluation can itself be part of a learning process through which diverse objectives and intentions can be reviewed and revised; and
- reinforce vision, because the initial visions of partnerships will often need to be refocused as program implementation advances.

Evaluation as Management

Accountability and management are among the most commonly identified purposes of evaluation. One of the major and most problematic transitions that occur once a partnership has been established is the shift from associates brought together by shared goals and visions to an executive body with day-to-day management responsibilities. An evaluation that begins at the design stage by explicating assumptions and clarifying goals can become a powerful ongoing tool for reinforcing this transition within partnerships.

Evaluation as management allows us to do the following:

- monitor progress, because an ongoing evaluation will produce regular outputs in relation to plans and targets;
- provide feedback, because evaluation in a partnership context will need to engage with a broad cross-section of partners as well as program managers;
- support reflection, because for decisions to be made on the basis of monitoring and feedback, information must be interpreted and reframed and the implications of actions understood; and
- enable accountability to external stakeholders and the broader constituencies from which partners are drawn, because such stakeholders will wish to receive progress reports along the way.

Evaluation as Explanation

To learn lessons and improve performance across different programs and partnerships, program evaluators need to explain as well as describe. It could be argued that this requirement crosses the boundary between evaluation and research, and the nature of explanation in evaluation and in the social and economic sciences more generally is today the subject of vigorous debate (Pawson and Tilley 1997; Davies, Nutley, and Smith 2000).Without entering this debate, I would simply assert that evaluation and evaluation research activity that aspires to explanation share a number of common elements.

Evaluation as explanation allows us to do the following:

- specify evaluation questions, because such questions should be the basis for an explanatory exercise, the development of hypotheses, and the choice of methods;

- develop models and hypotheses to pick causal pathways and mechanisms that are assumed to influence effectiveness;
- gather systematic data, probably triangulated, because of the importance of cross-checking and validating findings, especially in complex multi-actor programs; and
- compare similar inputs across different contexts and different inputs in similar contexts, or in the classical formulation of "realist" evaluation (Pawson and Tilley 1997), to understand mechanisms in context.

Partnership as Means or End?

There is broad agreement within the evaluation and policy communities that, while processes and implementation mechanisms are important, the justification for public policy interventions is that they deliver real results to their intended beneficiaries (Hanna and Picciotto 2002; Roche 1999). In this context, partnerships are commonly thought of as a means rather than an end.

In international development, however, the distinction between means and ends is often unclear. David Ellerman (2002) has argued that development assistance "must be autonomy-compatible," and that "transformation can come only from within." This view is consistent with the Comprehensive Development Framework introduced by the World Bank and with much of the work of the OECD Development Assistance Committee (OECD DAC 1998). In relation to partnerships, we can reasonably regard processes that help beneficiaries to formulate their own development strategies, that encourage ownership and commitment, and that help create a development consensus that involves governments, the private sector, and civil society, as contributing to the goals of development.

In long-term development initiatives, there is often a need to identify intermediate outcomes along the chain of anticipated and planned results, whose achievement would signal the success of partnership arrangements. This arguably would support regarding the evaluation of partnerships as in part addressing ends as well as means.

Conclusions and a Modest Proposal

The underlying rationale of this chapter is the belief that the evaluation of partnerships in international development, as in other domains, could be advanced by insights derived from organizational theory. Using these insights would allow us to design better partnerships by opening up the black box of partnership, working to improve partnership effectiveness and to learn lessons for the future.

I conclude with a modest proposal: that we develop the framework for partnership evaluation outlined in this chapter in collaboration with practitioners and development agencies active in international development partnerships. Taking this forward in a collaborative and action research mode would offer the prospect not only of applying theoretical insights about partnerships in the world of international development, but also of developing new theories and understandings through the experience of practitioners. The results could be of value to everyone, across many public policy domains, who works with partnerships.

References

Adler, Paul S. 2001. "Markets, Hierarchies, and Trust: The Knowledge Economy and the Future of Capitalism." *Organizational Science* 12(2): 215–34.

Alter, Catherine, and Jerald Hage. 1993. *Organizations Working Together*. Newbury Park, Calif.: Sage.

Arvidsson, G. 1986. "Performance Evaluation." In F-X. Kaufmann, G. Majoney, and V. Ostrom, eds., *Guidance, Control and Evaluation in the Public Sector*. Berlin, Germany: De Gruyter.

Chelimsky, E. 1997. "Thoughts for a New Evaluation Society." *Evaluation* 3(1): 97–109.

Cibbora, C., and G. F. Lanzarra. 1994. "Formative Contexts and Information Technology: Understanding the Dynamics of Innovation in Organizations." *Accounting, Management and Information Technology* 4(2): 61–86.

Davies, H. T. O., S. M. Nutley, and P. C. Smith. 2000. *What Works? Evidence-Based Policy and Practice in Public Services*. Bristol, U.K.: Policy Press.

Ellerman, D. P. 2002. "Helping People Help Themselves: Autonomy-Compatible Assistance." In Nagy Hanna and Robert Picciotto, eds., *Making Development Work: Development Learning in a World of Poverty and Wealth*. New Brunswick, N.J.: Transaction.

Emery, F., and E. L. Trist. 1965. "The Causal Texture of Organizational Environments." *Human Relations* 18(1): 21–32.

Evans, P. 1996. "Government Action, Social Capital and Development: Reviewing the Evidence on Synergy." *World Development* 24(6): 1119–32.

Evans, R. G., and G. L. Stoddart. 1994. "Producing Health, Consuming Care." In R. G. Evans and T. R. Marmor, eds., *Why Are Some People Healthy and Others Not?* New York: De Gruyter.

Gambetta, D. 1988. "Can We Trust Trust?" In D. Gambetta, ed., *Trust: Making and Breaking Cooperative Relations*. Oxford: Blackwell.

Gwatkin, D. R. 2000. "Health Inequalities and the Health of the Poor: What Do We Know? What Can We Do?" *Bulletin of World Health Organization* 78(1): 3–18.

Hanna, Nagy, and Robert Picciotto (eds.). 2002. *Making Development Work: Development Learning in a World of Poverty and Wealth*. New Brunswick, N.J.: Transaction.

Hannan, Michael T., and John H. Freeman. 1977. "The Population Ecology of Organizations." *American Journal of Sociology* 82: 929–64.

Johnston, R., and Paul R. Lawrence. 1991. "Beyond Vertical Integration: The Rise of the Value-Adding Partnership." In G. Thompson, J. Frances, R. Levacic, and J. Mitchell, eds., *Markets Hierarchies and Networks: The Coordination of Social Life*. Thousand Oaks, Calif.: Sage.

Lamming, Richard. 1993. *Beyond Partnership: Strategies for Innovation and Lean Supply*. Englewood Cliffs, N.J.: Prentice-Hall.

Lave, J., and E. Wenger. 1991. *Situated Learning: Legitimate Peripheral Participation*. New York: Cambridge University Press.

Maxwell, Simon, and Tim Conway. 2002."Partnerships." In Nagy Hanna and Robert Picciotto, eds., *Making Development Work: Development Learning in a World of Poverty and Wealth*. New Brunswick, N.J.: Transaction.

OECD DAC (Organisation for Economic Co-operation and Development's Development Assistance Committee). 1998. "Strengthening Development Partnerships: A Working Checklist." Washington, D.C.: World Bank.

Olsen, M. 1965. *The Logic of Collective Action*. Cambridge, Mass.: Harvard University Press.

Pawson, R., and N. Tilley. 1997. *Realistic Evaluation*. London: Sage.

Picciotto, Robert. 1998. *The Logic of Partnership*. Washington, D.C.: World Bank.

Putnam, R. 1993. *Making Democracy Work: Civic Traditions in Modern Italy*. Princeton, New Jersey: Princeton University Press.

Roche, C. 1999. *Impact Assessment for Development Agencies*. London: Oxfam.

Scott, W. R. 1981. *Organizations: Rational, Natural and Open Systems*. Englewood Cliffs, N.J.: Prentice-Hall.

Stern, E. D. 1993. "Ongoing and Participative Evaluation." *Research Evaluation* 3(2):75–82.

Stern, E. D., J. Cullen, and J. Kelleher. 1992. "The Evaluation of Artisan (Telematics and Rural Development)." European Commission Working Paper.

Tavistock Institute. 1999a. "The Thematic Evaluation of the 'Partnership Principle' in European Union Structural Funds." Brussels: Commission of the European Communities.

———. 1999b. "Evaluation of New Deal for Young Unemployed People: National Case Studies of Delivery and Impact." London: Employment Service.

———. 1996. "The Evaluation of the FORCE Programme of Continuing Vocational Training." Brussels: Commission of the European Communities.

Weick, K. E. 1995. *Sense-Making in Organizations*. Thousand Oaks, Calif.: Sage.

Zucker, L. 1986. "Production of Trust: Institutional Sources of Economic Structure 1840–1920." *Research in Organizational Behavior* 8: 53–111

5

Evaluation of, for, and through Partnerships

Robert Klitgaard

Partnerships are growing rapidly in business, international development, and public policy generally. This phenomenon brings daunting but exciting challenges for evaluators. The first problem is defining just what *partnership* might mean.[1] As Robert Axelrod pointed out earlier in this book, there may be analogues to the Prisoner's Dilemma, where proceeding without partnership leads both participants to worse outcomes than they might have achieved had they properly taken into account their strategic interaction. Partnerships may be analyzed in terms of gains from trade, where one party is good at wheat, the other at iron, or complementarities, where one is good at marketing, and the other at production, and we decide to join forces. In all these situations, one can speak of potential gains to be had from recognizing strategic interdependence, and therefore not thinking like myopic individuals.

Enthusiasm for these potential gains is widespread. The World Economic Forum's annual report describes a partnership craze in business. The CEO of Hewlett-Packard explained that "companies are functioning more like living organisms in an ecosystem of other organisms. Corporations can no longer be self-sufficient. They must be constructed around partnerships." The CEO of Merrill Lynch observed: "For over a hundred years, Merrill Lynch never did a thing that wasn't strictly Merrill Lynch. In the past three to five years, [we] have developed more joint ventures and partnerships than you could count" (McAdoo 2001, p. 40).

In international development, too, talk of partnerships abounds. The word partnership has been applied to relations between rich and poor countries, between donors and recipients, especially recently but also in the past. The World Bank's president, James Wolfensohn, has been among the most eloquent advocates: "I cannot stress enough the importance of partnerships. The

---

Robert Klitgaard is professor of International Development and Security, Rand Graduate School

task ahead is too formidable for any single institution or set of institutions to tackle. Every one of us has a role to play. Halving poverty by 2015 is possible, but only if we concert our efforts in a new way."[2] The flavor of some of the rhetoric is captured in the title of a recent report: Partnership Alchemy (Copenhagen Center 2000).[3]

In public policy around the world, partnerships are becoming increasingly prevalent. More and more, the challenge is to enable the institutions of government, of the private sector, and of civil society to work together (see, for example, Weisbrod 1997; Boris and Steuerle 1999; and Vaillancourt Rosenau 2000). Moreover, evaluation is seen as crucial for these partnerships to work. Consider these examples:

- Better schools will be forged through partnerships of communities and education providers, including both public schools and the private sector. Results-oriented education demands excellent evaluation, including better measures of quality, the design of incentive systems, and the design and management of interactions of the public sector, citizens, and the private sector.
- Health care will become fairer and more efficient by becoming more client-driven, more sensitive to competition, and more accountable for results. Again, it becomes crucial to forge and manage effective partnerships between the public, private, and nonprofit sectors and the consumers of health care and to evaluate these partnerships carefully.

From roads to water supply, from electrification to environmental projects, infrastructure increasingly involves partnerships of the public and private sectors in their design, finance, and management. Communities also play a key role in deciding what is done and how, and in monitoring progress. These partnerships require evaluations of the first order, including excellent economic and engineering analyses, policy frameworks, information systems, and data analysis.

International security increasingly involves partnerships of many kinds. Operations other than war involve the military in deeper relationships with civil society, government, international organizations, and business. Moreover, defense policy requires greater understanding of public-private collaboration to deal with terrorism, organized crime, and the vulnerability of the information infrastructure. What kinds of partnerships between businesses, communities, and government seem most promising for what kinds of security risks? What are the dangers and costs of such partnerships?

Research suggests that the trend toward partnerships will continue (Purcell forthcoming; Bobbitt 2002). One driver is technology, including the communications revolution, which enables partnerships within and across borders (Antón, Silberglitt, and Schneider 2001). Other drivers are more difficult to measure, and they may be dependent rather than independent variables—for example, changing perceptions about the role of the state (Treverton 2001; May 1997).

If partnerships between government, business, and civil society are the wave of the future, what does this mean for policy research and evaluation? It means three things. We will be doing more evaluations of partnerships. We will be doing more evaluations for partnerships. And we will be engaging in more partnerships to do our evaluations.

Evaluations of Partnerships

Let us begin by distinguishing three levels of evaluation questions regarding partnerships.

Level 1. Benefits and Costs for a Specific Partner

The first-level question focuses on a particular partner. It asks, "How good is this kind and degree of partnership for this partner?"

The evaluation asks about the benefits and costs of the partnership, compared with alternatives. Familiar evaluation problems of selection bias,[4] intervening variables, and power[5] can be expected to be severe here. We will focus on another matter: What are the relevant benefits and costs?

The benefits may be of many kinds. A recent publication of the World Bank's Business Partnership and Outreach Group lists eight possible benefits for business, among them "to enhance or rebuild brand image/corporate reputation" and "to address public accountability issues or market failures." Among the seven possible benefits for "communities/our clients" are efficiency, effectiveness, equity, and sustainability (World Bank 2000b).[6]

Some supposed benefits often are not enunciated publicly, including prestige, political insulation, and co-optation. These motives have, I believe, been dominant in many recent business–NGO partnerships and, perhaps, in "the partnership craze" at the World Bank, where partnerships can be an effort "to enhance or rebuild brand image/corporate reputation."

Costs are also important, if frequently forgotten in exhortations to partnership.[7] One begins to hear worried voices among those being asked to enter partnerships. The mundane transactions costs of interacting, coordinating, and partnering can loom large in practice. These costs have been highlighted in internal World Bank studies that interviewed managers involved in partnerships. (One is reminded of the adage "No one likes to be coordinated.")[8]

There are also opportunity costs. For example, last year at the World Bank, an initial survey found that the Bank was a member of eighty-seven global and regional partnerships. Worried about the costs of too many partnerships, the Bank's management asked how such partnerships could be evaluated.

How should the Bank decide in advance which partnerships to join and how to participate? In response to this question, a "discussion note" laid out these evaluation criteria:

> To ensure that the Bank fulfills its mission, it needs to be able to be selective in its role and only participate in initiatives with the greatest possible development impact, the best leverage of resources, and the strongest synergies with other partners. A clear direction for the Bank then is to make sure that its work at the global level contributes to poverty reduction and builds on its core expertise—developing and helping to implement country-based programs. (World Bank 2000c)[9]

Other costs are important but difficult to measure. NGOs, for example, have been fearful of partnerships diluting their mission, silencing their voices, and bureaucratizing their cultures (Hulme and Edwards 1997). Similar worries have been expressed about government institutions being undermined by outsourcing, public–private partnerships, and even by regulation. Consider the phenomenon of "regulatory capture," wherein regulatory agencies are diverted from their public purposes through their interactions with the regulatees (Laffont and Tirole 1991).

Level 2. Evaluating Partnerships as a Whole

A second level of evaluation focuses on the overall results of a partnership and on the allocation of tasks within it.

At one level, the evaluation question is to estimate the benefits and costs accruing to the partnership as a whole, as compared with alternatives. As with evaluations at level 1, empirical estimation will be plagued by a lack of controlled experiments and, therefore, by the problems of correcting for selection bias, of choosing appropriate independent variables, and of getting a large enough sample to enable a useful measure of confidence.

The evaluator may be asked to identify where and how public–private–nonprofit partnerships of specific kinds are likely to make sense. Can an evaluator look at intermediate or proxy variables where theory or experience suggests correlates of successful partnerships? For example, what are the analogues to gains from trade? When does it pay to make, versus buy? What are the pros and cons of horizontal integration?[10]

Recent work adds new insights. What does government do, what does business do, what do NGOs and civil society do—and of course, for foreign assistance, what do donors do? Robert Picciotto uses economic classifications of goods (such as their excludability and their jointness in consumption) to derive the distinctive advantages of government hierarchy, decentralized market, and civil society cooperation (Picciotto 1995; see also Savas 2000). Some kinds of goods seem particularly suited to provision by one or another of these institutions; for example, public goods by government, private goods by the market, and common pool resources by NGOs. Picciotto's framework also permits the analysis of intermediate goods, such as toll goods, which should involve both state and market. And most interestingly for our problem, it suggests new ways to analyze partnerships for addressing complicated issues. For example, to enable new seeds to make a difference in Malawi, it has been suggested that some parts of the solution belong to the state (funding research and development), some to the market (distributing new seed varieties), and some to NGOs (mobilizing farmers to enable group credit). Other new work is suggestive for evaluators. Dennis Young analyzes metaphors of interaction between NGOs and the state, including substitutes, adversaries, and complements (Young 1999). There also is promise in applying contract theory to partnerships among government, business, and civil society, where a key area to evaluate is the allocation of residual rights (those that cannot be specified in the partnership "contract") (Hart, Shleifer, and Vishny 1997; Besley and Ghatak 1999).

On a more practical level, the Prince of Wales' Business Leaders Forum provides guidelines for evaluating partnerships (IBLF 2000). It presents useful lists of things to evaluate for the partnership as a whole and for each of the partners: needs, inputs, process, and outputs.

Even so, the lists leave out some of the most important motives and outcomes. On the positive side, partnerships may build trust, enable negotiation, reduce violence, undergird a social contract, inhibit government discretion, and enable freer flows of information.[11] On the negative side, partnerships may enable corruption and cronyism, reduce diversity, and inhibit innovation.

For example, Jose Edgardo Campos and Hilton Root studied various public–private policy partnerships in East Asia, especially "deliberation councils" involving people from industry, the government, academia, and in some cases, the press, consumer groups, and labor (Campos and Root 1996). Campos and Root extolled the benefits mentioned in the previous paragraph as the key to the East Asian economic miracle. In contrast, after the East Asian economic crisis of 1997, some critics cited these same partnerships as catalysts of crony capitalism and corruption, which rendered these countries more vulnerable. The evaluator's lesson is to look for both the benefits and costs of partnerships, and for many varieties thereof.

Level 3. Evaluating the Enabling Environment

A third level of the evaluation question concerns the environment in which partnerships of various kinds emerge or do not emerge and function well or function badly.

Consider the analogy of industrial policy. A level 2 question is: "What sort of industry should a government subsidize (in other words, what kind of partnership is beneficial, given the alternatives)?" The level 3 question is "How can government create an environment in which industries will develop optimally over time?"

At Rand we are asking: "Under what conditions will what forms of hybrid governance tend to function well?" We are exploring how partnerships are affected by:

- better measures of quality of service and quality of life;
- better estimates of institutional performance;[12]
- how well incentives are aligned with performance, within and across institutions; and
- the cost of information flows, which in turn affects learning and feedback.

Thus we are struggling with another broad and important category of conditions, those having to do with the social and cultural setting of the partnership. Many contextual factors can affect the benefits and costs of partnerships and, indeed, whether partnerships emerge at all. How to grasp the many possible interactions between (aspects of) partnership and (aspects of) the social and cultural setting remains a daunting challenge, in theory and in practice (Klitgaard 1995, 1997).

Here one must also ask, what are the disabling conditions for hybrid governance? Partnership has a nether side, which may abet market power, cronyism, and corruption. Pranab Bardhan has pointed out the troubling persistence of dysfunctional institutions. He criticizes the benign view (he refers especially to institutional economics), which tends to "understate the tenacity of vested interests, the enormity of the collective action problems in bringing about institutional change, and the differential capacity of different social groups in mobilization and coordination" (Bardhan 2000).

There are two taboos in discussions of partnerships with developing countries that evaluation must confront. First, is the question of incompetence. One of the partners may not only have less capacity technically or managerially but may actually be incompetent. Technical assistance is sometimes woeful, as are so-called international experts; this much we are allowed to say.[13] But so-called local counterparts are often so poorly paid and so badly trained that partnering with them creates special challenges and perils. This much is taboo to say.

Second, is the problem of dysfunctional institutions. Calls for partnership and for local ownership ring hollow if the owners are systematically corrupt.

We are active in an imperfect world, and often the places where we are most called to action are those with the gravest problems of incompetence and the most dysfunctional institutions. To put it another way, some of those who advocate local ownership of aid simultaneously criticize examples of aid ownership by past politicians, for example in Indonesia, Peru, and Nigeria. Similarly, a renewed emphasis in donor circles on capacity building and on fighting corruption combines awkwardly with calls for local ownership, causing rhetorical and practical tensions in organizations such as Britain's Department for International Development, NORAD in Norway, and the World Bank.

Evaluation may actually enable local ownership under conditions of low capacity and dubious probity. Evaluations abet accountability. Objective, independent information about performance enables both sides of the partnership to make credible commitments. But any evaluation must be realistic about the levels of technical competence on all sides of the partnership, and must both countenance and counteract the real temptations for corruption, self-congratulation, and conceptual hectoring.[14] Evaluation can be part of the problem (when vitiated by incompetence or nullified by corruption), but it also can be part of the solution to both taboo topics.

An evaluation at level three should focus on such aspects as the availability of good information about quality of service and about performance, the incentives within and across organizations, and the (admittedly poorly theorized) social and cultural context. It should also frankly assess the capacities of the partners and the likelihood of abuse of power and corruption. Finally, it should recognize the possibly strategic role of evaluation in difficult settings: evaluations can, in fact, be enablers of productive partnerships and antidotes to abusive ones.

Evaluating for Partnerships

Now let us switch to a second dimension of evaluating partnerships, where the client or audience for the evaluation is a partnership. In the past, the clients of policy research and evaluations were mostly governments, including states and localities; this was true even when the actual sponsors were private foundations, consortia of companies, or the World Bank. Now the context is changing rapidly and sometimes dramatically. Increasingly, I believe, the clients for our evaluations will be multiple, just as the partners in development activities are multiple. We will be preparing evaluations for donors, governments, businesses, NGOs, and citizens of many stripes.

This prospect opens a huge area for discussion and learning. For example, what kinds of evaluation outputs are most useful for what kinds of people and groups; indeed, for what kinds of partnerships? How does the process of evaluation itself influence the partnership relationship?

Space does not permit an extended discussion, but I would like to provide an example of how the evaluation process can help partnerships develop and succeed.

In 1998, the "big three" U.S. automobile manufacturers—General Motors, Daimler-Chrysler, and Ford—and the United Auto Workers' union (UAW) decided to partner in an evaluation of forty-three managed care plans. The Rand Corporation was selected to help with this evaluation under a steering committee that included the three automobile companies, the UAW, the state of Michigan (as an employer and a purchaser of service for Medicaid enrollees), and the Greater Detroit Area Health Council.

The evaluation task was technically challenging. Quality has many dimensions, including quality of care, cost, and coverage, across many kinds of services; available data are sometimes incomplete; and the participants in the different managed care plans differ. More to the point I wish to make here, the client for the evaluation is a partnership—and one where distrust is endemic.[15] For example, the UAW suspects that the companies will be tempted to misrepresent different health plans in the interest of saving money. The ultimate audience for the evaluation, the auto workers, will need the results in a form they can understand and use.

So, how should an evaluation of forty-three health plans proceed? One approach might be this: Develop an empirical database for each health plan. Then standardize the dimensions of quality, cost, and coverage to the different populations each health plan serves—for example, different age groups and different regions, which may have different profiles of health service needs. Analyze the results and present the findings in a report.

This approach is fine as far as it goes, but it neglects two aspects of evaluating for a partnership:

- First, the results should be intelligible to all the partners. Rand and its clients worked hard to develop different ways of enabling workers to assess the quality of the different plans. We developed a scorecard with one to five stars in each of four categories of quality: access and service, doctor communication and service, staying healthy, and getting better/living with illness.
- Second, an evaluation can not only improve the choices of auto workers, it can also help the interactions among workers, companies, and government become more trusting, less conflict-laden, more transparent, and more effective. In fact, a key aspect of Rand's evaluation was a collaborative process. Every month, Rand researchers met with the steering committee to review objectives, explain interim results, get feedback, make changes, and assist the partners to work together on improving health.

In an interview this year, I asked the UAW representative what the most important benefit of the evaluation had been. He said, "The process and the information enabled all of us to negotiate better. It gave us a common ground, and it built trust." This sort of benefit may be more important in the long run than the better choices about health plans that the workers were able to make.

Evaluations through Partnerships

Evaluations through partnerships have a further element: using the comparative advantage of each partner.

This is not the place to discuss the benefits and costs of such areas as participatory evaluation. But I will say that I find some of the literature on this subject one-sided (emphasizing the benefits but not the costs)[16] and incomplete (the lists of benefits and costs both tend to leave out some of the most important dynamics).

Partners potentially can bring different strengths—legitimacy, technical capacity, local knowledge, funding, convening authority, and so forth—to the various stages of the evaluation process (such as setting the agenda, carrying out the study, interpreting the results, dissemination, and implementing change). In principle, the quality of the evaluation can be improved in many ways by combining forces.

However, evaluation partnerships also have costs of many kinds, including the aforementioned costs of coordination and various opportunity costs. Moreover, as we have already seen, partnerships can have broad impacts on the dynamics of each partner and on future iterations of the partnership relation. These can be good, as when they build trust and enable economies of coordination. They can also be bad, as when they co-opt weaker partners and subvert their missions and cultures and the competencies of individual partners, or when they reduce the diversity of views.

Recent articles warn that seeking consensus through partnerships can limit diversity and creativity. For example: "Although it does not ensure a fair and inclusive dialogue, the representation and exploration of dissensus helps to protect us from the false assurance of an articulated consensus that may under-represent, misrepresent, or exclude groups of voices within the community" (Moss and Schutz 2001; see also Gregory, McDaniels, and Fields 2001). Evaluation partnerships must be managed in a way that tries to value and preserve dissenting perspectives.

The message for evaluators is that these partnership issues are rich areas for hardheaded research.

Conclusion

What does the new age of partnerships mean for evaluation? It means a change of what we evaluate (partnerships), for whom we evaluate (partners as clients), and with whom we evaluate (with partners). In other words, we can anticipate changes in what we do, for whom we do it, what skills we need, and what products we produce. I do not pretend to be able to specify all these changes, but I have tried to suggest some of their characteristics, with an eye on thinking together about our priorities and how we might partner to pursue them.

Evaluation of Partnerships

Each partner will ask the evaluation question: "Is this partnership worth it for me?" Or a better question: "What are the costs and benefits to us and our mission from various kinds of partnerships; structured how; managed how?" Evaluators can think about answering this in two ways. One is the metaphor of the experimental trial. Another is the metaphor of theoretical analysis, where one might use economics, organization theory, and the analysis of bureaucratic politics to suggest guidance. One might also use hypotheses for middle-level generalizations.

Those engaged in partnerships, and those who fund them, regulate them, or permit them to exist, may ask a second question: "Is this partnership achieving its social objectives?" Or a better question: "What are the short-term and long-term social costs and benefits of various ways of structuring and managing various kinds of partnerships, given the task at hand and a host of contextual factors?" Again, one might imagine an empirical approach to this question based on an experiment, or on regression-style statistical analysis to control for the various intervening variables. Theory may also help, even though we are at a nascent stage.

There is a third important question: "What policies and contexts enable partnerships?" Or a better one: "Under what conditions do what kinds of partnerships tend to emerge for what kinds of issues, with what kinds of social consequences, in the short run and the long run?" These are difficult questions in the best of circumstances.

In all of these areas, I find blind spots. Advocates of partnerships tend to downplay costs. Lists of benefits tend to be incomplete, leaving out some of the most important ones. And the dynamics of partnerships, both positive and negative, are underemphasized.

Evaluations for Partnerships

Two new issues arise. First, different partners have different needs for information. Second, the way evaluations are done can lead the partnerships to new benefits. Evaluations are strategic, especially in situations in which trust is low, competence is limited, and corruption is present.

Evaluation through Partnerships

As more actors are involved in designing and implementing programs and projects, more actors will be involved in evaluating them. How should evaluations be optimally designed, given the attributes of the different partners? How should they be carried out, again to improve the partnership itself? How can joint evaluations avoid the risks of premature consensus and a loss of diversity?

Moving Forward

How should we begin to address these formidable challenges? There is what might be called the purist's dream. Here one imagines specifying and identifying the appropriate model of all the factors that affect the various benefits and costs of partnership, including endogeneity and dynamics (including path dependence). One imagines pulling together valid and reliable data on all the benefits and costs and intervening variables, including subjective and value-laden judgments and perceptions. One then dreams of having enough cases to be able to estimate the model—to say what partnerships work, in what senses, when—and therefore to be able to provide scientific guidance to the designers of and participants in partnerships.

Dream on. It hasn't happened, and probably never will. This admittedly sweet dream is useful only in reminding us of how incomplete are our own mechanical evaluations. There are, however, alternatives.

When I was a graduate student, I worked one summer in Peru's Institute of National Planning. The Peruvian government wanted to evaluate the foreign aid it received, as part of an effort to get ownership of the aid. There were more than 200 aid projects, ranging from rural roads to immunization to environmental protection to the development of the fishing industry. The dream evaluation would have been a social benefit–cost analysis of each project, then taking those results and adding variables about sector, donor, project design, participation, and who knows what, to get a model of when what kinds of aid projects work, in what senses, in and for Peru.

In the real world, of course, there were three people in our office and few funds. We had almost no data on social benefits, and only a few on costs. We couldn't even get the Peruvian policymakers to agree on what the metrics for "social benefits" might be.

After a couple of weeks, I wrote to one of my professors, the great statistician Frederick Mosteller. I described the task and its impossibility, and I implicitly laid that impossibility on the dream model of evaluation I thought I had been learning from him.

Professor Mosteller wrote back. In effect, he said: "People can never agree on what benefits and costs are. But they can and do agree on outrageous successes and outrageous failures. Find these among your projects. Study them. Compare them. Share your results, and learn some more."

We followed his advice. It worked, in several senses. The Peruvians and the donors used the results to stimulate their own knowledge and thereby to generate tentative conclusions about some of the ingredients of successful and unsuccessful aid projects. The donors were impressed and cut the Peruvians more slack in deciding what projects would be funded and how the projects should be structured. My Peruvian boss was promoted and then was plucked away by the United Nations Development Program to replicate this evaluation system for foreign aid in two Central American countries (Klitgaard 1975).

Can we also be inspired by Professor Mosteller's advice?[17] Might we together study examples of outrageous success (and, later, of outrageous failure) in the separable aspects of evaluations of partnerships, for partnerships, and through partnerships?

Can we locate excellent evaluations of partnerships, in the three senses mentioned above (from the perspective of a single partner, of the entire partnership, and of the enabling environment for partnerships)? Can we identify superb cases of evaluations for partnerships, where the way the evaluation was done and presented helped each partner and helped the partnership as a whole? And can we find examples of evaluations done through partnerships—where, for example, government agencies, business firms, NGOs, citizens, donors, and researchers have used their different resources to create joint learning?

As we find these examples, how might we then share them with one another and with those partners and see what kinds of creative insights they generate? Might such an undertaking be an early priority for the International Development Evaluation Association (IDEAS)?

Notes

1. For a review of recent usage, see Maxwell and Conway (2000) and Eriksson (2001). Three decades ago the Pearson report talked about partnership for development. This led to a stream of titles contesting aid as partnership; see, for example, Nelson (1971) and Albert (1973).
2. See *http://www.worldbank.org/partners/*.
3. The alchemy metaphor is designed, perhaps unsuccessfully, to refer to situations in which, in the words of the Center's Web site, "participants seek to achieve more than the sum of their individual parts by creating leverage and synergy based on and between key components of the partnership—context, purpose, participants, organization, and outcomes." See *http://www.copenhagencentre.org/TCCWEB/TCCWEB.NSF/K_Concepts/K222?OpenDocument*.
4. For example, if one compares partnerships with other situations in which partnerships have not been formed, one may not be able to control for unobserved variables that influence both the likelihood of joining a partnership and the success of that partnership. One's estimate of the productivity of being in a partnership will be biased.
5. Apparently the most detailed study of partnerships in a development context is the book *Evaluation and the Collaborative State* (Gray, et al. forthcoming). The study contains twenty-five observations, which is still too small to enable sophisticate statistical analysis.
6. It is of course a long way from a typology of benefits to their careful measurement in a specific case, and in international development I know of no exemplar.
7. The UK alliance InterAct "believes that the shift to a focus on collaborative processes is key to democratic renewal, social inclusion, sustainable development, and a vibrant civil society." InterAct also recognizes the importance of evaluation.

While its working paper lists many potential benefits, however, it details none of the direct and indirect costs (InterAct 2001).

8. A point once made by Robert Chambers could be made about "partnership" substituted for "coordination." "'Integration' and 'coordination' can be seen to have heavy costs as well as benefits. . . . The word 'coordination' provides a handy means for avoiding responsibility for clear proposals. It is perhaps the reason that it is much favored by visiting missions who are able to conceal their ignorance of how an administrative system works or what might be done about it by identifying a need for better coordination.' Indeed, a further research project of interest would be to test the hypothesis that the value of reports varies inversely with the frequency with which the word 'coordination' is used" (Chambers 1974).
9. The document later notes that "Key aspects of the Bank's comparative advantage are global reach and a broad developmental mandate, ability to mobilize and manage resources, and operational competence at the country level." Again, it is easier to list these aspects than to monitor and evaluate them across a range of potential partnerships.
10. For a framework for evaluating horizontal integration, see Klitgaard (1991).
11. InterAct (2001) lists as possible benefits increases in information and understanding, trust among stakeholders, ownership, capacity among stakeholders, openness and transparency, "representativeness of participation," and "level of understanding about the process and the specific project"—as well as "changes in values, priorities, aims and objectives" and new relationships between organizations, formal and informal. At a more practical level, it says to look for reduced vandalism, better maintenance, leverage for additional funding, and impact on the policy process. The document admits that "there remains insufficient hard evidence on these benefits for them to be widely acknowledged."
12. This builds on better measures of quality, but is separable from them. An example: Suppose we had a fuller set of measures of educational quality. To judge a school's performance, in the sense of value added, we would have to adjust for changes in the quality of the intake and for other features of the environment that affect the quality of education but are not under the school's control.
13. When in the 1960s Dudley Seers wrote an article called "Why Visiting Economists Fail" (Seers 1962), another economist responded that the real issue was "Why Failed Economists Visit."
14. By "conceptual hectoring" I refer to the self-serving, sometimes nobly motivated evaluator who has an agenda he or she wishes to serve (often a conceptual agenda such as "advancing the poor" or "preserving the environment," or a favored means such as "microcredit" or "public–private partnerships"). The evaluation is structured around findings that a variable seems to matter, or a difference exists, and around admonitions to take a favored something into account, without quite saying how. The result: conceptual hectoring.
15. A lack of trust is a general phenomenon in partnerships among business, government, NGOs, and international agencies, or subsets thereof. Consider this conclusion from a recent conference in Asia: "[P]erhaps the most critical requirement for bringing about a greater number of effective corporate–NGO partnerships in Asia Pacific is to do away with the traditional 'us against them' attitude that remains between corporations and NGOs." (Yamamoto 1999). On the distrust between donors and recipients, see Klitgaard (1992).
16. For example, the costs of evaluation partnerships are virtually unmentioned in *Knowledge Shared: Participatory Evaluation in Development Cooperation*" (Jackson and Kassam 1998).
17. For a development example of the same kind of logic, see Paul (1982).

References

Albert, Paul. 1973. *Partnership or Confrontation? Poor Lands and Rich.* New York: The Free Press.

Allison, Graham T., and Philip Zelikow. 1999. *Essence of Decision: Explaining the Cuban Missile Crisis,* 2nd ed. Reading, Mass.: Longman.

Antón, Philip S., Richard Silberglitt, and James Schneider. 2001. *The Global Technology Revolution: Bio/Nano/Materials Trends and Their Synergies with Information Technology by 2015.* Santa Monica, Calif.: Rand.

Bardhan, Pranab K. 2000. "Understanding Underdevelopment: Challenges for Institutional Economics from the Point of View of Poor Countries." *Journal of Institutional and Theoretical Economics* 156(1): 224.

Besley, Timothy, and Maitreesh Ghatak. 1999. "Public–Private Partnerships for the Provision of Public Goods: Theory and an Application to NGOs." Development Economics Discussion Paper Series, No. 17. London: London School of Economics. Available online at *http://econ.lse.ac.uk/staff/tbesley/papers/ngo.pdf*

Bobbitt, Philip. 2002. *The Shield of Achilles: War, Peace, and the Course of History.* New York: Knopf.

Boris, Elizabeth T., and C. Eugene Steuerle (eds.). 1999. *Nonprofits and Government: Collaboration and Conflict.* Washington, D.C.: The Urban Institute Press.

Campos, Jose Edgardo, and Hilton L. Root. 1996. *The Key to the Asian Miracle: Making Shared Growth Credible.* Washington, D.C.: Brookings Institution Press.

Chambers, Robert. 1974. *Managing Rural Development.* Uppsala, Sweden: Scandinavian Institute of African Studies.

Copenhagen Center. 2000. *Partnership Alchemy.* Copenhagen: The Copenhagen Center. Available online at *http://www.copenhagencentre.org/TCCWEB/TCCWEB.NSF/K_Concepts/K222?OpenDocument*

Eriksson, John. 2001. *The Drive to Partnership: Aid Coordination and the World Bank.* Washington, D.C.: World Bank.

Gray, Andrew, Bill Jenkins, Frans Leeuw, and John Mayne (eds.). Forthcoming. *Evaluation and the Collaborative State.* New Brunswick, N.J.: Transaction.

Gregory, Robin, Tim McDaniels, and Daryl Fields. 2001. "Decision Aiding, Not Dispute Resolution: Creating Insights through Structured Environmental Decisions." *Journal of Policy Analysis and Management* 20(3): 415–32.

Hart, Oliver, Andrei Shleifer, and Robert W. Vishny. 1997. "The Proper Scope of Government: Theory and an Application to Prisons." *Quarterly Journal of Economics* 112(4): 1126–61.

Hulme, David, and Michael Edwards (eds.). 1997. *NGOs, States and Donors: Too Close for Comfort?* London: Macmillan.

IBLF (International Business Leaders Forum). 2000. "Measures for Success: Assessing the Impact of Partnerships." IBLF, London. Available online at http://www.pwblf.org/csr/csrwebassist.nsf/content/f1d2a3b4c5.html

InterAct. 2001. "Evaluating Participatory, Deliberative, and Cooperative Ways of Working." Brighton, U.K.: InterAct.

Jackson, Edward T., and Yusuf Kassam (eds.). 1998. *Knowledge Shared: Participatory Evaluation in Development Cooperation.* West Hartford, Conn.: Kumarian Press.

Klitgaard, Robert. 1975. "On Assessing a Gift Horse." *International Development Review,* No. 4.

———. 1991. *Adjusting to Reality: Beyond State v. Market in International Development.* San Francisco: ICS Press.

———. 1992. "Poisonous Texts." *Negotiation Journal* 8(3): 215–19.

———. 1995. "Including Culture in Evaluation Research." *New Directions for Evaluation*, No. 67.
———. 1997. "Applying Cultural Theories to Practical Problems." In Richard J. Ellis and Michael Thompson, eds., *Culture Matters*. Boulder, Colo.: Westview.
Laffont, Jean-Jacques, and Jean Tirole. 1991. "The Politics of Government Decision Making: A Theory of Regulatory Capture." *Quarterly Journal of Economics*, 106(4): 1089–1127.
Maxwell, Simon, and Tim Conway. 2000. "Perspectives on Partnership." OED Working Paper Series No. 6. Washington, D.C.: World Bank.
May, Ernest R. 1997. "The Evolving Scope of Government." In Joseph S. Nye, Jr. et al., eds., *Why People Don't Trust Government*. Cambridge, Mass.: Harvard University Press.
McAdoo, M. R. 2001. "Tying the Knot: The Partnership Craze." In *Sustaining Growth and Bridging the Divides: A Framework for Our Global Future*. World Economic Forum Annual Meeting 2001 Report. Davos, Switzerland: World Economic Forum.
Moss, Pamela A., and Aaron Schutz. 2001. "Educational Standards, Assessment, and the Search for Consensus." *American Educational Research Journal* 38(1): 65.
Nelson, Joan. M. 1971. "The Partial Partnership: Trends in Multilateral Aid and Aid Coordination." *International Organization* 25(1): 79–96.
Paul, Samuel. 1982. *Managing Development Programs: The Lessons of Success*. Boulder, Colo.: Westview.
Pearson, Lester. 1968. *Partners in Development*. New York: Praeger.
Picciotto, Robert. 1995. *Putting Institutional Economics to Work: From Participation to Governance*. World Bank Discussion Paper 304. Washington, D.C.: World Bank.
Purcell, Randall. Forthcoming. "Good Practice in Global and Regional Programs: Engaging the Poor and Civil Society, Building Inclusion, Harnessing Markets, Working with the Private Sector, and Managing Donor Relationships." Washington, D.C.: Development Grant Facility, World Bank.
Savas, E. S. 2000. *Privatization and Public–Private Partnerships*. New York and London: Chatham House Publishers, Seven Bridges Press.
Seers, Dudley. 1962. "Why Visiting Economists Fail." *Journal of Political Economy* 70(4): 325–38.
Treverton, Gregory F. 2001. *Reshaping National Intelligence*. New York and Cambridge: Cambridge University Press.
Vaillancourt Rosenau, Pauline (ed.). 2000. *Public–Private Policy Partnerships*. Cambridge, Mass.: MIT Press.
Weisbrod, Burton. 1997. "The Future of the Nonprofit Sector: Its Entwining with Private Enterprise and Government." *Journal of Policy Analysis and Management* 16(4): 541–55.
World Bank. 2000a. "Partnership Oversight and Selectivity: A Discussion Note." Processed (Internal document).
———. 2000b. "Partnering with Business: Questions and Answers." Business Partnership and Outreach Group Briefing Note No. 2. Washington, D.C.: World Bank. Available online at *http://www.worldbank.org/business/files/note2.pdf*
———. 2000c. "Addressing Global Dimensions in Development." Discussion Note. Washington, D.C.: World Bank.
Yamamoto, Tadashi. 1999. "Corporate–NGO Partnership: Learning from Case Studies." In Tadashi Yamamoto and Kim Gould Ashizawa, eds., *Corporate–NGO Partnership in Asia Pacific*. Tokyo and New York: Japan Center for International Exchange.
Young, Dennis R. 1999. "Complementary, Supplementary, or Adversarial? A Theoretical and Historical Examination of Nonprofit–Government Relations in the United States." In Elizabeth T. Boris and C. Eugene Steuerle, eds., *Nonprofits and Government: Collaboration and Conflict*. Washington, D.C.: The Urban Institute Press.

6

The Logic of Partnership

Robert Picciotto

Partnership is a means to an end—a collaborative relationship toward mutually agreed objectives involving shared responsibility for outcomes, distinct accountabilities, and reciprocal obligations. Where there is no common vision of what the partnership is about, no mutual stake in the outcome, lack of clarity in task allocations, or imbalance in influence and unfairness in allocation of costs and benefits, the partnership is hollow.

In the business world, partnership has a specific and instructive meaning. It is a form of organization in which some or all of the owners accept unlimited liability for the organization's debt and jointly exercise management control. This form of organization meets all the criteria listed in the above definition. It is especially appropriate for professional service organizations in which (1) the most important asset is the knowledge and experience of the partners; and (2) reputation and teamwork are central to success. In fact, partnerships are the dominant form of organization in professional services industries.

In such knowledge-based industries, limited liability corporations are less effective than partnerships because shareholders and boards of directors are not especially good at monitoring the quality of intellectual work and also because capital requirements (better met through corporate forms of ownership) tend to be lower than in manufacturing. Peers are in a much better position than bosses to judge the quality of professional work and to monitor one another. Thus, under a partnership arrangement, free riding is discouraged and partners have both the incentive and the motivation to coordinate their activities and ensure professional excellence.

Robert Picciotto is former director-general, Operations Evaluation, The World Bank.

Partnership and Markets

In a modern economy, coordination of the billions of people and their choices among the infinite possibilities facing them is a mind-boggling problem. The problem is compounded when the operating environment is subject to change and permanent adaptation becomes necessary. The key to such adaptation is information, particularly about the best use of resources, available technologies, and the needs of consumers. Typically, this information is localized and dispersed throughout the economy.

Under central planning, the information is transmitted to a single point where it is processed and leads to decisions from the top. The resulting costs are prohibitive in a global, technology-intensive economy. The alternative is to decentralize decision making. This involves less information transmission and more delegation of authority. The challenge is to ensure that separately made decisions yield coherent results. Experience has amply demonstrated that the market is the most appropriate way of ensuring such coherence for private goods.

Competition is the key to effective market operation. But cooperation is also required. The need for cooperation arises out of the benefits of specialization. People can produce more if they cooperate, specializing in their productive activities and then transacting with one another to acquire the actual goods and services they desire. This requires special institutional arrangements to raise capital, secure a stable supply of labor and skills, and market the products. Such arrangements are called firms.

Adam Smith's famous example of the pin factory vividly shows the benefits of cooperation and specialization and the consequent need for coordination. The various stages of pin manufacturing are carried out by different people, each specialized in a single task—pulling the wire, straightening it, cutting it to the appropriate lengths, sharpening the point, attaching the head, and packaging the final product. Adam Smith demonstrated how the resulting volume of output was many times greater than it would have been if each person involved had done all the stages alone.

Coordination through markets and prices is remarkably efficient where markets are competitive and property rights are ensured. In an ideally functioning system of markets, all that anyone needs to know is his or her own capabilities and tastes and the prevailing prices. When conditions change, price variations transmit all the data needed to make efficient production and consumption decisions. For private goods, the market system also solves the problem of motivation so that by pursuing one's own interests, the public interest is automatically served through the providential "hidden hand."

On the other hand, there is no market within the firm where the principles of partnership must be pursued (consensus, coordination, specialization, and fairness) to meet the needs of the market. Paradoxically, then, competition outside the firm favors cooperation inside it. The very justification of creating a firm is to eliminate the need for market transactions among individuals engaged in a common enterprise. Similarly, alliances across organizations can minimize overall transaction costs and enhance the effectiveness of the participating organizations and can contribute to the public interest, provided they do not lead to restraints on trade.

Partnership and Public Goods

Outside the organization, the free-market model breaks down where public goods are involved. Clean air is the archetype of a public good. You cannot take away a pound of clean air and sell it on a market stall. It is nonsubtractable. And clean air is also nonexcludable—that is, you cannot prevent anyone from enjoying it whether they have paid to do so or not. Goods with either or both of these characteristics present collective choice problems.

When many people have the right to use a single shared resource, there is an incentive for the resource to be overused (the tragedy of the commons). Equally, it is difficult to make people pay for public goods, or otherwise contribute to their production. This is the free rider problem. It explains why public goods are typically undersupplied. Consider the case of an underground petroleum deposit with undetermined ownership rights. Each party will try to draw oil quickly so that the others do not get it all first. Excessive pumping raises the cost of extracting the oil and leads to rapid resource depletion. In such circumstances, collective action requires a mix of cooperative behavior and hierarchical decision making.[1]

Why do collective choices involve such tough dilemmas? For two main reasons: First, as Kenneth Arrow has proven, without an individual whose preferences become the group's preferences (in other words, a strong leader), it is impossible to aggregate the preferences of individuals so that the ordering of their preferences is respected. There must be give and take. Second, as Mancur Olson has shown, without special incentives to cooperate, there is no good reason for individual members of a large group to exert themselves on behalf of the group, since the personal benefits they would derive from doing so are infinitesimal.

Partnerships are designed to overcome both of these dilemmas.

They do so in different ways, depending of the nature of the good. While public goods enjoy neither excludability nor subtractability and private goods enjoy both, toll goods enjoy the first but not the second; and common pool goods the second but not the first. These characteristics have important implications for institutional design. Access arrangements for private and toll goods must rely on exit (market) mechanisms, whereas access to public and common pool goods depends on voice (participation) mechanisms. For their coordination and oversight, public and toll goods are, in different degrees, subject to hierarchy (the state) while private goods again rely on market forces and common pool goods are largely coordinated and overseen by voice mechanisms (participation).

Partnership Is Highly Relevant to Development

With the conceptual brush cleared, it is easier to appreciate why economic and social development is highly dependent on partnership. Sustainable development requires the creation of infrastructure, policies, and knowledge and the husbanding of natural resources in socially and ecologically responsible ways. This means that the production of private goods is inseparable from the complementary production of public, common pool, and toll goods in appropriate balance with private goods. Poor countries are by definition countries where such goods are exceedingly scarce. Thus, development consists in building the institutions capable of investing in basic infrastructure, designing appropriate policies, and producing the knowledge needed for a modern economy and an equitable society. Without an appropriate enabling environment, the private sector cannot function effectively. The rules of the game must be clear and they must ensure a level playing field.

There is mounting evidence that harmonious coexistence and collaboration among the private sector, the voluntary sector, and the state are characteristic of prosperous societies. Institutions designed to share financial risks and provide social safety nets are essential to encourage investment and ensure social harmony. The nurturing of appropriate customs and behaviors engendering social trust is another essential component of modernization. Thus, cooperation in the social sphere is twinned with competition and innovation in the private sphere. This is, ultimately, why partnerships are worth nurturing in developing countries. The advent of civil society in the new democracies of the South and the East facilitates the task. Hence, the development process is inseparable from the construction of partnerships capable of delivering the appropriate mix of goods needed for balanced, broadly based growth.

There are basic differences between partnerships in the development field and business partnerships. Typically, in a development venture, values and objectives differ sharply among participants and there is asymmetry of resources and capacities among them. This is why public consultations and participation are so crucial in the design and implementation of development projects and programs. Where one or more of the participants do not enjoy the organization and skills available to other participants, capacity building is a prerequisite of true partnership.

Partnership Can Be Evaluated

The prerequisites of an effective partnership are efficient specialization, competence, coordination, and motivation.

Specialization does not enhance productivity unless the partners have adequate skills and experience. Coordination matters because, without assurance that the preceding stages of production have been carried out in a timely way, the benefits of specialization are wasted. And without motivation to work as a team, coordination is not possible. To create coordination and motivation usually requires a mix of cooperation and authority.

The legal definition of partnership is revealing: joint rights and responsibilities in a common enterprise set up with the understanding that there shall be a "communion of profit" between the parties. This means that a partnership is justified only if the benefits exceed the costs and the net benefits are equitably assigned to the parties. In turn, this implies that the partnership is relevant, efficacious, and efficient from the perspective of the participants.

Relevance means that there is a bedrock of shared values and that the participants "own" the objectives of the partnership. There needs to be a judicious balance in the use of resources toward meeting the distinctive needs of partners.

Efficacy means that the design and operation of the partnership is appropriate and likely to lead to achievement of the joint objectives. The specific goals of the partnership may be broad and generic or highly particular and specific; highly demanding or extremely modest. Equally, the membership requirements may be too exacting (that is, keeping away those whose participation is needed to achieve results) or too loose (that is, undermining loyalty or favoring free riding). Operating protocols for the partnership may be such that they encourage creativity and innovation—or destroy them.

In assessing efficiency, care must be taken to distinguish monetary and nonmonetary costs and benefits. The metric of "doing good" may be hard to define, let alone reward. An efficient partnership is one that uses joint resources with economy and achieves substantial results at limited cost. Replicability and sustainability are the decisive tests of efficiency. Given the incommensurability of costs and benefits and the difficulty of quantifying such values as trust and loyalty, similarly oriented partnerships are best assessed in relation to one another through benchmarking.

Where the partnership is "one of a kind," counterfactuals (in other words, alternatives designed to achieve the same purpose) must be modeled. In all cases, the views of the parties need to be sought systematically. In the end, partnerships should be judged by their results. Accordingly, results-based management should include partnership as part of the results chain.

Five Prerequisites of Successful Partnerships

Evaluation findings highlight five prerequisites of successful partnerships:

- The goals must be adequately defined and fully owned by the partners.
- The partners must secure full consensus for the goals of the partnership within their organizations.
- The partners must demonstrate intellectual conviction through concrete upfront actions.
- The partners must reach out and engage in broad-based participation in support of partnership goals.
- Capacity development must be built into the partnership to ensure that the weaker members can participate fully and exercise influence.

These are demanding standards. The more specific the goals, the more likely they are to be achieved but the harder it is to achieve consensus among a large number of partners. There are distinct diseconomies of scale associated with partnerships: the larger the group, the more likely the risks of shirking by individual partners and the greater the need for strong incentives for participation and teamwork. For large groups, this implies a need for strong, even charismatic, leadership and selective incentives for participants. It also suggests that in a growing partnership, it may be best to upgrade the demanding-ness of goals only gradually, as measures to promote loyalty take hold among the participants. Moreover, it suggests that a piloting phase, during which trust can be nurtured among partners, may help build strong partnerships.

The need for full participation in the elaboration of partnership objectives by the individual partners (through voice) and the concrete upfront actions required to demonstrate commitment is consistent with the loyalty-building characteristics of cohesive groups. The importance of strong ownership of partnership objectives and the need for broadly based participation are especially critical where there are threats by outside groups to the integrity of a budding alliance. The capacity-building determinant of partnership success is consistent with the imperatives of fairness, reciprocity, and mutual respect that are characteristic of sustainable cooperative arrangements.

World Bank Partnerships

Three factors explain why partnership is part of the Comprehensive Development Framework promoted by the World Bank.

First, partnership can provide privileged access to knowledge in support of development. Given that globalization is a fact of life, access to knowledge requires international cooperation. In the private sector, connection to all kinds of global networks has become a business imperative. In the public sector, there is a need to connect development experience across countries and across sectors. The World Bank houses a unique concentration of knowledge about developing countries. Its field office network and information infrastructure connect developing member countries to one another, and to the rest of the world. Conversely, the World Bank acts as a platform for interaction and mutual learning between developed and developing countries, as well as between the public sector and the private and voluntary sectors, which have assumed a dominant role in development.

Second, partnership can help to enhance the efficacy of the overall development system. Development assistance has the characteristics of an international public good, whose effective delivery requires systemic cooperation. The World Bank occupies a special position in a development assistance system that has become unwieldy and fragmented. Overall transaction costs in the official aid system keep rising while resource transfers stay stagnant. Comparative advantages are not being tapped sufficiently. Coherence is lacking, just as global development challenges—global warming, deforestation, volatile financial flows, public health hazards, international crime—have become ever more injurious to the welfare of the planet. Fundamentally, development assistance is an international public good, and this is why it requires cooperation, coherence, and coordination instead of duplication and wasteful competition. This means businesslike cooperation—that is, mission-oriented partnerships.

Third, partnership has become essential to the World Bank's own development effectiveness because of recent shifts in the operating environment and the Bank's corporate priorities. As long as the World Bank conceived its role as largely that of a project-lending organization working through the public sector, the need for partnership with the private sector and civil society was limited. Today, the World Bank has many facets. It is a knowledge bank as well as a lending bank. It is equally concerned with economic growth, social equity, and environmental sustainability. While it invests a great deal in traditional investment projects, a rising share of its resources is being channeled to initiate and sustain policy reform and institutional development. While it works with and through governments, it is also reaching out to the private sector and civil society.

The Partnership Logic in Action

The World Bank itself may be viewed as a partnership. Its members provide unconditional guarantees for all Bank financial obligations. Elaborate processes are in place to secure consensus among members regarding the Bank's development agenda. Reciprocal obligations are clearly specified. Most decisions are reached by consensus.

Each Bank-financed *project* is a concrete and visible reflection of development partnership. Each project is backed by a cluster of agreements reflecting reciprocal rights and obligations between the Bank, the borrowing government, the implementing agency, the contractors and consultants, and increasingly the local authorities and nongovernmental organizations associated with the development venture. About 1,400 such projects are under implementation, worth $140 billion in commitments. Cofinancing ($5–6 billion a year) facilitates the building of management coalitions to implement these projects. New, adaptable lending products have been introduced to facilitate partnerships at the project and program level.

At the *country level,* a new vision of partnership is being piloted that puts the country at the center of its own development. Partnership is conceived as a process managed by the country rather than by any one institution or donor. It requires the government concerned and its people to develop a national development strategy. The process brings together all major actors—government, private sector, civil society, and development assistance agencies—to debate and agree on the best assistance program to support the strategy. Several elements of this vision are already in action through the Poverty Reduction Strategy program in low-income countries.

At the *regional and global levels,* development issues that transcend national boundaries are being addressed through multi-country partnerships. The Africa Program for Onchocerciasis Control demonstrates that a debilitating disease (river blindness) can be gradually eradicated through international cooperation. The partnership involves the ministries of health of affected countries, the World Bank, WHO, NGOs, and the private sector. Merck, a major pharmaceutical company, is providing a new drug free of charge to help control the disease. The Consultative Group for International Agricultural Research (CGIAR) brings together fifty-three public and private sector members that support a network of 16 research centers. FAO, UNDP, UNEP, and the Bank cosponsor the CGIAR. The Global Environment Facility was launched in 1991 to provide grants and concessional funds to recipient countries for activities that protect the world from depletion of the ozone layer, global warming, biodiversity depletion, and the pollution of international waters.

Alliances have also been formed to promote dissemination of information technology in developing countries, to increase the reach of micro-enterprise finance and tropical disease research, to protect cultural heritage, and to combat AIDS.

The World Bank provides a platform for collaboration through *fiduciary services.* About 800 trust funds are managed by the Bank to fund a wide variety of development ventures. The Bank also provides aid coordination services. It provides the secretariat for the Special Program for Africa and for thirty-four consultative groups. In post-conflict countries, the Bank helps to coordinate reconstruction assistance—for example, in Bosnia and Herzegovina and in the West Bank/Gaza.

The journey has only begun. The World Bank's development assistance programs are supportive of the Millennium Development Goals, which aim to induce greater coherence into the development system. Equally, the Bank's knowledge initiatives are being geared more systematically to the learning needs of the Bank's partners. In a nutshell, the poverty reduction mission of the Bank demands partnership.

Note

1. In practice, of course, where the state has surface and subsurface rights, there is a tight licensing system (regulated by the state) where customary rights are in the hands of communities.

Part 2

Partnerships in Practice

7

Partnership, Mutual Accountability, and Evaluation

Jean-Claude Faure

Partnership in development aid implies working together with national and local governments, civil society, and the private sector, in both donor and recipient countries, on programs that are based on a shared view of a country's needs, capacities, and goals. The principle of partnership recognizes that the main responsibility for combating poverty and fostering development lies with the governments and peoples of developing countries, and that the role of development cooperation is only to support those countries in the implementation of national policies that are based on self-reliance and responsibility.

For the past three years the international community has sought to put into practice this paradigm of cooperation toward poverty reduction. New and promising approaches to cooperation have emerged in the Comprehensive Development Framework, poverty reduction strategies, and new responses to conflict and post-conflict situations. Putting the paradigm into practice is a formidable challenge.

The key to all partnerships is shared values. To nurture shared values means that we must change the way donor agencies operate. We must move from a conditionality mode to a shared process, setting targets and using strategic indicators to measure progress and to judge success and failure. We must use dialogue to help set policies and to adapt decisions to changing circumstances. And in many cases, we must build confidence through strengthening the partner country's own capacity to diagnose and act on its development concerns.

Jean-Claude Faure is chairman, Development Assistance Committee, Organization for Economic Co-operation and Development.

Motivation is another key element of successful partnership. In its year 2000 policy statement, "Partnership for Poverty Reduction: From Commitment to Implementation," the donor community identified ownership as the foundation of cooperation in partnerships with developing countries. A strategy is emerging that goes beyond the building of a common framework for program implementation to a partner-led coordination that is more transparent and simpler. Harmonized procedures among donors will enhance the use of local capacities and permit aid to be untied. The Development Assistance Committee (DAC) has made progress toward this end: we are developing fewer isolated projects and more sector-wide approaches.

A third key element of genuine partnership is mutual accountability. If developing countries are to assume genuine ownership of development cooperation, transparency and accountability must be much stronger than has been the norm. To achieve this requires an effective monitoring and evaluation system—that both recognizes the leading role of the partner country and meets the legitimate requirements of the donor country as defined by its government and constituencies.

Achieving this mutual accountability may be the most difficult challenge of partnership, and it is one in which evaluation has a critical role to play. Those whose job it is to evaluate the successes and failures of development cooperation must ask the following questions: Is there enough country leadership and partnership? What is program effectiveness? Is there enough accountability within government and outside government? Is there enough accountability among the donors?

We should also look to evaluation as a mechanism to help understand how to treat poor performers. The partnership approach works only where governments are able and willing to assume ownership of the development process. Yet many of the poor live in countries with governments that lack the political will or ability to assume ownership. The international community cannot walk away from these so-called poorly performing countries.

Evaluation is also about learning, feedback, and the dissemination of knowledge. We must involve all stakeholders in the process of integrating evaluation results and a proper understanding of risks into partnership endeavors. This requires the active involvement, in a demand-driven manner, of developing-country partners, civil society, and the private sector, and as far as possible it means full coordination and joint evaluation.

Finally, we must reflect on the rationale, scope, and modalities of evaluation. In discussions of financing for development, including the implementation of the Millennium Development Goals, we need indicators, targets, figures, and timeframes to give substance to the concept of mutual accountability in North–South relations.

In the DAC, the evaluation community is alive, active, and well organized. We are working toward the mainstreaming of evaluation that we feel is needed both in the partnership implementation process and in our peer reviews. But we need to be much more consistent, and we need to inject the evaluation dimension into development partnerships much more than we do at present.

Different Perspectives and Types of Development Partnership

8

Global Public Policy Partnerships

Inge Kaul and Grace Ryu

More often than not, global public goods (GPGs) are neither readily nor successfully provided by markets or states. By definition, public goods are subject to market failure, but they are also subject to government failure. To meet the challenge of providing global public goods, the public is reemerging into public policymaking through innovative means and partnerships—notably, global public policy partnerships (GPPP). These trends mean that public economics needs to be systematically rethought if it is to continue to serve as a useful tool of public policymaking. This chapter explores the links between global public goods and global public policy partnerships.

The Changing World of Public Goods

According to economic theory, private goods are those that are excludable. That is, they can be produced and distributed according to demand, their ownership can be transferred for a price, and clear property rights can be attached to them.[1] Fortunately so, because many private goods tend to be rival in consumption—one person's enjoyment of a good may reduce or exhaust the utility of that good for others (a piece of cake consumed by A is no longer available for B's enjoyment). Because of these properties, the provision of private goods can normally be left to the market.

Public goods are often described as the counterpart of private goods, their main defining feature being non-excludability. This means that once public

---

Inge Kaul is director, Office of Development Studies, UNDP. Grace Ryu is policy analyst, Office of Development Studies, UNDP.

The views expressed in the chapter are the authors' and do not necessarily reflect the policies of the institution with which they are affiliated.

goods are produced, their benefits—and in the case of public "bads," their costs—are there for all to consume, often without the possibility of exit or escape. (Take the example of a traffic light. When we want to cross a busy street on foot, we may welcome the traffic light and happily consume the protection and opportunity to cross that it offers us. At other times, when we are in our car and in a hurry or on a little-traveled road, we may be less pleased by its existence.)

Public goods are goods in the public domain and can affect the public and its various parts quite differently. In terms of their utility, they are not distribution neutral. How useful—or detrimental—they are for one or the other segment of the public depends on the circumstances in which people find themselves. Stability in financial markets is a public good, but is much more important to the manager of a financial corporation than to a farmer in sub-Saharan Africa.

The recognition that people's individual and collective preferences for both public and private goods differ is critically important. Many studies stress that privateness or publicness is often a matter of policy choice, rather than innate properties of a good. It may therefore be appropriate to see public–private as a continuum along which goods can be moved; that is, goods can be made more or less private or public in their benefits and costs. For example, law and order can be made less public if police services are contracted out to private businesses (leaving fewer resources for the general public) or if police services are provided on a discriminatory basis to privileged groups. Or consider airwaves that are public in property but which are licensed for television or radio broadcasting and subsequently made excludable via signal scrambling. Pure public and private goods are rare—they are more of a theoretical construct to guide our analysis and understanding of different types of goods.

This raises some important questions. If a good's publicness is variable, who decides the extent to which it is a public good? What and how much of a good can be produced, and at what cost? What is the shape and content of the good? Before we attempt to answer these questions, we must examine the goods that exist in the public domain and how the composition of the public domain is changing.

The Changing Public Domain

There is much uncertainty and confusion about the notions of public and private—what they denote, and how they are linked. This is not surprising, given the tectonic shifts that have recently affected what we considered to be public and private. Three trends are of particular importance: privatization, openness, and policy convergence behind borders.[2]

Privatization of State Enterprises

The 1950s saw an era of state-led development in market economies as well as in the centrally planned socialist economies. The state and its activities—ranging from governmental core functions to public ownership of the means of production—constituted the public sector. Policymaking ranged from benignly democratic to dictatorial, suffocating private economic activity and intruding into people's private lives.

The strong political and economic role of the state during this era had diverse historical and contextual roots, including the social ills of early industrialization, the two World Wars, and the Great Depression of the 1930s. Natural monopoly situations had arisen in many countries because of an urgent need for physical infrastructure development. The public domain was territorially bound and often politically constrained, but it was also plentiful in terms of public goods, including publicly provided private goods (in other words, goods with essentially excludable properties that were made public in consumption by policy design).

The 1970s brought a shift in political sentiment toward economic liberalization and privatization. Financial markets expanded; state-owned enterprises, including social security schemes, were privatized; and state-provided services were increasingly subjected to marketization (that is, outsourced for delivery by private companies or organized on principles of cost recovery and user fees). Although neither universal nor pursued equally by all countries, the trend was widespread and left fewer deliberately created goods in the domestic public domain. The net effect of economic liberalization on people's lives is difficult to determine, but at the individual level it created distress among those who could not afford the now market-provided goods.

The state as the main mechanism for people's public economic interactions gave way increasingly to the market as the public space and coordination mechanism for the provision of goods and services. In addition, companies increasingly went public, obtaining capital from financial markets (and consequently from the general public) and creating an ever-denser web of relations between markets and people as consumers, workers, savers, and investors.[3]

Policy debates since the 1970s have focused on the balance between market and state as economic coordination mechanisms. Most of the debate has been on whether goods should be *produced* through the state or through the market, and how much the state should control the market. Until recently the critical issue of who should benefit from these various goods has been neglected. Should goods be—whether state- or market-provided—in the public domain and there for all to enjoy, or should they be left to the purchasing power of each individual actor?

Openness of National Borders

Concurrent with the trend toward less state intervention and fewer publicly provided private goods and services, the increased openness of national borders has swelled the volumes of cross-border economic activities such as trade, investment, travel, and communication. Promoting growth and development for some, the new openness has also entailed greater economic competition. Keynesian policies have been cut back, exposing people to adjustment pressures in industrial as well as in developing countries.

Cross-border activity has also functioned as a powerful conveyor of externalities, positive and negative. Positive externalities, such as spillovers of new knowledge and technology, have often been taken for granted, but negative externalities, such as infectious diseases, food safety concerns, financial contagion risks, air pollution, and international crime, have become sources of public concern.

A new sense of publicness—that of being dependent on the actions and policy choices of others, at home and abroad—has in fact emerged. Unfortunately, the greater weight given in the public consciousness to the negative aspects of openness has at times overflowed into expressions of xenophobia, demands for protectionism, and anti-market and anti-business sentiments.

Further to this negative perception of open borders is the growing awareness of the scarcity of the services provided by the global commons—notably the atmosphere, but also water and biodiversity. The feeling that there are limits to growth has introduced new competitiveness and a strengthened sense of privateness into the increasingly interdependent global community's psyche, adding a North–South, rich–poor divide to the prior East–West divide of the Cold War.

Policy Convergence behind Borders

Market integration depends on two ingredients: openness of national borders and policy convergence behind national borders. The structural adjustment programs of the 1980s and early 1990s unleashed changes along both these lines. In fact, the policy prescriptions of the "Washington Consensus" were aimed at achieving a harmonization to the Western model of such hitherto country-specific national public goods as legal frameworks, judiciary systems, and financial regulation and supervision. The pressures for this type of policy convergence came from some industrial countries, directly or via intergovernmental bodies such as the Bretton Woods institutions, and from "the market," in the form of perceived or real market discipline, often reinforced by the work of private credit rating agencies.

Intriguingly, part of the demands for policy convergence was a demand for more democracy and more accountable and transparent government performance. This goal was shared by business, the Western industrial countries, and many civil society organizations, including women's and human rights advocacy groups. The civil society organizations often joined forces across borders and pressed their concerns in international forums. By campaigning against the misuse of government sovereignty (in the form, for example, of human rights violations), these groups contributed to a general narrowing of governmental policymaking sovereignty. Political pluralism and the practices of representative democracy rapidly swept across much of the world, especially after the end of the Cold War in the late 1980s, opening up important new space for public participation in policymaking.[4,5]

In sum, the period from the 1950s through the 1990s showed a growing trend toward an interlocking of national public domains, often resulting from externalities and top-down, market-oriented globalization, rather than bottom-up, public policy choices. Where once the state was the public sector, in today's multi-actor world private companies have become more public, civil society has reemerged politically, and expectations of governance, state accountability, and legitimacy have grown. We live now in a world of more global public awareness but, according to many, of fewer positive public goods and more negative externalities, and of more public goods for markets and business than for the general public.

Global Public Policy Partnerships

These trends have put back on the policy agenda the issue of what will be the shape and content for the public domain, nationally and internationally.[6] They have also resurrected the issue of the private/public benefits of goods, raising awareness that public goods are not distribution neutral in their net benefits, and that they have different utility for different groups of people.

The critical issues now are what public goods to provide, how much of each to provide, at what net cost to whom, and how precisely to shape them. Periodic elections are too crude an instrument to make these finer, more precise choices—there are simply too many factors of government failure that can drive a wedge between the mandates electorates provide to governments and the outcomes of government policy.[7] There has instead been a virtual explosion of civil society organizations (CSOs) in recent years, with the number of international CSOs estimated now to stand at about 29,000. There are a further 20,000 transnational CSO networks and countless national CSOs. India alone is estimated to have more than a million national CSOs (Edwards 2000).

CSOs have introduced a new issue focus into policy debates at all levels. Often, they are single-concern organizations, focusing on a particular public bad that they wish to see turned into a public good (for example, environmental degradation into sustainable development). Many CSOs work either nationally or internationally in pursuit of greater government responsiveness to public concerns. Since governments increasingly cite market or other outside pressures as a reason for not providing certain policy outcomes, CSOs often intervene with multilateral bodies to assist intergovernmental cooperation on public concerns and to minimize the risk of "rivalry among states" (Strange 1996).

Acknowledging the role of markets and the influence of business on the state, CSOs also direct their actions toward corporations and private firms. Through the exercise of consumer pressure, private business can be made to internalize the costs of externalities, conform to labor norms, and comply with environmental regulations. And when business does meet its public obligations, credit awaits for showing "corporate citizenship" and social responsibility.[8]

The civil society focus on intergovernmental bodies and corporations, individually and collectively, is so strong that business, government, and the media are raising questions about the accountability and legitimacy of CSOs. This has led in turn to proposals for a CSO code of conduct. But driven by the work of CSOs, the increasing desire of virtually all actors to be (and to be seen to be) publicly concerned has provided a new and important basis for partnerships, including global public policy partnerships.

Revisiting the Concept of Public Goods

We would like now to return to the concept of public goods.[9] Five modifications seem to be warranted to take today's realities into account.

1. Recognizing Global Public Goods

It is important to recognize explicitly the existence of global public goods (GPGs). These are goods with benefits that are strongly universal in terms of accruing to multiple countries, several—preferably all—population groups, and to current and future generations (Kaul, Grunberg, and Stem 1999b).[10]

Multilateral development assistance is not in itself a good. It may serve as a tool to help foster GPG purposes, but generally it is a transfer mechanism from richer to poorer countries, serving the interests of the recipient and possibly also of the donor. Given the scarcity of resources, it is, moreover, rival in consumption.

2. Elements in the Public Domain

The public domain contains four basic elements: (1) preexisting goods, such as the natural commons; (2) human-made goods, such as an efficient financial market; (3) externalities, existing in the public domain either by design or by default; and (4) private goods made public by design. The dividing lines between these different elements are significant, but not always clear. The standard definition of public goods as nonexcludable does not capture the many externalities of private activities, or capture goods and externalities made public by design, such as basic education or health care. Using nonexcludability as our defining characteristic risks losing sight of the fact that the privateness or publicness of a good often is not an innate property but a policy choice.

It would be more appropriate to define public goods as goods in the public domain; or, better, to start with a public policy debate about the desirable properties of the public domain and then ask economists how to build that domain. This would bring into sharper focus the special category of non-rival goods, such as many parts of our knowledge stock. Often, these goods could be made public by design, at high net benefits to society as a whole, while preserving incentives for continued activity by private knowledge producers.

3. Preference Revelation

A substantial literature addresses the problems of preference revelation that are often associated with public goods. In large measure, it begins with an assumption that policymakers face a self-interested, free-riding electorate as they seek to answer questions of allocative efficiency. In practice, however, rather than hide its preferences, the public is struggling to find the ear of government. CSOs are demanding space alongside business at the decision-making table.

4. Addressing Inclusiveness

For the public, it is often as important to have been consulted as it is to achieve a particular policy outcome. The fairness of the process of decision making about public goods is a key element of their public properties—for the reason that fairness of process is presumed to lead to fairness of results. However, many goods in the public domain are shaped by international "clubs," such as the World Trade Organization (WTO) or the G10, engendering a perception that GPGs often benefit business interests and richer countries more than they do other stakeholders.

To take into account the expanded space of public policymaking and concerns about equity and justice, public goods should be subjected to two further tests to determine (1) the extent to which they are the product of a process marked by publicness in decision making, and (2) the extent to which their net benefits are public (in other words, benefiting all). Of course, not all public goods must, or can, benefit all. It is therefore important to have the additional notion of a public domain that is at least relatively equitable.

5. Diversification of Production

The state increasingly is just one of several actors involved in the production of public goods. This diversification is essential. Given the level of globalization, openness, and cross-border movements, GPGs can no longer be produced through domestic policy action alone but are the product of international cooperation, over and above multi-actor cooperation. This renders the production of public goods much more complex than is depicted in the state-centrist models of public economics—so much more complex, in fact, that the complexity can only be flagged here and not yet answered.

In sum, it would appear desirable to define public goods as goods that are public in consumption or, put differently, that are in the public domain. For each good, we must ask why it is there and whether its degree of publicness is optimal. We should also ask if, by making some goods (notably non-rival private goods) more public by design, we might enable the public domain to make a greater contribution to economic growth and development.

In addition, we need to acknowledge the growing importance of GPGs and, it seems, that of regional public goods.

The GPG Concept: A Guide for and to Global Public Policy Partnerships (GPPPs)

GPPPs play a role in setting global policy agendas, negotiating issues, and implementing joint endeavors. They tend to gather around issues, often focused on a global public good (GPG) whose inadequate provision adversely affects the lives of people around the world, and whose more efficient provision can be achieved only through horizontal and vertical cooperation.

GPPPs and their supporters should ask whether the partnership seeks primarily to address the provision of a GPG or whether it is bound merely by shared private concerns, as in the case of a club, say, for international lawyers, doctors, or meteorologists. The incentive structures of the participating members and the functioning of the partnership are in each case quite different.

For those GPPPs that address GPG concerns, an examination through a GPG lens of their structure and functioning could be critical to their success. The advantages that such a perspective would bring to the process include the following:

- *A shift in emphasis from reducing a bad to producing a good.* International cooperation efforts are often satisfied with merely keeping bads under control (for example, containing a political conflict or financial crisis). Often little effort is made to remove the root causes of a crisis and construct a corresponding good (for example, to move from conflict prevention to peace or from financial crisis control to financial stability and market efficiency). An explicit GPG focus would require partnerships to state their objectives clearly in constructive terms.

- *Issue/GPG specificity*. There is extensive literature showing how the properties of a good—that is, the exact nature of its privateness or publicness—determine the cooperative behavior of different actors. The message of this literature is that each public good, including GPGs, tends to follow its own good-specific production path. There is no "one size fits all" approach to the design and organization of public policy partnerships and goods.
- *The dual nature of the provision process*. In the case of private goods, markets will ex post reveal the preferences and demands of each individual. In the case of public goods, prioritization has to happen ex ante. Accordingly, the provision of public goods can be envisioned as two closely intertwined processes: (1) the decision making about which goods to produce, in what quantities, at what cost, and with what distribution of net benefits, among the parties concerned; and (2) the actual production process. GPPPs sometimes deal with only one of these processes. It is important to clarify which partners are engaged in which process, because the concerned parties may not necessarily be the same in each.
- *The need for an issue manager for a GPG*. The Global Alliance for Vaccines and Immunization, the Landmines Campaign, and the Commission on Dams all demonstrate what can be achieved with a strong driving force in place. On many development issues, however, it is unclear who is in charge. We are still exiting the era of geographical, sector-, or country-focused development—horizontal or layered development—and have yet to fully realize the type of vertical-plus-horizontal development that successful issue management requires. We need also to move away from bureaucratic development to a public entrepreneurial effort. Effective GPPPs and the enhanced provision of GPGs require a multi-actor, multisector, and multilevel approach—that is, matrix management. This may in many instances be too complex a task for partnership members to attempt using a decentralized committee approach. A CEO and staff may be required.
- *The financing of GPGs and GPPPs*. Neither GPGs nor GPPPs should be seen only as an "aid tool" for development. They are critical to the well being of people worldwide, in industrial as well as in developing countries, and are thus in the mutual interest of all. This should be reflected in their financing modalities. The Global Environmental Facility (GEF), for example, specifically addresses global environmental sustainability, but its work may also help alleviate poverty. To the extent that public funding is required, that funding should therefore come out of the budgets of the national sector ministries concerned. For example, money for the GEF should come mainly out of the budgets of environment ministries, but funding for the implementation of codes and standards

should come from central banks, which would stand to benefit from the seigniorage generated by the work done. Where global public goods are produced through GPPPs, there should be opportunities to raise public money to leverage private finance.

- *Anchoring GPGs and GPPPs.* Global public policy partnerships often emerge spontaneously, placing themselves between various actor groups. If we accept them as a pragmatic and practical response to the limitations of each individual actor, and hence as a desirable and necessary tool of policymaking, then it is necessary to define clear rules to link them to other actor groups. Failure to do this may result in GPPPs complicating rather than resolving problems of public policymaking and GPG provision.

Conclusions

We have entered a new era of policymaking. People's lives are increasingly affected by global public goods (GPGs), a large and growing number of which present themselves as negative cross-border externalities. GPPPPs, galvanized by civil society organizations, are responding to this trend. GPGs and GPPPs, together with the broader changes toward more direct democracy in which they are embedded, are growing in importance. The character of public goods has changed and requires a fresh conceptualization.

An appropriately updated conceptualization of GPGs would serve as an important tool for strategy and policy development by global public policy partnerships and by the international organizations that facilitate and support them.

The issues we are facing present new challenges of globalism, which demand that we work together across borders for common concerns, and new challenges of publicness. We must recognize that the public domain is indeed public and is there for all. The state is the public's visible hand; it is not the public. The same holds true for intergovernmental organizations. The defining role of the GPPP is to bring together civil society and business—the key elements of the public sector—with the two main coordination mechanisms: the state and the market.

Notes

1. See, for example, Acocella (1998), Cornes and Sandler (1996), Musgrave and Musgrave (1984), and Stiglitz (2000).
2. This discussion draws on a wide range of sources, including Albrow (1996); Arrighi (1996); Bhagwati (1999); Anheier, Glasius, and Kaldor (2001); Dunning (1999); Galbraith (1994); Held (1995); Heilbroner and Milberg (1995); Keck and Sikkink (1998); Keohane and Nye (2000); Lindblom (2001); Megginson and Netter (2001); North (1990); Nye and Donahue (2000); O'Rourke and Williamson

(1999); Reich (1988); Rodrik (2000); Scholte and Schnabel (2001); Swanson (1992); and Walzer (1983).

3. We are suggesting here that the market itself is a public good. Its entry barrier—it is open in principle to all, but in practice only to those that have purchasing power—constitutes an access problem rather than an exclusionary quality. Markets can even be seen as a pure public good, because they also have the property of non-rivalry in consumption. In fact, a larger number of participants makes markets more competitive and more efficient.
4. Norms such as equity or gender equality constitute a public good in the sense that they are non-rival. My being treated equitably or equally does not subtract anything from your enjoyment of such a principle; on the contrary, my being treated equitably and/or equally confirms the validity of the norm and enhances the likelihood that you will enjoy the same right. See Rao (1999) for a more detailed discussion of this point. A system of representative democracy would also constitute a public good if it claimed to apply to all adult citizens of the polity. If it finds public acceptance, then it assumes an increasingly nonexclusive/nonexcludable character. Since it is non-rival in consumption, it even constitutes a pure public good, as many regimes do.
5. Contrary to other pressure groups, civil society organizations often meet top-down globalization with bottom-up pressures.
6. For an overview study, see Reinicke (1998); Reinicke and Deng (2000).
7. The sources of government failure can, besides outright corruption, be linked to a host of factors, including, for example, principle-agent problems. In addition, people in many countries have, of course, had quite traumatic experiences with autocratic government behavior, which are difficult to forget and therefore encourage people to take concerns into their own hands rather than entrust them to the state, or to the state alone, even if it is a democratically elected one. See, in particular, Arendt (1958).
8. Based on such CSO-business agreements, it has often been possible for governments to proceed with corresponding legislation.
9. The discussion draws on Kaul (2001); Kaul and Mendoza (2003); and Kaul, Grunberg, and Stem (1999a.).
10. It is important not to confuse GPGs with goods that are situated at the international level and which may or may not have global public benefits. For example, the United Nations is not a GPG; as a meeting place it is merely a contributor to the production of GPGs, such as peace or environmental sustainability.

References

Acccella, Nicola. 1998. *The Foundations of Economic Policy; Values and Techniques*. Cambridge, Mass.: Cambridge University Press.

Albrow, Martin. 1996. *The Global Age: State and Society beyond Modernity*. Stanford, Calif.: Stanford University Press.

Anheier, Helmut, Marlius Glasius, and Mary Kaldor. 2001. *Global Civil Society Yearbook 2001*. New York: Oxford University Press.

Arendt, Hannah. 1958. *The Human Condition*. New York: Doubleday.

Arrighi, Giovanni.1996. *The Long Twentieth Century: Money, Power and the Origins of Our Times*. London: Verso.

Bhagwati, Jagdish. 1999. "Third World Intellectuals and NGOs: Statement against Linkage." *The Earth Times* 8(17).

Cornes, Richard, and Todd Sandler. 1996. *The Theory of Externalities, Public Goods, and Club Goods* (2nd ed.). New York: Cambridge University Press.

Dunning, John H. (ed.). 1999. *Governments, Globalization, and International Business*. New York: Oxford University Press.

Edwards, Michael. 2000. *Future Positive: International Cooperation in the Twenty-First Century*. London: Earthscan.

Galbraith, John Kenneth. 1994. *A Journey through Economic Time: A Firsthand View*. New York: Houghton Mifflin.

Held, David. 1995. *Democracy and the Global Order: From the Modern State to Cosmopolitan Governance*. Stanford, Calif.: Stanford University Press.

Heilbroner, Robert L., and William S. Milberg. 1995. *The Crisis of Vision in Modern Economic Thought*. New York: Cambridge University Press.

Kaul, Inge. 2001. "Public Goods: Taking the Concept to the Twenty-First Century." In Daniel Drache, ed., *The Market of the Public Domain*. London and New York: Routledge.

Kaul, Inge, Isabelle Grunberg, and Marc A. Stem (eds.). 1999a. *Global Public Goods: International Cooperation in the 21st Century*. New York: Oxford University Press.

______. 1999b. "Defining Global Public Goods." In Inge Kaul, Isabelle Grunberg, and Mar Stern, eds., *Global Public Goods: International Cooperation in the 21st Century*. New York: Oxford University Press.

Kaul, Inge, and Ronald U. Mendoza. 2003. "Advancing the Concept of Public Goods." In Inge Kaul, Pedro Conceição, Katell Le Goulven, Ronald U. Mendoza, eds., *Providing Global Public Goods: Managing Globalization*. New York: Oxford University Press.

Keck, Margaret E., and Kathryn Sikkink. 1998. *Activists Beyond Borders*. Ithaca, N.Y.: Cornell University Press.

Keohane, Robert, and Joseph Nye. 2000. "Introduction." In Joseph Nye and John Donahue, eds., *Governance in a Globalizing World*. Washington, D.C.: Brookings Institution Press.

Lindblom, Charles E. 2001. *The Market System: What It Is, How It Works, and What to Make of It*. New Haven, Conn.: Yale University Press.

Megginson, William L., and Jeffrey M. Netter. 2001. "From State to Market: A Survey of Empirical Studies on Privatization." *Journal of Economic Literature* 39(2): 321–89.

Musgrave, Richard Abel, and Peggy Musgrave. 1984. *Public Finance in Theory and Practice*. New York: McGraw-Hill.

North, Douglass. 1990. *Institutions, Institutional Change and Economic Performance: Political Economy of Institutions and Decisions*. New York: Cambridge University Press.

Nye, Joseph, and John Donahue. 2000. *Governance in a Globalizing World*. Washington, D.C.: Brookings Institution Press.

O'Rourke, Kevin H., and Jeffrey G. Williamson. 1999. *Globalization and History: The Evolution of a Nineteenth Century Atlantic Economy*. Cambridge, Mass.: MIT Press.

Rao, J. Mohan. 1999. "Equity in a Global Public Goods Framework." In Inge Kaul, Isabelle Grunberg, and Marc Stern, eds., *Global Public Goods: International Cooperation in the 21st Century*. New York: Oxford University Press.

Reich, Robert B. 1988. *The Power of Public Ideas*. Cambridge, Mass.: Harvard University Press.

Reinicke, Wolfgang H. 1998. *Global Public Policy: Governing without Government?* Washington, D.C.: Brookings Institution Press.

Reinicke, Wolfgang H., and Francis Deng. 2000. *Critical Choices: The United Nations, Networks, and the Future of Global Governance*. Ottawa, Canada: IDRC Publishers.

Rodrik, Dani. 2000. "Governance of Economic Globalization." In Joseph Nye and John Donahue, eds., *Governance in a Globalizing World*. Washington, D.C.: Brookings Institution Press.

Scholte, Jan Aart, and Albrecht Schnabel (eds.). 2001. *Civil Society and Global Finance*. Tokyo: United Nations University Press.

Stiglitz, Joseph E. 2000. *Economics of the Public Sector* (3rd ed.). New York: W.W. Norton.

Strange, Susan. 1996. *The Retreat of the State*. Cambridge, Mass.: Cambridge University Press.

Swanson, Judith A. 1992. *The Public and the Private in Aristotle's Political Philosophy*. Ithaca, N.Y.: Cornell University Press.

Walzer, Michael. 1983. *Spheres of Justice: A Defense of Pluralism and Equality*. New York: Basic Books.

9

Regional Partnerships in the European Union

Anastassios Bougas

In Europe, for more than ten years, partnership has been a fundamental principle for implementing structural interventions in general, and regional policy in particular. Taking the European Union as a case study, this chapter examines the evolution of regional partnerships over time, evaluates their performance and impact, and draws some lessons.[1]

In the mid-1980s, it was widely recognized that Europe needed a new and more participatory delivery system for its regional policy, to increase the effectiveness of the policy and to reduce the internal disparities of the enlarged European Union (EU).[2] After experimentation in the context of the Integrated Mediterranean Programs of France, Italy, and Greece, a new delivery system was introduced, based on four principles: indicative programming; concentration of measures and financial resources on limited priorities and objectives; additionality of EU resources; and partnership.

Partnership offered a means to achieve close cooperation between the Commission and the national, regional, and local authorities in each member state, covering the whole cycle of the policy process from preparation, planning, implementation, and monitoring through to evaluation. The EU Commission hoped that partnership would operate as a lever for institutional change and capacity building, and that the new arrangements would "change the aims and associated decision-making paths and patterns within the national administrations in order to improve their quality as a delivery mechanism" (Hall, Smith, and Tsoukalis 2001).

Evolution of EU Regional Partnerships

Over time, regional partnerships have become progressively more inclusive, shaped by efficiency concerns, an evolving concept of the European

Anastassios Bougas is Head of Evaluation, Regional Policy DG, Directorate A-Coordination of Evaluation, of the European Commission.

model of society and participatory democracy, and reactions to the demand for more participation by emerging actors. (Box 9.1 describes the partners involved.) It is useful to distinguish four phases:

1986–89: Experimentation

The experimental phase sought to explore a new method of work, taking dialogue and cooperation/consultation as the key areas in which to measure the success of programs (European Commission 1988). The approach taken consisted of program-based financing, joint identification of measures, involvement of the European Commission in the monitoring committees, and assumption by the regional authorities of a key role during the negotiation and implementation phase. Flexible programming was introduced, to be managed and continually adapted by the partners.

1989–93: Flexible Introduction of the Principle and Shared Responsibilities

Reform of the structural funds in 1988 put the partnership principle into general use.[3] The new regulations remained quite vague, enabling them to be flexibly interpreted and applied to different institutional and administrative contexts. The regional authorities were confirmed as key partners, but the member states did not involve them in the negotiation phase with the European Commission. There was no clear distinction between the responsibilities of the key partners concerning issues such as implementation, evaluation, control, or accountability.

1994–99: Inclusive Partnership Based on Subsidiarity

This phase saw the first clear differentiation between decision-making and consultative partners. With the 1993 reform of the structural fund, partnership became more inclusive with the integration of social partners, but its dynamic and perspective remained limited by the partners' need to comply with their respective national institutional, legal, and financial provisions. This development echoed debates at the EU level in the early 1990s on the definition of a European model of society and the delimitation of competencies between the different institutional levels, based on the subsidiarity principle.

2000–06: Redefinition of Responsibilities and Roles

With the 1999 reform of the structural funds, partnership has become more inclusive, welcoming new members such as environmental authorities and opening up to NGOs and associations working on gender equality. The accession of Sweden and Finland was the catalyst for action on gender and the environment. Subsidiarity was reinforced, too, with the European Commission renouncing its role as a full member of the monitoring committees and leaving the steering of subnational partnerships to member states.

Box 9.1
The EU Partners

•The European Commission has maintained an important position within the partnership structure. Although considered an external protagonist with its own priorities, the Commission helps the "internal" partners to formulate and present coherent positions. Its role has become more strategic: giving advice and instructions, and ensuring compliance with the rules. As a partner, the Commission has important leverage in regional policy, through its access to independent information and its legitimacy (even if this is not unconditional) (Marks, Hooghe, and Blanc 1996). Its role as a strategic partner depends on its capacity to use diverse contacts, its ability to anticipate and meditate demands, its decision-making efficiency, and its internal cohesion, which must enable it to move quickly on key issues of economic and social cohesion.

•The member states—the EU's dominant partners—set the strategy, jointly with the Commission, for negotiations on assistance to regions; they define national priorities for policy conception and articulation; and they negotiate programs with the Commission. Within the national context, they nominate vertical and horizontal partners; they decide the management and payment authorities and guarantors of the functions of control, audit, conformity, and accountability; and they diffuse information and guidance to lower administrative levels.

•The regional authorities have maintained an intermediary role as full partners, but more is now expected of them. Their role has evolved from responsibility for straightforward executive tasks to providing a more tangible input into policymaking. Their competencies depend on national institutional and administrative frameworks. In centralized member states they are an executive partner operating on behalf of the member state and assuming some of its functions, while in federal states they take on some comparable responsibilities.

•Municipal authorities are increasingly influential but not universally recognized within the structure of EU regional partnerships. The importance of towns in regional development and the creativity of urban partnerships have led to a call for real and systematic integration of municipal authorities into regional partnerships, but many regional authorities have sought to restrict the role of municipalities as they consolidate their own position.

•Social partners are systematically present in a consultative role throughout the program cycle, but consultation with them is most effective at the pre-negotiation phase and in the specification and development of programs. Their contributions vary, depending on the existence of technical support, the intervention field (for example, employment, social inclusion, or training), and the tradition of corporatism within the member state or region concerned. With a view to upgrading their role and commitment, the legal requirements of the structural funds now oblige the member states to state explicitly in their plans the arrangements for consultation with social partners, and to integrate their views in the plans.

•Environmental authorities, NGOs, and representatives of civil society and stakeholders are progressively being integrated into the partnership. It is expected that their contribution will relate most to the goals of the programs, taking account of any potential for conflict of interest. The need to ensure that regional development patterns favor sustainable development will enhance the role and impact of these latecomers to regional partnerships.

The structural fund regulation of 1999 provides a clear differentiation of partners' roles. Three forms of partnership have emerged:

- Strategic partnership concentrates on programming, negotiation, evaluation, and performance. The strategic partners are the member states and the European Commission.
- Operational partnership concentrates on implementation, control, and accountability. The operational partners are the member states and to some degree the regional authorities.
- Consultative partnerships are active before and during programming, as well as during program implementation. They are under the control of the member states.

Europe has implemented the partnership principle pragmatically, to avoid blockages in decision making. As the Tavistock evaluation pointed out, for reasons of flexibility, of competencies defined in national contexts, and of experience and capacity, "there are significant differences in the participation of partners in the programming cycle, with a more important role for more partners at the planning and project selection stage, a variable role for different partners for various operational tasks, and a less developed role for the full formal partnership in terms of monitoring and evaluation" (European Commission 1999).

The first regional partnerships were oriented more to implementing goals than to defining them. Since most were put in place after programs had been conceived and drafted, their initial function was to oversee the implementation of national priorities at the regional level. They carried out mutual surveillance, and their existence encouraged transparency in financial flows and provided a supplementary guarantee to the member states that were major contributors to the EU budget.

As the regional partnerships evolved, they became a key communication channel for information and knowledge, which encouraged the development of new perspectives on program strategy. Ongoing evaluation was developed, intensive discussions took place between partners at both the formal and informal levels, policy priorities were identified, and debate began on the causes of achieving or not achieving expected results. Progressively, an interaction developed between programming and implementation needs, with the regional partnerships becoming, to some extent, what Schon (1994) defines as an "organizational learning mechanism."

Some negative side effects of partnership have also emerged over the ten-year period. Tasks and competencies were initially the joint responsibility of the vertical institutional partners—the Commission and member states—and this resulted in some confusion in accountability.

Another source of problems is the fact that the regional partnerships do not all have the same capacity for learning and adaptation; this makes the procedures for partnership time-consuming. Furthermore, in the many member states that continued with their own political agendas on decentralization, the co-existence of two management systems—the results-oriented system of the structural funds and national systems of public expenditure—also created tension, linked to the subsidiarity principle.

Shaping Factors for Partnerships

The fact that a common model has quite successfully been applied to different institutional, administrative, and social regulation contexts prompts the question: What factors shape partnership, and are they common to the different phases—launch, development, and functioning—of partnership? My feeling is that they are not, and that the best way to establish partnerships is not necessarily from the bottom up.

In the EU's experience the major shaping factor has been the work of a single partner—the Commission—which catalyzed the establishment and development of a large-scale partnership. Such a partner should have a broad vision, be able to lead the partnership, offer technical assistance and support for the empowerment of partners, and have the capacity and credibility to launch the operation. The work of this one partner in setting the framework, supporting empowerment, and providing leadership in particular can be beneficial for regions without tradition and experience in these areas. In Europe, "in many cases the Union initiatives . . . [have] encouraged a strong regional mobilization, together with the emergence of the new actors," and new partnerships themselves may also emerge (Keating 1998).

A second shaping factor in the EU has been the national context in the individual member states. This is often dominant, particularly during the operational phase and in the definition of each partner's room for maneuver. As noted by the Tavistock Institute evaluation, "the degree of decentralization and the de-concentration occurring in the different member states shapes the relations between key actors within partnerships" (European Commission 1999).

Other shaping factors are the nature, content, and type of intervention, and in some cases the physical geography. Regional programs, urban programs, cross-border programs, social inclusion programs, territorial employment pacts, and so forth require partnerships with compositions and practices that correspond to the specific objectives of the intervention or the territory and the agents being mobilized. Some regional partnerships have difficulties in communication posed by physical geography and lack of territorial continuity. This is even more problematic in cross-border regional partnerships, which have additional problems associated with the multiplicity of legal and administrative contexts and practices.

Finally, experience suggests that the greater the tradition of cooperation among civil society, stakeholders, and beneficiaries, the more creative a partnership tends to be. Engagement among these actors counterbalances the vertical dimension, which has a tendency to institutionalize and sometimes to bureaucratize the partnership function (Putnam 1993).

Performance and Impact of Regional Partnerships

Achievement of Primary Objectives

Better strategy. The rationale for regional strategy is now clearer and better justified. The coherence among needs, priorities, and objectives has been progressively strengthened as it has been challenged at different levels.

Project selection has gradually improved. The selection criteria for projects are published in the programming documents and are subjects of discussion and approval in the monitoring committees. Project selection is more transparent than in compartmentalized administrations, resulting in projects that better fit their purposes and better mobilization of local agents and project promoters.

Increased capacity to absorb funds. Partnership functions as a permanent alert mechanism, in which each partner has its own reason to accelerate financial flows and their absorption. Within the monitoring committees, and often based on ongoing evaluation, the debate is about what does and what does not work. This reflective approach to problem solving influences both strategic and operational concerns, including the absorption of funds.

Partnership operates as a communication channel, helping to improve coordination across sectoral administrations and the different vertical levels. Each partner is invited to demonstrate coherence within and across its areas of responsibility. Both horizontal and vertical coordination have improved. Coordination at the EU level, though there is still room for improvement, has been enhanced through common priorities, joint negotiation teams, shared participation in the monitoring committees, tighter management practices, and common evaluations.

Partnership aids transparency. Not only are the underlying reasons for program goals and project selection more transparent, but public procurement at national and regional levels also has become more open and reached greater conformity with European directives.

Secondary Effects

The delivery mechanism for the structural funds in general and partnership in particular has contributed to some other key developments:

Partnership operates as a lever for institutional change and capacity building. Member states were obliged to set up or to develop institutional capacity to assume the new responsibilities of regional programming, monitoring, and management at a decentralized level (European Commission 1999). For some member states the new delivery system for regional policy and the decentralized partnership initiated or accelerated decentralization and/or the deconcentration reforms, while others recast and reshaped their existing institutional and administrative patterns.[4] The new environment encouraged new actors to emerge: politicians, environmental authorities, municipalities, social partners, and NGOs (Marks, Hooghe, and Blanc 1996).

Partnership is helping to maintain a permanent and relatively stable structure of program implementation. This often was absent in the past; in many less-developed regions, lack of attention to implementation resulted in "sleeping projects" and billions of euros in unabsorbed credits.

Partnership influences regional economic development patterns through integrating beneficial new developments. The political priorities of higher levels and the work of local actors are transforming traditional regional economic patterns, introducing more positive attitudes to the environment, gender equality, and innovation, and thus increasing the potential for intangible investments, financial engineering, and public–private partnerships.

Partnership, functioning as a mechanism for positive integration, reduces the need to produce regulations and legal clauses that reduce flexibility. Working together facilitates explanation, understanding, interpretation, and the identification of appropriate solutions within a legal framework.

Partnership is a driver for modernization of regional policy management. The delivery system of the structural funds has introduced a results-oriented management system.

Partnership has produced real progress on evaluation. The learning curve on evaluation has been extraordinarily steep. In the period 1990–2000, working in partnership made possible the development of methodologies for program evaluation and the launching of hundreds of evaluations. The European Commission began creating the demand a decade ago, and has maintained the pressure for evaluation, emphasizing "learning by doing" in this regard. Today, the regions and all the member states have concrete experience in ex ante and ongoing evaluation. Evaluation tasks are now organized in a network so that each partner learns from the activity of others and all partners work to improve evaluation practice[5] and the quality of regional program strategies and implementation. Informal technical evaluation groups function at the levels of the EU, member states, and many regions. The regional partnerships have different levels of knowledge and innovation capacity, but each, according to its own rhythm, is progressing toward a convergent evaluation system.

Balancing Consensus with Efficiency, and Other Concerns

The literature on European integration converges toward the view that the most effective and democratic form of governance is multilevel governance. Multilevel governance is more effective "because partners and institutions are better committed to achieve goals and objectives for which they have already contributed to the definition and specification."[6] It is more democratic for reasons of proximity (Polack 2001).

On the downside, critics see the lengthening of the decision-making process for regional policy as a loss of efficiency. "Europeanization" and decentralization have also challenged national and regional patterns and their territorial interaction, and often required time-consuming adaptations and arbitration (Benz and Eberlein 1999). The partnership principle and the desire for consensual decisions could lead in such cases to what has been defined as the "joint decision trap" (Scharpf 1988).

In practice it appears that the benefit obtained through partnership—a better fit of the priorities and greater ownership of the program goals—outweighs any detrimental effects of the more protracted decision-making process. Close observation of the structural funds' multilevel decision-making process reveals a sort of "safety valve" that establishes equilibrium between the search for broader consensus and the need for efficiency. High-level decisions are taken at an intergovernmental level, where negotiators have the necessary institutional legitimacy and capacity for fast decision making. Partnership in this context is really proactive. In turn, decisions on program priorities and objectives are made through a hierarchy that gives an impetus to the conception of programs and reprogramming.

Furthermore, there is a clear safeguard mechanism of mutual adjustment in relation to negotiation and implementation. The monitoring system has a periodicity that prevents the postponement of progress checks (it includes biannual monitoring meetings, an annual progress report, and an annual overview of execution and problems between the Commission and the management authority of the program). A critical path sets time limits for policy conception and articulation, as well as for consultations and negotiations. A performance reserve[7] has been introduced to promote the achievement of key operational goals and improvement in the quality of the entire management, monitoring, and evaluation system. Any committed funds not used within two years are automatically de-committed, with no compensating credit. In addition, there is an obligatory timetable for the mid-term evaluation and adaptation of programs and for the closure of program activities.

Efficiency gains result also from the reduction of potential conflicts by working through partnerships. Partnerships, particularly those that are proactive, strengthen the internal coherence of the program (needs, priorities, and broad and specific objectives) and its external coherence (EU, national, and regional priorities), thus facilitating smooth implementation.

Several other criticisms have appeared during the EU's ten years of partnership development.

First, the "Europeanization" of regional policies poses the risk of some organizations losing some of their competencies to the national and European levels. This concern is understandable, given that member states and the European Commission define the legal clauses, but there is no major evidence of such a development.

Second, the Court of Auditors has criticized the European Commission for irregularities and insufficient application of rules by the lower levels. Some of these criticisms resulted from the lack of a clear definition and identification of the responsibilities and tasks of each partner, and to some degree they highlight a refusal to consider that for each innovation with good results, there were others that introduced risks and errors. Insufficient human resources, circumstances, and the human factor can feed into such criticisms, with a resulting need to redefine the roles and structure of partnerships.

The third criticism, lack of cost-effectiveness, seems to be justified for some small programs from which the system requires new processes and more data collection. More generally, the problem relates to the fact that two parallel management systems continue to operate: the member states that are beneficiaries of the structural funds are reluctant to adapt their own systems to those required under the funds, increasing to some degree the transaction costs.

Some Lessons of Experience

Partnerships Should Be Considered Mid- to Long-term Investments

The use of partnerships should be allowed to develop progressively, to ensure the integration of partners in a shared, common approach that will prove efficient in the operational phase.

Partnership Requires Partnership Capacity

Capacity building takes time, and needs differ among regions. Partnership in lagging regions that lack experience, practice, or appropriate technical assistance needs a learning period of three to five years to produce results that add value to the quality of programs. This type of partnership requires animation, steering, and leadership. Strategic partners should allow new partners the possibility to use technical assistance to develop appropriate monitoring and evaluation systems. At this stage, partnerships are less reflective, and thus they should have less demanding timetables for program design and reprogramming.

Partnership in declining industrial regions needs to be oriented away from defensive and/or corporatist attitudes. Evaluation can make an important contribution for partnership effectiveness and reflectiveness: opening these partnerships to representatives of municipalities and other stakeholders creates an impetus for their reshaping and performance.

Partnerships in developed and dynamic regions are rapidly effective and dynamic. Their main problem is the absence of flexibility in the program boundaries and the obligation to respect top-down priorities. They need space to exercise their high capacity for innovation.

Different Partners Make Different Contributions

The roles, participation, and added value of different partners vary. It should be accepted that the stronger partner should have more responsibility, as the driver for capacity improvement, and for supplying technical assistance to help the weaker partner perform its role. Lack of confidence or excessive enthusiasm can be counterproductive; pragmatic partnerships with responsibilities defined corresponding to the real capacity of partners seem most successful.

Responsibilities Must Be Clear

In all cases, successful partnership requires a good definition of the individual partners' responsibilities and tasks. Lack of definition of what should be done, who initiates what, which partner is accountable for what, and what comes under partnership and what does not are some of the key factors behind inefficient partnerships. Lack of clarity also generates tensions among partners.

Rapid Rotation of Personnel Is Risky

Valuable experience is often lost because of changes in personnel. During the launching and development phase of partnership, notably in the less-developed regions, rules, practices, procedures, and information are not always written down and preserved for future use. Rapid rotation disadvantages weaker partners and leads to the establishment of dominant partners or relationships of dependence, and the asymmetry of knowledge between partners reduces partnership performance.

Quality and On-time Information

Last but not least is the requirement for appropriate quality information and data systems. In many cases, the setting up of partnerships precedes the establishment of procedures and the collection of the necessary data. Such a situation leads to unsuccessful partnership.

Conclusions

In the context of EU structural policies, partnership has had a significant impact on efficiency, institutional development, and capacity building. It has encouraged the emergence of new stakeholders that have strengthened the work of endogenous development.

Partnership functions as an integrative mechanism based on an understanding of the needs, priorities, and capacities of the different partners. Thus it is a tool for flexibility and coherence and for lasting mutual adjustments to manage this flexibility. Where partnership is absent or reduced, legal clauses and regulations multiply and introduce rigidity and distance to decision making.

Partnership influences regional development patterns. Such patterns have evolved to integrate the needs of more competitiveness related to the opening of the European economy; to ensure better integration of local needs; and to support sustainable development. The more regional partnerships are open, inclusive, and dynamic, the more regional strategy and programs will be innovative.

Partnership has been the key mechanism used to introduce new instruments with which to manage regional and public policies. The diffusion and promotion of evaluation practice is a representative example.

Notes

1. Much of this chapter is informed by a high-quality evaluation by the Tavistock Institute on behalf of the European Commission (European Commission 1999). There is a double controversy in economic and political science literature over the degree to which the European structural funds contribute to the reduction of regional disparities, and over the degree to which partnership, as a multilevel decision-making tool, reinforces the decentralization and regionalization of public policies. Having in mind that this debate should continue, the conclusions I draw in this chapter should be treated with caution: perhaps they are best seen as a basis for further discussion, and for the reevaluation of regional partnerships.
2. The procedure used was project-based budgeting, national priorities, and financial resources distributed on the basis of national quotas.
3. The structural funds comprise the four instruments for co-financing activities within the member states: the European Regional Development Fund, the European Social Fund, the European Agricultural Guidance and Guarantee Fund, and the Financial Instrument for Fisheries Guidance.
4. For Greece, Portugal, and recently Sweden and Ireland, this is a question of launching the decentralization process.
5. Competencies for evaluation have been reorganized to maximize the benefits. Programming authorities are responsible for ex ante evaluation, mid-term evaluation is a shared responsibility of partners, and the ex post evaluation is the responsibility of the European Commission. Technical evaluation groups operate at the level of the European Commission and the member states as well as many regional levels.

6. This is one of the key conclusions of the Tavistock Institute evaluation of partnership (European Commission 1999).
7. Four percent of the financial allocations corresponding to each program has been set aside. It forms a common pot to distribute in the middle of the period to the performing programs.

References

Allen, D. 2000. "Cohesion and the Structural Funds." In *Policy Making in the European Union*. Oxford: Wallace and Wallace.

Benz, A., and B. Eberlein. 1999. "Regions in European Governance: The Logic of Multi-Level Interaction." *Journal of European Public Policy* (June).

Crozier, M. 1994. "Le Problème de l'Action Collective: L'Éducation du Regard." In *L'Analyse Stratégique*. Paris: Seuil.

European Commission. 1988. "Activity Report of 1986/87 on IMPs." Brussels: European Commission.

———. 1996. "First Report on Economic and Social Cohesion." Office for official publications of the European Communities.

———. 1999. "The Thematic Evaluation of the Partnership Principle." Tavistock Institute on behalf of the European Commission.

Hall, R., A. Smith, and L. Tsoukalis. 2001. "Competitiveness and Cohesion in EU Policies." Oxford: Oxford University Press.

Keating, M. 1998. "Is There a Regional Level of Government in Europe?" In *Regions in Europe*. London: Routledge.

Marks, G., L. Hooghe, and K. Blanc. 1996. "European Integration from the 1980s: State-Centric versus Multi-Level Governance." *Journal of Common Market Studies* 3 (September).

Polack, A. 2001. "Evaluation ex ante de la Réforme 1999 de la Politique Régionale de l'UE: Renationalisation ou Gouvernance à Plusieurs Niveaux?" Thesis, Collège d'Europe, Bruges, Belgium.

Putman, R. D. 1993. "Making Democracy Work." Princeton, N.J.: Princeton University Press.

Scharpf, F. W. 1988. "The Joint Decision Trap: Lessons from German Federalism and European Integration." *Public Administration* 66.

Schon, D. A. 1994. "Quelques Questions à propos du Concept d'Apprentissage Organisationne." In *L'Analyse Stratégique*. Paris: Seuil.

Smith, Andy. 1988. "The Sub-Regional Level: Key Battleground Level for the Structural Funds." In *Regions in Europe*. London and New York: Routledge.

———. 1995. "L'Europe Politique au Miroir du Local: Les Fonds Structurels dans les Zones Rurales en France, en Espagne, et au Royaume Uni." Paris: L'Harmattan.

10

Country-Focused Partnerships—Lessons from Experience

Kwesi Botchwey

This chapter offers a few words of caution about the practice of partnership.

The partnership approach to development is not new. What is new is that it has become widely accepted as the most effective and viable framework for development cooperation. The factors that have shaped the evolution of this approach include the following:

- The end of the Cold War and resultant changes in the political interests and priorities of donor countries.
- Rising public interest in partnerships in both donor and recipient countries. This has manifested itself in the emergence of militant civil society advocacy groups, in the practice of development assistance against a background of new constraints on aid budgets, and in an increasingly recriminatory debate about the impact and effectiveness of aid.
- The quest for greater effectiveness in the allocation, management, and use of aid.
- An international focus on the global dimensions of development and on the need to evolve sustainable solutions to global challenges, such as those in trade, financial markets, and public health.

Giving Partnership an Operational Meaning

The World Bank has done a great deal of work in recent years to help give the concept of partnership an operational meaning. The work has also sought to allay concerns, noted particularly among recipient countries, that the talk of partnership is just empty rhetoric.

Kwesi Botchwey is director of Africa Research aand Programs, Center for International Development, Harvard University.

Despite the multiplicity of initiatives, there is a remarkable convergence of views—that an effective partnership must include the following components:

- Country ownership of the development agenda. This is broadly defined as leadership by the recipient country in setting the agenda, mobilizing and coordinating external support for it, and sustaining it through the intellectual and political commitment of the government and the broad support of stakeholders, based on their participation in the policymaking process and understanding of key development objectives.
- Support, by donors, of the national development agenda through an adaptation of their programs and administrative procedures to the recipient country's national strategy and local conditions. This should be achieved through a consultative process, preferably conducted in the recipient country.
- A rationalization of donor programs and projects within the overall framework of the national agenda, a harmonization of donor administrative procedures to ease the pressure on country capacity, and the decentralization of decision-making authority away from donor capitals to the "field."

Any Progress?

These basic conditions for partnership are meant to address the weaknesses of previous development assistance frameworks.[1] They are broadly consistent with the views and expectations of the recipient countries. In 1998, the Development Assistance Committee (DAC) of the Organization for Economic Co-operation and Development convened a forum of development partners and five developing countries to discuss ways of improving partnerships. The forum reportedly identified a need to strengthen national ownership through improved aid coordination and the harmonization and simplification of donor procedures. This finding is broadly consistent with the recommendations of a number of position papers by bilateral donors and independent studies.

The partnership agenda has been advanced by the World Bank's Partnership Initiative and by the commitment of the International Development Association to move matters beyond a declaration of intent. Progress has been made in rationalizing donor programs, harmonizing donor procedures, decentralizing decision-making authority to the field, and fostering the involvement of stakeholders in recipient countries in policymaking and debate. The Bank's partnership strategy has been put into practice in a number of countries.

Progress has not been unobstructed, however. Obstacles on the donor side include the influence of commercial (and, to a lesser extent, political) interests in donor aid decisions, which have encouraged derogation from national investment strategies and/or competition with other donors; and the tendency for aid agencies and offices to compete rather than collaborate in support of national strategy.

Obstacles on the recipient country's side include the tendency to exaggerate capacity and failure to identify capacity weaknesses. Both of these inhibit the exercise of national ownership. Even where there has been reasonable progress, such as the broadening of stakeholder participation, new problems have arisen.

Where Are We Now?

The Poverty Reduction Strategy Paper/Comprehensive Development Framework (PRSP/CDF) initiatives and processes have advanced the partnership agenda, but they have also exposed a number of pitfalls. It is generally recognized that successful partnership depends on national ownership, and that this in turn depends on national capacity and effective aid coordination. It is worth taking a look at the lessons we can draw from our short experience with the PRSP/CDF processes.

National Capacity

Lack of capacity has been a major constraint on the preparation and timely submission of PRSPs. It is important to view this problem from the perspective of the recipient countries. The decision to adopt the PRSP—initially as the trigger mechanism for access to the resources available to heavily indebted poor countries and now for all development assistance—was taken without consultation with the countries that would be expected to complete the document. The decisions on the structure, form, content, and timeframe for the submission of PRSPs were also made without consultation.

The PRSP was introduced into ongoing active aid relationships, with all their complexity and their calls on scarce capacity. The prevailing conditions clearly did not adequately shape the launching of the new process. To further confound the issue, a torrent of donor-funded consultants descended to offer assistance before the target countries could digest the full import of the PRSPs or mobilize to lead the process. Given these circumstances, it is hardly surprising that lack of capacity has become a constraint on country-led PRSP processes.

Donor and Bank policies have tended to be ineffectual, costly, and mostly supply-driven—and in many cases they have tended to weaken capacity at the national level. It is instructive that although donor enthusiasm for it has grown in recent times, the Partnership for African Capacity Building (PACT), now part of the expanded mandate of the African Capacity Building Foundation (ACBF), remains peripheral to the capacity-building programs of donors and the IDA itself. Equally instructive, the IMF has remained outside the PACT and, regrettably, is reportedly contemplating a new initiative of its own.

Aid Coordination

Aid coordination and country ownership of the partnership process are dialectically related. Better aid coordination, achieved through the harmonization of donor programs and procedures, legitimizes the central place of nationally determined strategies and investment priorities, and eases pressure on national capacity. It thereby facilitates the exercise of national leadership in the technical as well as the political aspects of the PRSP process. Donor support of the PRSP process as the definitive framework for country-led programs is often less than wholehearted, however, with some donors reportedly preferring to use more conventional vehicles to route their funding. The continuing uncertainty over the place of sector-wide approaches in the PRSP has not been particularly helpful in this regard.

There has been no shortage of alternative ideas for a partnership framework. The CDF, for example, could have served as a vehicle for pursuing the goals that inspired the PRSP process. Some progress has been made, not least in relocating coordination mechanisms such as the consultative group to recipient countries and in ensuring broader stakeholder participation in policymaking and implementation. But the empirical record of development assistance shows that there is still a substantial gap between the partnership rhetoric and the reality on the ground.

The mood in recipient countries is one of "pragmatic engagement"—a euphemism for resignation—with many countries simply going through the motions to get development assistance. There is growing cynicism over a succession of initiatives and mechanisms that tax national energies and capacities without providing real relief, and popular sentiment in many donor countries is becoming just as cynical.

The Greatest Challenge

The greatest obstacle to the realization of effective partnership is the inability of the partner country to provide the required leadership. This incapacity has persisted despite near-unanimous agreement on the need for strong national leadership. In truth, however, recipient countries have little space to exercise leadership. Within many partnerships they have little or no political leverage, and such capacity as they have is often undermined by pressure from the aid relationship.

Many countries lack the resources (or are so immersed in the aid-dependency psychology that they are unable to prioritize the use of their resources) to convene meetings to coordinate their position with their donor counterparts. For many, their only meetings are those convened and led by donors or donor-sponsored institutions. The international community thus sets the international development agenda, targets, and performance benchmarks, and the issues that are current in the international development discourse dominate the national development debate.

Policymakers are usually so preoccupied with managing relations with donors and with the multilateral development banks that little or no time is left to reflect on long-term structural issues other than those raised in the framework of donor relations. In these circumstances, the presence of decentralized donor staff in the field and the participation of civil society and private sector actors may serve to further scatter the focus of policymakers and cripple government leadership.

Conclusion

I do not seek to imply that recipient countries are blameless victims of an overbearing donor relationship. Nor would I suggest that the situation cannot be fundamentally changed, as the partnership initiative portends. I would simply summarize my argument as follows:

We must remind ourselves from time to time that in our zeal to see results we often unwittingly cripple local initiative and creativity. East Asia would never have wrought its miracle if it had been subjected to such a phalanx of donor initiatives and ideas. Countries that are in receipt of aid need to be more proactive, and donors need to allow more space and time for national debate. Policymaking should be guided by a thorough understanding of both the universality and the particularity of the development challenge. We must recognize that responsibility for the realization of development outcomes is primarily that of the country concerned. It is not a shared responsibility of country and donor.

Beyond these concerns for space and national leadership facilitation, the unfinished agenda for aid coordination and the role of conditionality will need to be addressed if country-led partnerships are to become a reality.

Note

1. At a meeting convened in 1995 by the Secretariat of the Task Force on Multilateral Development Banks (MDBs) with thirty-two African participants from government, civil society, and the private sector, the participants reportedly described the "old" assistance framework quite predictably as a train whose destination and speed of travel are determined by donors and the MDBs.

11

Country and Donor Partnerships

Stuart Salter

As a representative of a bilateral aid agency, I bring a perspective to the aid partnership debate not yet represented in this book. There are some things we do well and others where we have some work to do.

The Canadian International Development Agency (CIDA) is an agency of the government of Canada mandated to support sustainable development activities that aim to reduce poverty and contribute to a more secure, equitable, and prosperous world. CIDA has its own minister, the Minister of International Cooperation, and operates as an independent ministry under the aegis of the Foreign Affairs Department.

CIDA is involved in 170 countries around the world. This is a direct result of Canada's unique position in the global community. Canada is part of the British Commonwealth and also a part of the Francophonie; we are a Pacific Rim country, and we also maintain a North–South relationship. CIDA has four geographic branches, a multilateral branch, and a policy branch that reaches back into the government.

In practical terms, we are set up as a line department that delivers programs. Our funding comes from the Canadian government, and we are subject to all of the government's rules and regulations, as embodied in our treasury board. We also must comply with the Canadian Environmental Assessment Act. The money we spend comes from taxpayers, and we must therefore spend it in ways the people of Canada want.

The Evolving Challenge of Partnership

Our approach to partnerships has been traditional, but we see that this must change. We do not believe that the organization and the structures we operate under permit us to do the kind of things we want to do or ought to be doing.

Stuart Salter is director, Scientific, Technical, and Specialist Resources Division, Canadian International Development Agency.

The most serious of our problems concerns the nature of the programs we support. At present, our accountability is assessed according to short-term financial regulations. Once a year, the Auditor General's office comes and looks over CIDA's operations, to make sure we are following Canada's rules and regulations. We have to show where our money goes and how it is spent. Because of this, we have been judging programs not by their long-term effectiveness, but on the way they look during Canada's annual audit—and many long-term programs, looked at in the short term, seem to acomplish very little. The short-term reporting requirement thus shapes the way we fund and set up development initiatives, and in many cases discourages us from undertaking sound projects simply because their annual bottom line is not attractive enough.

Another problem CIDA faces is familiar to many development agencies: money. In the last decade, our budget has decreased from US$3 billion a year to US$2 billion.

A third problem, and again one shared by lots of development agencies, is what happens to that money.

We recently polled Canadians, asking what they thought of international development. The results showed almost unconditional support for humanitarian assistance and complete support for such international agencies as the Red Cross.

For bilateral country projects, however, there was much less support. One reason for this, to put it bluntly, is that in some of the countries that Canada has aided, the money has not gone to aid projects, it has simply disappeared. CIDA must demonstrate to Canadians that we are spending their money well. If they are discontented with the way we spend money, Canadians will stop supplying that money.

Communications

I should point out here that our taxpayers' support also depends on our communication skills. I believe CIDA's performance evaluation group does an excellent job technically, but we fail to get the message across to the people of Canada about the real goals of development and the successes that our efforts achieve. I also think Canada suffers from the "global mill syndrome"—that is, every time a project goes wrong, the news of it hits the front page and another regulation is created telling us what to do. If we were in better control of the way we inform the public about our work, we could prevent such complications.

Coordination

CIDA often is involved in projects with other donors. Joint projects can impose a terrible burden on aid recipients: every agency has its goals, and every agency has its reporting structure and a set of rules it must follow. Many of us must also conform to an incentive structure. This can result in ten partners working on the same project with ten different results-frameworks and ten missions jetting into town, all with their own consultants. Of course, the government of each partner expects a report only about what its own particular agency has achieved. The sum of the aid provided by the ten donors may be US$100 million, but the fact that every single agency must cleave to its own rules and regulations means the whole is much less than the sum of its parts.

Let me give an example. In the Caribbean, we and a number of other agencies have been trying for some time to get an HIV/AIDS project off the ground. It could be a terrific project. Everybody agrees it is the right thing to do, and everybody agrees on the methodology. However, with more than ten donors involved in planning the project, it is weighed down by so many complications it is almost impossible to see how we will ever get it off the ground.

Adapting for the Future

The context of international development is changing, and many aid agencies are reviewing their approaches, structure, and policies. At CIDA, we have realized that we need to make a number of changes. In particular, we see that our future development projects must operate with new drivers. The most important ones are as follows.

A Strategic, Results-based Approach

To start, we need to look critically at our projects to make sure they fit within a broad context. Currently they are simply not strategic enough: though taken individually they appear to make sense, when we ask what we have achieved in a particular country or region, it is difficult for us to say.

Let me use an example our president has cited. Recently, he visited several countries in which a key political issue is land reform. In those countries, CIDA has supported two micro-enterprise endeavors—agricultural projects with such goals as improving crop yields. Those programs were good in and of themselves, but did they advance the vital issue of land reform? No. Did the programs work with those of any other donors—that is, were they part of some greater regional or sectoral framework? No. I suspect that these programs were created in part because of the structure of our agency, and the emphasis that we place on short-term results. Future CIDA programs and projects will likely need to be situated within an overall sector or regional framework.

Local Ownership

Another of the new drivers we must put in place is local ownership within our client countries. It is our experience that projects that do not have the engagement of a local entity fail, almost by definition. At the same time, it is also amply clear that the successful projects begin with the engagement and support of local civil society. This is a truism now to the development community. In the future, we expect it to become more and more difficult to obtain financial support for partnerships that do not have a strong element of local support.

Accountability

The next area we need to revise is that of accountability. Clearly, development agencies need to be able to report back to their own governments to account both for the substance of their development programs and for their use of funds. We want to change the rules of the game: we no longer want to judge the success of an aid project by short-term financial rules. Nor do we want a multiplicity of domestic reporting requirements to tie us up when we should be concentrating on the task in hand.

If we are to ask the auditor general and the government of Canada to change the rules, however, we shall need a new, very clear notion of accountability. We cannot toss out the old rules without putting in place a better alternative.

Reporting and Feedback

We need to create new mechanisms for reporting and feedback. We need to frame both projects and programs within a results structure that can be monitored, measured, and communicated. These new mechanisms must focus not on our agency but on our clients. There are three key issues here:

- The new framework must give CIDA a way to show clear results. It must employ good technical evaluation skills to show how the program is achieving its intended goals.
- Our future reporting and feedback mechanisms must provide clear lines of accountability. I hesitate to recommend this, because I understand the possible risks and dangers of using a pure, results method of accounting. I remain flexible about the ways we might decide to define "results."
- We must improve our communications skills, so that we can keep Canadians informed of the goals and purposes of our aid projects. I think our goal of redefining our accountability will be helped by the sensitivity and understanding of the people of Canada. I think they are willing to listen to us and understand this very important change.

New Partnerships

CIDA will also need to keep itself open to new forms of partnership. For example, sometimes CIDA might find that the best partner for a project is a foundation. We might even find that the best partner is someone in the private sector. The definition of potential partners is changing, and we must change in response.

Information and Communication Technologies (ICT)

Use of ICT is another driver that is essential to the new context of development agencies. ICT may enable us to continue with our familiar projects—more efficiently—but it also will allow us to contemplate aid work that hitherto may have been impossible. It will also permit us to engage a much broader base of stakeholders.

Stewardship of Funds

Finally, we must respect our stewardship of funds. Transparency is vital to aid partnerships. We need to show Canadians that we can take better care of the money they entrust to us—that we can operate with a superior degree of stewardship. We also need to explain why it is important that we revise the way we carry out our operations. When we talk to Canadians about our programs and plans, we need to talk not only about the moral imperative—on which most Canadians already agree—but also about the long-term benefits of aid programs for the world as a whole.

12

Partnerships for Knowledge Creation

Laurence Prusak and Salvatore Parise

This chapter examines how private sector companies are adapting to today's realities by expanding their knowledge resources and capabilities through alliances and partnerships. Based on recent research, we emphasize the key importance of the relational or social aspects of collaborative partnerships: building trust, awareness, and transparency with the partner; articulating and communicating alliance learning objectives; and managing partnerships holistically as well as individually.

There is little doubt that alliances and partnerships will be a critical component of strategic management in the twenty-first century. A recent study showed that highly successful companies expect 35 percent of their revenues by 2003 to come from alliances, up from 21 percent in 1998 and 15 percent in 1995 (Harbison and Pekar 1998). The same study revealed that the most active alliance participants achieved a 17 percent return on equity, which is much higher than the average returns for Fortune 500 companies and for the companies least active in alliances.

Alliances are a critical mechanism by which a company can acquire knowledge resources to complement its own internal capabilities (Hamel 1991; Hagedoorn and Schakenraad 1994; Stuart 2000). The types of resources that companies exchange in alliances include employee expertise, technological know-how, and customer knowledge, in addition to such physical resources as equipment, property, and products. The true test of an alliance depends less on *what* is exchanged, however, and more on *how the alliance manages its shared resources for joint value creation.* A learning capability is both an important component of partnership success and a differentiating factor among partnering companies.

Laurence Prusak is executive director, IBM Institute for Knowledge Management.
Salvatore Parise is a research consultant, IBM Institute for Knowledge Management.

Motivations for Forming Alliances

Just as an alliance or partnership can be structured in many different ways (for example, joint venture, marketing agreement, or license), there are many reasons why companies should form an alliance (Thompson 1967):

- Pooled interdependence exists when partners pool their resources to achieve a shared goal. The motivation is usually to improve operations by sharing high costs or by replacing expensive internal resources with more efficient partner resources.
- Sequential interdependence describes alliances in which a particular product or resource is transferred unilaterally from one partner to another. The motivation for these alliances is to gain access to the partner's knowledge resources. Software vendors, for example, often partner with system integrators or consulting companies to gain access to corporate markets. Sequential alliances are also used to manage risk and to hedge bets: large technology companies will partner with several smaller companies working on competing technologies to hedge their bets on which technology will win out in the marketplace.
- Reciprocal interdependence has the potential to create the most value. Reciprocal alliances involve the sharing of knowledge resources for innovation and joint product development, and require a high degree of integration and coordination between partners. An example is the mid-1990s alliance between Intel and Hewlett-Packard to develop a 64-bit chip. The reciprocal alliance also provides the greatest learning opportunities. Corning Glass began forming alliances in the 1970s with telecommunication companies and research firms to develop a commercial fiber-optic solution. The company found that one of the benefits of these alliances was collecting information that enabled it to establish a second series of alliances with manufacturers of its emergent products (Gomes-Casseres 2000).

Alliances can succeed, but they also can fail. Some researchers have cited success rates of lower than 50 percent (Harrigan 1988; Bleeke and Ernst 1985). Poor alliance design often gets the blame because benefits weighted too heavily in favor of one partner have caused the other partner to be dissatisfied. Changes in the marketplace can also cause partners to rethink their alliance, thus bringing about its premature demise.

Relational and Social Aspects of Alliances

Increasingly, however, the critical component of partnering is seen to be relationship management. Ertel, Weiss, and Visioni (2001), for example, conclude that the high failure rate of alliances is due to poor working relationships among partners. Hutt and others (2000) find that close attention to personal relationships can accelerate learning and lead to a more effective alliance. This aspect of alliances is frequently neglected after papers are signed, when the person who structured the alliance assigns the contract to a new employee who is unfamiliar with the partner.

Finally, studies suggest that the way partners manage the collective learning process can play a central role in the success or failure of an alliance (Larsson, et al. 1998). We believe that the creation of knowledge is a social activity, and that the structure of an alliance should be created with its social context in mind. An alliance between long-time competitors, for example, will require a structure that is different from an alliance between companies that have worked together in the past.

Key Components of a Successful Alliance

We believe that several factors are important in making a partnership work (Table 12.1). These factors were identified from research conducted at the IBM Institute for Knowledge Management and other recent research.

Develop a Relationship that Fosters Trust

Trust is perhaps the most critical component of an effective partnership. Trust performs two functions: (1) it reduces transaction costs by eliminating the need to monitor the partner constantly and put everything into a contract; and (2) it creates a working environment of collaboration and sharing. Trust enables partners to collaborate without fear of opportunism or misappropriation. Ideas and insights can be shared quickly, without the need to formalize every exchange. An alliance can be effective without trust, but in place of trust there must be contracts and documentation.

What can we do to build trust with a partner? Trust usually grows from interacting with the same partner over time; in other words, "trust builds trust" (Cohen and Prusak 2001). Research confirms that both trust and previous ties with a partner predict alliance formation (Garcia-Pont and Nohria 1997; Gulati 1995). All things being equal, it is thus best to seek as a partner a company with a reputation for trustworthiness.

The important question remains of how to build trust with a new partner. First impressions are critical, and the behavior of the two companies during the negotiating phase can go a long way toward building a trusting relationship. Negotiations in which both partners act in good faith to establish a "win-win" outcome can provide a basis for trust, whereas competitive negotiations can lead to resentment. Effective dialogue can also help establish clear objectives, purpose, and commitment, reinforcing the trust between partners. The participants on the alliance team should be carefully selected. Ideally, they should be familiar with the partner's products, culture, and values, and they should have good interpersonal skills. Previous experience with alliances can also be an advantage.

Table 12.1
Alliance Success Factors and Associated Actions

Success Factor	Associated Action
Foster and maintain trust	• Target companies with a reputation as a preferred partner • Start to build trust during negotiations • Staff alliance teams with personnel who are familiar with the partner and possess effective interpersonal skills
Build awareness and transparency	• Document information requirements early in the alliance process • Have frequent meetings with partner • Introduce the role of knowledge intermediary • Understand partner's language and culture
Develop learning objectives	• Define learning objectives • Communicate learning objectives both internally and with partner • Create structures and processes to capture and disseminate alliance knowledge • Understand similarities with partner's knowledge domain
Manage partnerships holistically	• Understand partner's role (for example, supplier, competitor, customer, complementor) • Assess interdependencies among partners • Ensure alignment between business strategy and alliance strategy

Build Awareness and Transparency

Awareness and transparency are both important to knowledge-sharing partnerships. Awareness is the ability of one partner to understand or be cognizant of the goals, values, and resources of the other partner, while transparency is a measure of the opportunity to learn from the other partner (Doz and Hamel 1998).

All too often, the alliance objectives formally documented in a contract are ineffectively communicated to partners. Our study of research and development alliances found that one of the major obstacles during the implementation phase was that of not knowing whom to turn to for information or expertise. There was a clear lack of awareness of the research being done both in the respondent's own company and in the partner organization.

One way to build awareness is for each partner to document its information and knowledge requirements at the beginning, and to assess which internal groups might complement the alliance's work. Frequent review meetings should be held to discuss any awareness issues that arise. Another solution is to appoint a knowledge intermediary as a bridge between the two organizations. This person is responsible for directing alliance team members to good sources of information and knowledge. A portal can be established as a repository for all alliance documents.

Transparency is a measure of how easy it is to obtain information, knowledge, and skills from a partner. It is governed in large part by the social aspects of the relationship. It is important, for example, that partnering companies share the same language. The use of different terms to describe the same technology or product, for instance, can cause confusion and a breakdown in communication. Trust affects transparency by affecting the willingness of partners to share information and knowledge. Indeed, some long-standing partnerships are so transparent that the companies are able to shape their business strategy based on what they see of their partner's strategy.

Develop and Communicate Learning Objectives

Another key finding from our research is the importance of clearly defining and communicating the learning objectives of the alliance. Doz and Hamel (1998) point out that the key difference between U.S. companies and Japanese companies engaged in alliances has been a serious intent to learn. In U.S.-Japanese alliances, Japanese firms typically have viewed alliances as a way to learn. U.S. firms, in contrast, have used alliances as a way of taking advantage of their partner's greater competitive skills, resulting in erosion of their own skills and ultimately in competitive disadvantage.

Alliance learning can take several forms. Content learning describes acquisition of the skills and expertise of the partner. Process learning refers to understanding and sharing what went right and what went wrong with the alliance process. Partner-specific learning denotes the building of social capital with the partner; this involves learning the partner's values, culture, and work routines, and using this knowledge to build a more effective relationship.

The learning objectives should be discussed during the negotiation phase of an alliance, in case cross-training between partners is required. Once defined, learning objectives should be communicated both internally and to the partner. Internal alliance team members should be cognizant of the different skills and know-how they need from the partner, and a structure and process should be established to acquire and disseminate this knowledge.

An alliance in which learning is heavily one-sided probably will not succeed in the long run. Partners that are perceived as entering into an alliance for the sole purpose of learning as much as they can, without regard for a "win-win" objective, also run the risk of developing a reputation as a poor partner.

A company's ability to learn from its partner ultimately depends on its ability to recognize the value of new information, assimilate it, and apply it to commercial ends (Cohen and Levinthal 1990). Absorptive capacity is a function of how closely related the knowledge domains of the partners are. For example, a firm that collaborates with a partner from a different industry might not have the level of understanding needed to internalize a new knowledge domain. Alliances between competitors, on the other hand, often present an ideal learning situation, since the knowledge domains of the partners are similar (Parise and Henderson 2001).

Manage Partnerships Holistically as well as Individually

The fourth key factor for a successful alliance is the use of a holistic approach to alliance management. Most companies are involved with many partners simultaneously. Just as product managers must use a portfolio approach when developing, pricing, and marketing their products, alliance managers must understand interdependencies when developing alliances. In other words, the partnering company should have an overall strategy on partnership in addition to a strategy for each individual alliance.

Potentially, a single organization may have several alliances with the same partner—for example, across different departments and business units. Alliance managers should be aware of all such partnerships, since a company's conduct in one alliance can affect how the partner company behaves toward it in other alliances. Alliance managers often told us that if they had known that their company already had an existing alliance with a partner, they would have behaved differently toward that partner.

How should a company design its portfolio of partners? One approach starts by considering the role of a potential partner relative to the markets the company serves. Partners can be competitors, complementors, suppliers, or customers from different industries. Alliances with competitors can be used to learn or reduce risk; with complementors and customers, to help develop products; with suppliers, to improve efficiency and integration; and with companies in different industries, to help create new markets. A recent study of the alliance portfolios of Dell Computer and Sun Microsystems concluded that Dell's strategy centered on its supplier partners and Sun's on its complementors (Parise and Henderson 2001).

Once the role of each partner is clear, the relationship manager can think holistically about the different goals addressed by the portfolio. The key, especially when the objective is to learn and create new knowledge, is to try to maintain a complementary or synergistic portfolio. While parallel partnerships with competing companies might be seen as a viable strategy to reduce risk, there is a danger that those companies will be reluctant to share their knowledge. A portfolio of partners promoting similar rather than competing solutions would be considered a complementary portfolio.

A holistic approach to alliance design and management can enable better alignment of alliance strategy with business strategy, but recent research indicates that this is still a major challenge. The alliance managers we interviewed repeatedly complained that they had no clear idea of what their companies' business strategy was. This was in large part due to their own positions in alliance functions that were often localized, with no formal process for communicating with the business strategy group. In other instances, the company had set up a separate group to generate new business, with alliances playing a major role, but the new group would be isolated from the main company and would face major difficulties in allocating resources and staffing alliance teams.

Conclusion: Building an Alliance Capability

Firms today are competing to build their alliance capability to the level where they become preferred partners. Recent findings suggest that companies that use best practice to capture and implement effective alliance processes have the highest success rates (Harbison and Pekar 1998). IBM, for example, has established a PartnerWorld program for its software partners, offering co-marketing, education and certification, technical support, incentives, and relationship management. Eli Lilly, a leading pharmaceutical firm, has created an Office of Alliance Management that is responsible for developing and implementing best partnering practices, training Lilly's staff to work with partners, and assessing cross-cultural differences with the partner.

To summarize, alliances and partnerships will remain an important source of learning and innovation in the knowledge economy. We have emphasized the relational or social aspects of developing collaborative partnerships: building trust, awareness, and transparency with the partner; articulating and communicating alliance learning objectives; and managing partners holistically as well as individually. Building alliances cannot be accomplished by following a list of generic steps. While there are some basic design rules that all companies should follow, successful collaborative relationships ultimately depend on a company's unique ability to build social capital with its partner.

References

Bleeke, J., and D. Ernst. 1995. "Is Your Strategic Alliance Really a Sale?" *Harvard Business Review* 73: 97–105.

Cohen, D., and L. Prusak. 2001. *In Good Company*. Cambridge, Mass.: Harvard Business School Press.

Cohen, W. M., and D. A. Levinthal. 1990. "Absorptive Capacity: A New Perspective on Learning and Innovation." *Administrative Science Quarterly* 35: 128–52.

Doz, Y. L., and G. Hamel. 1998. *Alliance Advantage*. Cambridge, Mass.: Harvard Business School Press.

Ertel, D., J. Weiss, and L. J. Visioni. 2001. *Managing Alliance Relationships*. Boston, Mass.: Vantage Partners.

Garcia-Pont, C., and N. Nohria.1997. "Local versus Global Mimetism: The Dynamics of Alliance Formation in the Automobile Industry." Paper presented at the Academy of Management, Boston, Mass., August 10-13.

Gomes-Casseres, B. 2000. "Alliances and Risk: Securing a Place in the Victory Parade." *Financial Times* 6–7 (May).

Gulati, R. 1995. "Social Structure and Alliance Formation Patterns: A Longitudinal Analysis." *Administrative Science Quarterly* 40(4): 619–52.

Hagedoorn, J., and J. Schakenraad. 1994. "The Effects of Strategic Technology Alliances on Company Performance." *Strategic Management Journal* 15: 291–309.

Hamel, G. 1991. "Competition for Competence and Inter-Partner Learning within International Strategic Alliances." *Strategic Management Journal* 12: 83–104.

Harbison, J. R., and P. Pekar. 1998. *Smart Alliances: A Practical Guide to Repeatable Success*. San Francisco: Jossey-Bass.

Harrigan, K. R. 1988. "Strategic Alliances and Partner Asymmetries." In *Cooperative Strategies in International Business*. Lexington, Mass.: Lexington Books.

Hutt, M., E. Stafford, B. Walker, and P. Reingen. 2000. "Case Study Defining the Social Network of a Strategic Alliance." *Sloan Management Review* 41(2): 51–62.

Larsson, R., L. Bengtsson, K. Henriksson, and J. Sparks. 1998. "The Inter-Organizational Learning Dilemma: Collective Knowledge Development in Strategic Alliances." *Organization Science* 9(3): 285–305.

Parise, S., and J. Henderson. 2001. "Knowledge Resource Exchange in Strategic Alliances." *IBM Systems Journal* 40(4): 908–24.

Stuart, X. 2000. "Inter-Organizational Alliances and the Performance of Firms: A Study of Growth and Innovation Rates in a High-Technology Industry." *Strategic Management Journal* 21: 791–811.

Thompson, J. D. 1967. *Organizations in Action: Social Science Bases of Administration*. New York: McGraw-Hill.

13

Partnerships: The Critical Role of the State[1]

Jorge Braga de Macedo

Recent experience and contributions to the literature show that we can achieve better development partnerships by reconsidering the role of the state. This chapter discusses the critical issue of maintaining an active role for the state—in other words, the World Bank's client—within the Comprehensive Development Framework (CDF). In implementing the CDF, with so many partners engaged in so many issues, it is easy to lose sight of the essential contributions of the state in the policy reform process.

I shall propose a model in which the state is regarded as a combination of actors—government, parliament, auditors—for whom the annual budget is the exclusive locus of conflict resolution (Branson, Braga de Macedo, and von Hagen 2001). The budget is an area in which a strong case can be made for doing more work in connection with CDF principles and results orientation. A well-defined budget is a critical component of success because markets and voters need credible signals of discipline. Without those signals, markets will not adjust and reforms will be short-lived.

This model has been implemented successfully in industrialized countries and can be adapted for application within a development context. The program of work of the OECD Development Center for 2001/2002 is dedicated to the interaction of globalization and governance (see, for example, Bonaglia, Braga de Macedo, and Bussolo 2001). Like Williamson (1994) and World Bank (1992, 2002) it supports the idea that we can realize better partnerships by revising our view of the role of the state. The "new authorizing environment for development," whereby developing countries assume ownership of improved policies and governance reforms while developed countries increase their development assistance and open their markets, also implies a central role for the state (Picciotto 2002c).

Jorge Braga de Macedo is president, OECD Development Center.

Reformist pressures—the topic of the next section—underline the evolution of governance in response to globalization, including the European and especially the OECD experience with peer pressure. This evolution suggests specific points about adapting to local circumstances, defining the government budget as the locus of conflict resolution, and increasing transparency as a way of enhancing policy credibility.

Reformist Pressures

Policy reform must be accompanied by attention to its impact on poverty, inequality, and social cohesion. Policies of poverty alleviation take on a salience in poor and rich countries that middle-income countries may find surprising and often confusing. On the one hand, the dynamics of the process of development are so intense in an emerging economy and society that widespread alleviation may seem impossible or undesirable or both, and have been often ignored, especially in recent years with the focus on creating appropriate incentives. On the other hand, especially after mass consumption is achieved, poverty alleviation becomes a moral imperative of civil society, so much so that economic incentives in recipient countries are often forgotten in the rush to provide humanitarian aid.

Among international organizations, a broad reformist approach originated in the report by Pearson (1968) and became part of the "basic needs" approach, but it was largely forgotten until the CDF was launched (World Bank 1999, 2001). Possibly influenced by this reformist approach, and encouraged by favorable public opinion, aid donors tended to give increasing prominence to poverty reduction until they agreed on the development goals listed in OECD (1996).

The ways in which the complementarity between national governance of economic actors and global competition works itself out varies across countries and over time, enhancing growth in some cases and stifling it in others. This is why creating new institutions, capable of delivering the desired role of the state in economic life, remains a matter for national choice. Preferences vary widely, and initial conditions—economic, social, and political—are equally diverse. A reformist government being replaced by a nationalist or populist one will change the policy response to globalization, for example.

But, as Krugman (1994) has vividly illustrated, reforms are often rhetoric rather than a revelation of a plan or a genuine commitment on the part of policymakers. The reason for this antireform bias pertains to a possibly perverse interaction between voters and the media, whereby new initiatives are broadly rewarded but entitlements are fiercely defended by those who benefit. In addition, since the losses are clearer than the gains, even though these may potentially be much larger, uncertainty about the political redistribution mechanism may also impart a "status quo bias," as illustrated in the context of protection by Fernandez and Rodrik (1991).

The ability to redistribute power and real resources to the population at large suggests that some social groups are able to distribute external resources among themselves in a more or less coordinated fashion. For some purposes, groups can be identified with parts of the government, in particular spending ministries (for instance, public works, education, health), possibly in alliance with industry or union lobbies (construction, teachers, pharmaceuticals). In other cases, groups can be identified with traditional institutions, such as the church, the military, the judiciary, and the like. This group influence on the tax/transfer mechanism implies some form of "common access" to the aggregate capital stock, when taxable sector coincides with exports whereas the "informal" sector involves import or import-substituting production. Each powerful group ignores the effect of the transfer it extracts on the taxes levied to balance the government budget.

As a consequence of each group's voracity, Tornell and Lane (1999) show that aggregate transfers rise more than proportionately and that better coordination among powerful groups, perhaps owing to a unitary rather than a divided government, decreases the "voracity effect." They also show that the associated "fiscal euphoria" has dissipated terms of trade improvements in many countries, especially those with weaker institutions. When an increase in the rate of return to capital in the taxable sector leads to a more than proportional increase in discretionary redistribution, the power of vested interests is perverse for society as a whole.

Adapting to Local Circumstances

Given the widespread awareness of reform rhetoric and of the resilience of vested interests, currents departing from mainstream development thinking have become more difficult to classify neatly in terms of method and ideology. The CDF is seen as a response to the perception that globalization leads to increased poverty. Successful development assistance reflects four principles: long-term, holistic strategy; country ownership; partnership (with business interests and civil society); and results orientation (as opposed to stress on inputs such as the percentage of aid in GDP). None of the principles is new, and they all raise difficult choices.

Nevertheless, the joint articulation of the four CDF principles as a framework to promote coherent aid programs linked with poverty reduction strategies has been influential in the development community. A broad group including major bilateral donors, other international organizations, civil society, and business is evaluating the extent to which the CDF principles have actually been implemented (Picciotto 2002a). In this evaluation the antecedents of poor policy performance, aid dependence, debt sustainability, and conditionality are being examined. It is already clear that judicious adaptation of the CDF principles to diverse country circumstances is critical to success.

First, the precise definition of "long-run" goals varies considerably from one country to another. Solvency constraints, within both the current account and the budget, are significant variables in the definition of appropriate time horizons for strategic planning.

Second, donor/lender conditionality versus client country ownership is an area of active debate. Within a large body of work that the OECD has done in this area, a recent report on the World Bank and aid coordination (Ericksson 2001) confirms the validity ownership principle according to which the country should lead the decision making with respect to its development priorities and the design of poverty reduction strategies. This still leaves room for conditionality, for instance when a country owns the wrong policies (Williamson 2000).

Branson and Hanna (2000) suggest that with the client in the driver's seat, conditionality can be regarded as a commitment mechanism for the Bank, much as ownership is a commitment mechanism for the country. The challenge then is to find country-specific ways of ensuring that the two mechanisms are compatible and that they work. The persistent belief that conditionality is necessarily wrong diverts attention from the need to meet this challenge, and does a disservice to the development community. What we must remember is that many myths about conditionality have come to be regarded as valid in general, when in fact they refer only to a specific conditionality.

Third, partnerships often make policymaking more difficult owing to various forms of transactions costs. As argued by Abraham and Plateau (2000), there are instances in which the granting of more power to communities and to lower levels of government has actually decreased the quality and efficiency of aid. Plateau's "chamber of horrors" (though this is not his term for it) of community participation contains a list of cases of what we would call "regulatory capture." As demonstrated by the European experience, supranational and international mechanisms can provide excellent defenses against this danger.

Fourth, results orientation by itself cannot overcome the voracity effects mentioned above (see also Azam 2001). Moreover, in the past, donors and lenders have given more attention to the share of budgets allocated to "fashionable" sectors than to the capacity of domestic institutions to make effective use of such budgets and deliver quality results (Picciotto 2002b). We must guard against a return to this "input" oriented approach to aid allocations.

Defining Budgets

To ensure the long-term success of reforms, the data relevant to the budget must be accepted by all. In the European Union, fiscal policy is the domain of the individual EU countries, but authority over the data on budgets, debt, and related metrics lies with the European Commission. This creates a situation in which securing the data is the responsibility of a third party. (Another example is the macroeconomic monitoring group established among the Mercosur member countries, together with Chile and Bolivia; see Braga de Macedo 2001.)

Another model worth examining is that of the Uganda Debt Network, which was the subject of a report at the 2001 OECD Partnership Forum. Here we see an example of building a budget through discussions with civil society.[2] Although Uganda's is an important innovation, it does not yet make perfect practice, however. The private sector is not involved in the process, which is a major weakness. The report also identifies some wishful thinking, particularly in terms of recommendations for staffing and raising the salaries of local government officials; enhancing monitoring activities; improving transparency; and allocating resources to lower levels, such as sub-counties. Additionally, the response by the Uganda Debt Network to corruption has involved nothing more effectual than letters to various officials.

Transparency of Governance

Governance is an issue not only for states or corporations, but also for NGOs and for international organizations.

The idea that "soft power" is now more important suggests that an organization's credibility relates directly to its transparency (Keohane and Nye 2000). Whether the transparency is perceived or real is a separate question. It suffices to say that improving transparency and thus enhancing the credibility of information can help to prevent some of the problems that have occurred in the past.

Business associations (as distinct from major businesses, which can be quite different in nature) often are essential intermediaries in the fight against corruption. There are many instances in which a government working alone or in partnership with NGOs has degenerated into something from which no solution can emerge. By adding nonprofit business associations to the mix, we add a component that understands the extent to which business is the victim of corruption. Coalitions that include civil society organizations and business associations should expect difficulties. But when business associations feel as though they are participating, they are more at ease.

It is relatively easy to apply norms to macroeconomic variables, such as deficits and debts, because these variables are easy to measure. The same is not true of structural policies. Even the European mechanisms of surveillance of structural issues have not overcome the danger of procrastination—and the interaction of surveillance with the election cycle can significantly delay reforms. For example, the voracity effect mentioned above remains operative even when external pressure brings government budget deficits under control. It may even be stronger than peer pressure, a possibility known as the "Euro hold-up" (Braga de Macedo 2001).

A related recommendation concerns the budgetary process and the social safety net. Viewing the ministry of social affairs not as the enemy of the ministry of finance but as a ministry that is part spending and part revenue could greatly improve budgetary procedure (Lucena and Braga de Macedo 1997).

Conclusion

The creation of partnerships with components from both above and below the government level does not weaken the state. Rather, it reinforces accountability and can facilitate development of the consensus that is essential for development progress. Further support for the view that consensus is important for investors can be found in Collier (2000).

The CDF reflects an interaction between globalization and governance that needs to be made specific in order to be useful for evaluators and policymakers. In this regard, a specific interaction emerges from the OECD and European experience with peer pressure. As mentioned at the outset, these procedures may be used more broadly as long as their basic values are shared among countries, even if these countries are located outside Europe.

Notes

1. I am grateful to conference participants, to Enver Kamal, and to Bob Picciotto for comments but remain responsible for the text, which does not reflect the opinions of the OECD, its Development Center, or its member countries.
2. One conference participant commented that Uganda's record on tracking government budgetary commitments was more impressive than that of the OECD.

References

Abraham, Anita, and Jean-Philippe Plateau. 2000. "The Dilemma of Participation with Endogenous Community Imperfections." Centre de Recherche en Economie de Développpment, University of Namur, August.

Azam, Jean-Paul. 2001. "Statecraft in the Shadow of Civil Conflict." OECD Development Centre and African Development Bank, February.

Bonaglia, Federico, Jorge Braga de Macedo, and Maurizio Bussolo. 2001. "How Globalisation Improves Governance." CEPR Discussion Paper no. 2992, October.

Braga de Macedo, Jorge. 2001. "Globalisation and Institutional Change: A Development Perspective." In Edmond Malinvaud and Louis Sabourin, eds., *Globalization: Ethical and Institutional Concerns*, Proceedings of the Pontifical Academy of Social Sciences, Vatican City, pp. 223–67.

Branson, William, Jorge Braga de Macedo, and Jurgen von Hagen. 2001. "Macroeconomic Policy and Institutions in the Transition towards EU Membership." In Ronald MacDonald and Rod Cross, eds., *Central Europe towards Monetary Union: Macroeconomic Underpinnings and Financial Reputation.* Boston: Kluwer Academic Publishers, pp. 5–30.

Branson, William, and Nagy Hanna. 2000. "Ownership and Conditionality." OED Working Paper No. 8, World Bank, Washington, D.C. Available at *www.worldbank.org/html/oed.*

Collier, Paul. 2000. "Consensus Building, Knowledge and Conditionality." The World Bank, Washington, D.C., April.

Eriksson, John. 2001. "The Drive to Partnership: Aid Coordination and the World Bank." The World Bank, Washington, D.C.

Fernandez, Raquel, and Dani Rodrik. 1991. "Resistance to Reform Status Quo in the Presence of Individual Specific Uncertainty." *American Economic Review* 81: 1146–55.

Keohane, Robert, and Joseph Nye. 2000. "Power and Interdependence in the Information Age." In Elaine Ciulla Kamarck and Joseph Nye, eds., *Democracy.com? Governance in a Networked World.* Hollis, N.H.: Hollis.

Krugman, Paul. 1994. *Peddlers of Prosperity.* New York: Basic Books.

Lucena, Diogo, and Jorge Braga de Macedo. 1997. "Reforming Social Security: Efficiency and Governance." In *Sustaining Social Security.* New York: United Nations.

OECD. 1996. *Shaping the 21st Century: The Contribution of Development Co-Operation.* Paris: OECD/DAC.

Pearson, Lester. 1968. *Partners in Development.* New York: Praeger.

Picciotto, Robert. 2002a. "OED's Renewal 1992–2002." The World Bank, Washington, D.C.

———. 2002b. "The Global Challenge of Development Evaluation." The World Bank, Washington, D.C.

———. 2002c. "The Need for IDEAS." The World Bank, Washington, D.C.

Tornell, Aaron, and Philip Lane. 1999. "The Voracity Effect." *The American Economic Review*, March, 22–46.

Williamson, John. 1994. *The Political Economy of Policy Reform*, Washington, D.C.: Institute of International Economics.

———. 2000. "Country Ownership, the CDF and Participation." The World Bank, Washington, D.C., October.

World Bank. 1992. *Governance and Development: A World Bank Policy Research Report.* New York: Oxford University Press.

———. 1999. "Towards a Comprehensive Development Strategy." Operations Evaluation Department Précis, no. 197, autumn.

———. 2001. *Partnerships and Development, A World Bank Policy Research Report.* New York: Oxford University Press.

———. 2002. "Globalisation, Growth and Poverty: Building an Inclusive World Economy." Washington, D.C.

14

Challenges for Governance in Partnerships for Delivering Services[1]

Maria Barrados

Government programs and services in many countries were traditionally delivered mainly through government departmental organizations reporting directly to a minister who was seen as accountable for the organization and its activities. The organizations were part of the government, staffed by government officials, and hence controlled by the government.

This tradition is changing significantly in many countries. Governments, including the federal and provincial governments in Canada, are increasingly entering into partnerships with independent agencies to deliver public goods and services.[2] These arrangements go beyond contracting out the delivery of service and increasingly involve other levels of government, as well as the private and/or the nonprofit sector in policy formulation, planning, design, and decision making about how and to whom government services are delivered. The tools being used are collaboration, networking, and delegation.

This chapter focuses on governance challenges in collaborative or partnership arrangements for delivering services in Canada. It presents a framework for evaluating these arrangements and the results of an audit of the governance structures of ten collaborative arrangements.

The Setting

The traditional approach to delivering government services and programs had the advantage of being relatively clear about accountability, transparency, and the public interest. Ministers were accountable, citizen redress was ensured through appeal to local elected officials, a policy on transparency was ensured through whatever "access to information" regime government

---

Maria Barrados is assistant auditor general, Office of the Auditor General of Canada.

had in place, and public officials were bound by traditional public service ethics and conflict-of-interest rules. Though each of these may often have been criticized as inadequate, the framework for addressing these governance issues was in place and reasonably well known and understood.

Today's trend of involving others in governing raises issues that are not addressed by the traditional managing and governing frameworks. A recent OECD report (1999, p. 7) points out that "management systems that are disaggregated, decentralized, and devolved need a new framework to guide behavior." Many observers have raised issues of accountability, transparency, and the public interest for these new arrangements, and auditors general have also raised concerns.[3]

New Governance Arrangements

Under the new governance arrangements, some or all of federal governance can be shifted to outside entities that are not accountable to ministers and the legislature. Arrangements through which the federal government shares policy formulation, risk, and operational planning, design, and management with another party or parties that deliver programs and services are called collaborative arrangements or partnerships. As pointed out in a study by the Office of the Auditor General,[4] these arrangements have three main features:

- The federal government and its partners pursue common objectives and results that have a public policy purpose.
- The participating organizations share governance related to public policy as well as to the way in which the arrangement itself is governed.
- Written agreements between the parties on governance and financing spell out the collective effort to steer as well as to control the use of resources.

The Need for a Governing Framework

Those developing such arrangements need a framework to ensure that issues of accountability and the public trust are adequately dealt with. Such frameworks are appearing in a number of jurisdictions and situations. I referred earlier to the accountability regime recommended by the Australasian Council of Auditors General (1997) to address the issue of commercial confidence in public-private arrangements. Recently in Canada, a Panel on Accountability and Governance in the Voluntary Sector (1999) made recommendations for improving governance and accountability in the voluntary sector, dealing with issues of transparency, publicly available reporting to government, and the need to focus reporting on performance. In the United Kingdom a number of reports and inquiries have addressed the issue of appropriate governance arrangements for nongovernmental bodies (Chancellor of the Duchy of

Lancaster and the Financial Secretary to the Treasury 1996; Committee on Standards in Public Life 1996, 1997; U.K. Cabinet Office 1998).

Essential Elements of a Governing Framework

In 1999, the Auditor General of Canada proposed a framework for new governance arrangements,[5] based on earlier work[6] that had examined collaborative arrangements. The framework has been modified slightly in the criteria for a follow-up audit being carried out by the Auditor General for reporting to Parliament in April 2002. Box 14.1 sets out this framework, which includes the elements of accountability (separated into reporting and accountability mechanisms), transparency, and protection of the public interest. Within each element are a number of specific attributes.

Reporting

Credible reporting to government and legislative bodies on what the arrangement has accomplished is an essential aspect of democratic governing. This reporting needs to include the following:

- *Clear statements of the public objectives* and the key strategies to achieve them.
- *Concrete statements of performance expectations.*
- *Appropriate measurement and reporting on progress* to the parties involved, the ministers responsible, the legislatures, and the public.

To achieve credible reporting on the arrangement's overall performance, the data each partner collects and reports must be relevant, accurate, verifiable, of good quality, and sufficiently comparable with other partners' data. Where several parties are involved, a common problem concerns ensuring that the data collected by the different partners are reliable and compatible. Of course, data sharing may be constrained by legitimate concerns for individual privacy, commercial confidence, and future negotiations between levels of government. Any such restrictions should be spelled out explicitly.

Accountability Mechanisms[7]

Existing federal mechanisms for accountability do not apply to new governance arrangements (or, when they do, they apply only to the ongoing federal portion of collaborative arrangements) unless specific provision is made. But many features are needed for accountability to be rendered:

- *Roles and responsibilities* of each of the parties involved in new arrangements must be clear, in relation to those of government and legislatures.

Box 14.1
A Governing Framework for New Arrangements

To ensure credible *reporting:*

- Clear public objectives *and key strategies* *
- Concrete performance expectations
- Appropriate measurement and reporting regime

To establish effective *accountability mechanism:*

- Clear roles and responsibilities
- Performance expectations that are balanced with capabilities
- Appropriate monitoring regime
- Partner dispute resolution mechanisms
- Procedures to deal with non-performance
- Specific evaluation provisions
- Appropriate audit regime

To ensure adequate *transparency:*

- Public access to information
- Communication of information on key policies and decisions

To protect the *public interest:*

- Citizen complaint and redress mechanisms
- Public consultation/feedback mechanisms
- Policies to promote pertinent public sector values

* *Italicized* portions were added in 2001 to the 1999 framework.

Source: Auditor General of Canada (1999b, 2002).

- *Performance expectations must be realistic,* given the resources, personnel, and authorities of the new arrangement.
- *Well-defined management structure:* The new arrangement is managing public monies, assets, and/or public authorities. It must have a well-defined structure to manage and govern—such as corporate boards, professional management, and financial controls—so that it can fulfill its public obligations.
- *Appropriate monitoring regime:* The federal government needs to have an adequate monitoring regime in place to know whether the arrangement is accomplishing what is expected.
- *Partner dispute-resolution mechanisms:* If the arrangement involves partners, then agreement is needed at the outset on how disputes among the partners are to be settled. Some might argue that putting dispute-

resolution and sanction mechanisms in place would be onerous (it would, for example, slow down and overly formalize relations among the partners); "pushing accountability too hard" may be thought to undermine trust and thereby weaken accountability further. Though we appreciate these concerns, dispute-resolution mechanisms are an important aspect of managing with partners and are quite common in the private sector. The success of collaborative arrangements, in particular, depends on all partners fulfilling their respective responsibilities, including the responsibility to hold others to account and take corrective action when necessary.

- *Procedures to deal with non-performance:* For example, how can the arrangement be terminated? If such issues are not dealt with upfront, then the government may have no way of keeping the arrangement on track or holding it to account.
- *Specific evaluation and audit provisions:* After a period of time, the success of the arrangement and its appropriateness as a tool of public policy should be evaluated. Audit and evaluation findings should be reported in a timely manner to government and the legislature.
- *Appropriate audit regime:* In collaborative arrangements, there is no easy way for legislatures to have a single audit undertaken of the whole arrangement. The Auditor General of Canada (1999b) suggested the need for an independent audit of the performance information that is reported to government and the legislature from these bodies.

Transparency

To the public and to users trying to obtain information, collaborative arrangements often appear to be a maze since they involve several organizations and governments.

Public access to information: With several different partners involved in a collaborative arrangement, some with their own access-to-information regimes and others perhaps with none, specific formal provision should be made for consistent and compatible rules on transparency.

Communication of information on key policies and decisions: For similar reasons, it is reasonable to expect information on key policies and decisions to be actively communicated to stakeholders and the public.

Protecting the Public Interest

Research conducted by EKOS Research Associates in 1998 found 63 percent of Canadians favoring the notion that "too much focus on private sector practices will weaken government's ability to protect the public interest." Canadians appear to recognize the need to protect the public interest in the exercise of government functions.

Citizen complaint and redress mechanisms: When Canadians feel aggrieved by the decisions or actions of their governments, they can appeal for redress through their elected representatives. An appeal mechanism short of litigation is needed for citizens affected by the discretionary decisions of bodies that exercise federal authority but are independent of federal control. There are a variety of ways to provide for redress.

Public consultation/feedback mechanisms: Public consultation and feedback on government services and programs is expected now and ought to be in place for new arrangements.

Policies to promote pertinent public sector values: Canadians expect federal authority to be exercised with fairness, impartiality, equity, honesty, prudence, and openness. They expect those who use federal authority to respect the public good and the rule of law, along with federal standards such as providing services in English or French where demographics warrant, and values such as personal privacy and cultural diversity. Canadians also expect that those who exercise public authority will not abuse their power or influence. As a result, codes of ethical conduct and conflict of interest in the public sector are traditionally more demanding than in the private sector. Private sector bodies that deliver public services to Canadians on behalf of the government need codes of conduct and conflict-of-interest rules that reflect public sector ethics.

These elements of the governing framework and their attributes are stated as general conditions, and their particular application to each new governance arrangement will need to be considered. On the one hand, given the wide range of arrangements, a "one size fits all" approach will not work. On the other hand, by their very nature these arrangements step outside—and hence cannot necessarily be expected to rely on—the federal government's established regimes of public management, administration, and accountability (for example, human resource management regimes, the framework of Canada's Financial Administrative Act, and the traditional role of a minister). In each arrangement, those involved need to develop an appropriate governing framework to address the essential elements.

Collaborative Arrangements in Canada: Audit Findings

The results of the audit of ten collaborative arrangements examined by the Office of the Auditor General are presented in Figure 14.1.

Performance Reporting is Occurring

The audit found some form of reporting in these collaborative arrangements, but performance measurement practices (as set out in the framework) needed attention. In addition, reporting to the legislature was generally weak and sometimes absent.

Figure 14.1
Key Figures Present in the Ten Collaborative Arrangements Examined

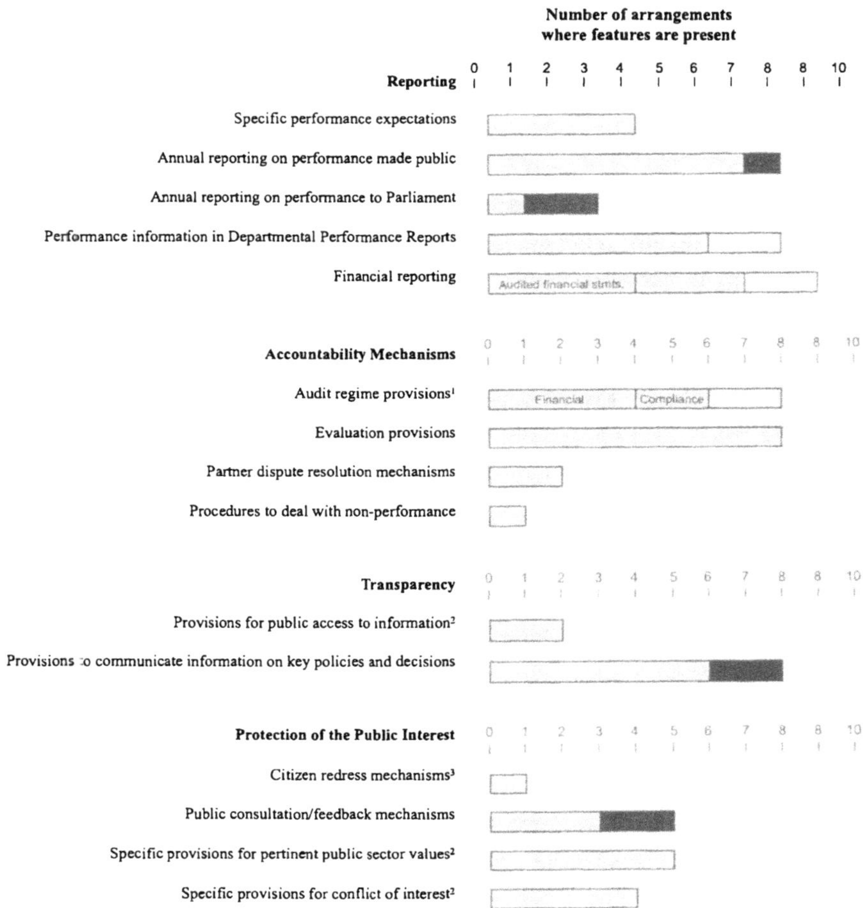

Notes: [1] Audit provisions in addition to value-for-money audits of the federal partner.

[2] Refers only to formal requirements in the arrangements. Relevant federal and provincial legislation/policies also apply.

[3] Refers only to the federal component of the arrangement. Provincial or private sector partner may have redress mechanisms.

☐ Yes, formal requirement or feature ■ Yes, voluntary ☐ Not applicable

Source: Auditor General of Canada (1999b).

Public objectives were found to be clear but specific expectations were not—they tended to focus on outputs and not the accomplishments expected of each partner.

The audit found that partners often had difficulty in comparing their data and in judging whether each others' data were reliable and compatible. The credibility of reporting on such arrangements requires that the data each partner collects and reports be relevant, accurate, verifiable, and sufficiently comparable with other partners' data.

Many Essential Accountability Mechanisms Are Not in Place

The audit found that while some of the elements set out in the framework were in place, many important mechanisms to ensure accountability were not. Partners' roles were generally spelled out clearly, but the assessment of partners' ability to deliver was inadequate. Without such assessments an arrangement is at risk, especially if there is no dispute mechanism in place. Only two of the arrangements provided for dispute-resolution mechanisms. None had a way to deal with nonperformance.

Evaluation provisions were in place. By contrast, the audit arrangements in place were fragmented and not specified in the agreements. Nor was there provision for coordinated or joint audit work, or for reliance on the audit work of a partner.

Transparency Needs Attention

Different partners may have different policies on access to information. Few of the arrangements set out adequate provisions for public access to key information. The arrangements generally lacked provisions for publicizing information on their key decisions.

Mechanisms to Protect the Public Interest Are Often Weak

Though all the arrangements made some provision for protecting the public interest, none had all the essential provisions. These provisions are particularly important when partners have different views on the public interest. Gaps or inconsistencies among jurisdictions may need to be addressed in negotiating arrangements.

While most arrangements regularly consulted their stakeholders, only one specifically provided for redress of citizens' grievances.

Accountability at Risk

It is a challenge for either the private sector or the voluntary sector to adhere to the traditional principles of accountability and good governance while simultaneously gaining flexibility by partnering with government. Collaborative arrangements among government partners are bound by legislative mandates that may impose constraints, as well as by political imperatives. In these cases, care is needed in coordinating the different components of the arrangement to ensure that the whole is well managed and able to report on the achievement of its objectives. If provincial governments are involved, then their own accountability requirements come into play.

Trust and Goodwill Are Essential and Present, but Are Not Enough

The new governance arrangements we examined are working without drawing noticeable public attention or complaint. Several officials we interviewed attributed this to the competence, dedication, and sense of public service exhibited by the managers of these arrangements, whether from inside or outside the federal government. Enthusiasm, client goodwill, and the determination of appointees to gain public confidence and to make the arrangements succeed may offset weak accountability infrastructures in the short term, but in the long term they cannot be counted on alone for success.

For example, the Canada Infrastructure Works Program (total expenditure of $8.3 billion Canadian) is a collaborative arrangement among three levels of government, designed to help maintain and develop infrastructure in local communities and to create employment. An audit by the Auditor General of Canada (1999c) concluded that the program did not appropriately balance the need for administrative flexibility with adequate accountability for the way the money was spent and for the results that the projects achieved. From a federal perspective, the audit concluded that program was essentially "running on trust" with better accountability required.

Conclusion

This chapter draws heavily on work carried out in Canada, but a number of other countries face similar concerns about the strength of the governing frameworks of new arrangements. The work being done by the Office of the Auditor General of Canada points to the risks for Parliament and the public in establishing these new arrangements. The governing frameworks for the arrangements established in Canada were fragmented with significant gaps, raising questions about Parliament's ability to scrutinize the implementation of public policy in these arrangements.

Canada's experience shows that alternative ways of providing public services and programs can increase efficiency and quality, but that measures need to be put in place to ensure that there is credible reporting, that effective accountability mechanisms are established, that there is adequate transparency, and that the public interest is protected.

Notes

1. Parts of this chapter were co-authored with John Mayne, Robert Cook, and Patricia MacDonald—and first presented to the IIAS Conference on Public Administration and Globalisation: International and Supranational Administrations, Bologna, Italy, June 19–22, 2000; International Public Sector Management Symposium, Mannheim, Germany, June 21–22, 2001; and Evaluation and Development: The Partnership Dimension, July 24, 2001, World Bank, Washington, D.C. The material used in this chapter comes mainly from work published by the Office of the Auditor General of Canada. The author is wholly responsible for the analysis and views expressed in this chapter.
2. A few countries, such as Sweden, have had independent agencies delivering services for many years.
3. (Bemelmans-Videc, forthcoming). For example, the Dutch Audit Office has published several audits on new arrangements (Autonomous Administrative Authorities in 1995, Covenants in 1995, and Supervising the Execution of Public Tasks in 1998). The Australasian Council of Auditors General (1997) published a statement of principles dealing with commercial confidence and the public interest. In December 1999, the Auditor General of Canada tabled a report in the House of Commons titled "Involving Others in Governing: Accountability at Risk."
4. Reports of the Auditor General of Canada to the House of Commons, chapter 5, "Collaborative Arrangements: Issues for the Federal Government," April 1999 and chapter 1, "Placing the Public's Money Beyond Parliament's Reach," April 2002.
5. Auditor General of Canada (1999b).
6. Auditor General of Canada (1999a).
7. Five elements for good accountability were identified by the Office of the Auditor General of Canada and the Treasury Board Secretariat in a 1998 paper. The list here provides more detail in the context of new governance arrangements.

References

Auditor General of Canada. 1999a. "Collaborative Arrangements: Issues for the Federal Government." In *Report to the House of Commons,* Chapter 5. Ottawa: Auditor General of Canada. April.

______. 1999b. "Involving Others in Governing: Accountability at Risk." In *Report to the House of Commons,* Chapter 23. Ottawa: Auditor General of Canada. November.

______. 1999c. "Canada Infrastructure Works Program: Phase II and Follow-up of Phase I Audit." In *Report to the House of Commons*, Chapter 17. Ottawa: Auditor General of Canada. September.

———. 2002. "Placing the Public's Money beyond Parliament's Reach." In *Report of the House of Commons*. Ottawa: Auditor General of Canada.

Australasian Council of Auditors General. 1997. "Statement of Principles: Commercial Confidentiality and the Public Interest." Civic Square, ACT: Australasian Council of Auditors-General. Available at http://www.acag.org.au.

Bemelmans-Videc, M. L. Forthcoming. "Audit and Evaluation in the Collaborative State: The Role of Supreme Audit Institutions." In Andrew Gray, Bill Jenkins, Frans Leeuw and John Mayne, eds., *Sharing Power: Evaluation and Management in the Collaborative State*. New Brunswick, N.J.: Transaction Publishers.

Chancellor of the Duchy of Lancaster and the Financial Secretary to the Treasury. 1996. *Spending Public Money: Governance and Audit Issues*. London: Chancellor of the Duchy of Lancaster and the Financial Secretary to the Treasury.

Committee on Standards in Public Life (Nolan Report). 1996. *Standards in Public Life: Local Public Spending Bodies.* London: Committee on Standards in Public Life.

______. 1997. *Standards in Public Life: Review of Standards of Conflict in Executive NDPBs, NHS Trusts and Local Spending Bodies* (Second Report). London: Committee on Standards in Public Life.

OECD. 1999. "Performance Contracting: Lessons from Performance Contracting Case Studies—A Framework for Public Service Performance Contracting." Paris: OECD. Available at *http://www.olis.oecd.org/olis/1999doc.nsf/LinkTo/PUMA-PAC(99)2.*

Office of the Auditor General and Treasury Board Secretariat. 1998. *Modernizing Accountability.* Ottawa: Office of the Auditor General and Treasury Board Secretariat.

Panel on Accountability and Governance in the Voluntary Sector (Broadbent Panel). 1999. "Building on Strength: Improving Governance and Accountability in Canada's Voluntary Sector." Final Report. Ottawa: Panel on Accountability and Governance in the Voluntary Sector.

U.K. Cabinet Office. 1998. *QANGOS: Opening Doors.* London: U.K. Cabinet Office. Available at *http://www.open.gov.uk.*

Case Studies

15

Partnership for Poverty Reduction: ActionAid Ethiopia

Akalu P. Tumebo

This chapter describes how a country branch of an international NGO uses partnership in designing and implementing its work against poverty.

ActionAid Ethiopia (AAE) is one of more than 300 officially registered NGOs operating in Ethiopia. These organizations are of both local and international origin and religious as well as secular orientation. Many of them have forged collaborative partnerships with local communities, traditional local institutions, and government organizations. For most of them, as for AAE, the guiding objective is poverty alleviation.

AAE's parent organization is the third-largest United Kingdom–based international NGO, with a presence in more than thirty countries in Africa, Asia, and Latin America. AAE's stated mission is to work, in collaboration with propoor partners and directly with poor and marginalized people, to eradicate absolute poverty and improve social equity.

From 1988 to 1993, the group was largely engaged in direct implementation of sectoral projects. In 1994, with the publication of its first country strategy paper, AAE decided to increase its presence in Ethiopia, working mainly through partnerships with community-based organizations, governmental organizations, and other NGOs. AAE's 1999 country program review reinforced the strategic importance of partnerships, and in its second country strategy paper in 2000, AAE made partnerships a strategic goal.

AAE's Partnerships

AAE is now engaged with many different partners. They are listed here in order of priority, starting with the group that presents the greatest challenge:

Akalu P. Tumebo is a program advisor, ActionAid Ethiopia.

- *The poor and the socially and politically marginalized.* These are the primary partners of AAE. All suffer from lack of or insecure access to such resources as land, oxen, farm tools, and credit. They have little or no access to basic preventive and curative health care, to education, or to potable water. Within this group, minorities, women, and women-headed households seem to fare the worst. AAE has made significant progress in targeting and addressing the needs of this group by initiating different development programs in specified development areas. Interventions in health, water supply, education, food security, and credit have returned clear benefits.
- *Communities.* Community members working in AAE-funded development areas belong to a variety of groups, including community project management councils, anti-AIDS youth clubs, water committees, and women's development associations. Most of these groups are led by volunteers selected by community members.
- *Government offices.* AAE works in partnership with local government, which is now so close to the NGOs that the gap between the two is almost indistinguishable. AAE has also exerted some influence on government thinking at the zonal and regional levels.
- *Ethiopian NGOs (ENGOs).* Since 1993, when it was working alone in just two development areas, AAE has extended its work to include long-term support of Ethiopian NGOs in eleven more development areas. It also supports many ENGO projects on a short-term basis, and partners with others on a non-project basis. AAE sits on the executive committee and chairs some networking groups of the Christian Relief and Development Association, an organization of more than 165 NGOs.
- *Multilateral and bilateral agencies.* Historically AAE has received little support from multilateral and bilateral funding donors, but donor agencies are increasingly committing themselves to engagement with NGOs. AAE now has partnerships with the European Union and the U.K. Department for International Development, and has obtained some funds for its poverty eradication initiatives in Ethiopia.
- *International NGOs (INGOs) operating in Ethiopia.* AAE works in partnership with international NGOs to research the impact of economic reform on poor households in Ethiopia. Through sharing its local experience with international groups, AAE contributes in part to the adoption of appropriate cost-effective centers of education within the school system, an alternative primary education model supported by INGOs.

ActionAid Ethiopia uses two main criteria when selecting partners: compatibility of vision, mission, and values with those of AAE; and willingness to work in the Ethiopian poverty belt. The organization uses a core process to direct the establishment and working of its partnerships (see Figure 15.1), whether formal and informal, with NGOs or community-based organizations.

Figure 15.1
AAE Core Process

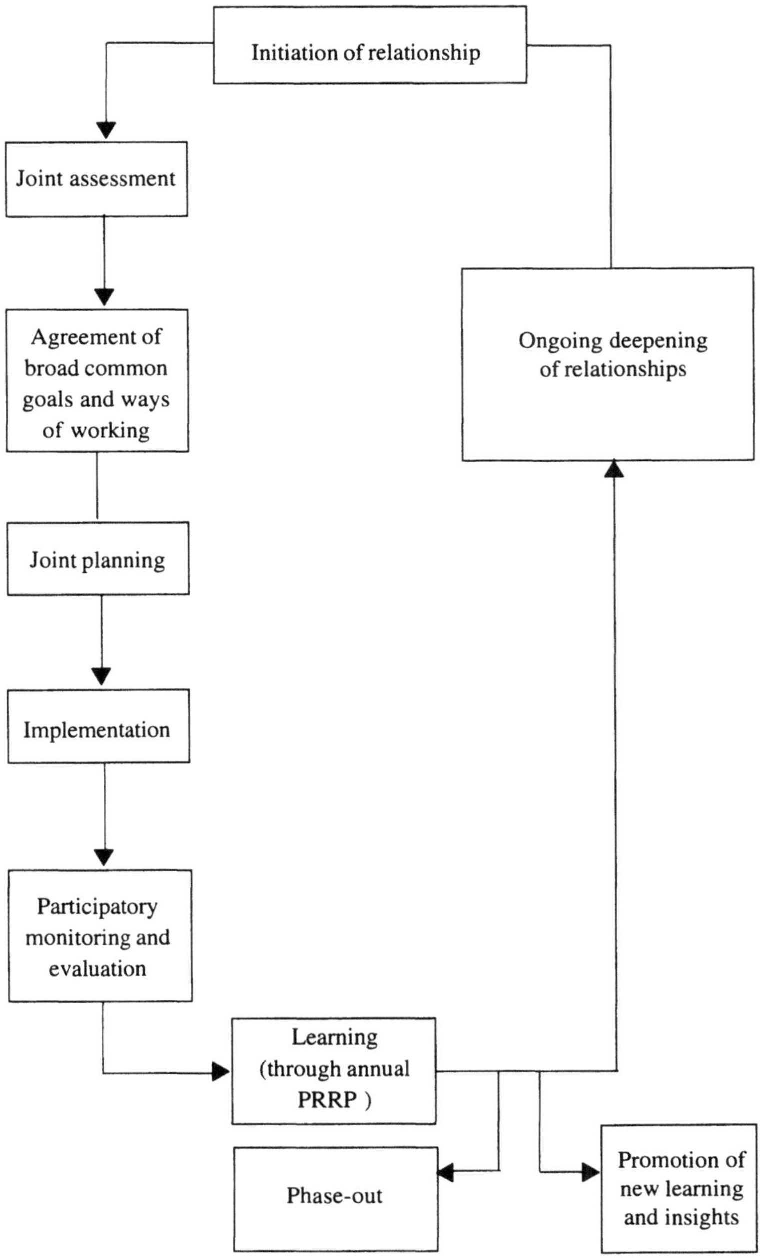

Box 15.1
The AAE–WISE Partnership in Addis Ababa

Of the 15 percent of the population of Ethiopia made up of urban dwellers, about 25 percent lives in Addis Ababa, a city of 2.5 million. Poverty is rampant. Women constitute about 51 percent of the city's population. More than 65 percent of the city's population is engaged in informal sector activities.

In 1997, the Organization for Women in Self-Employment (WISE) was established as an indigenous NGO with a vision of eradicating urban poverty by providing assistance to self-employed women. AAE is the sole financer of WISE's programs, but also supports WISE by making its training programs available to WISE members, sponsoring attendance at national and international training programs, and by providing logistical support.

WISE has four key objectives: to help self-employed urban women increase their income and improve their quality of life; to help these women improve their line of trade and secure their employment; to create better employment opportunities; and to bring women together to discuss their problems and strategic needs, helping them find ways of improving their quality of life.

To achieve these objectives WISE uses a three-pronged strategy:

• *Organizing* to bring poor, self-employed women together for purposes of support and to build the institutions that will sustain their development efforts. The different organizations created by WISE fall into three categories: (1) cooperatives, which ultimately are intended to become formalized and obtain the support of government; (2) groups trading similar goods and services; and (3) market unions, to bring together traders who operate in the same marketplace.

• *Training* in entrepreneurship and business and leadership skills.

• *Financing,* by mobilizing savings using the cooperative model, a low-interest, flexible lending scheme with no loan ceiling. The financing program also aids women in securing an allotted space in the market and constructing a shelter there; it supports the design, manufacture, and distribution of tools within a cost-sharing mechanism; it funds sanitation work both at home and in the business place; and it funds small-scale studies designed to provide technical advice to beneficiaries.

Program Achievements

Since it began operations in 1998, WISE has reached an estimated 2,500 women, about 1,800 of whom are still active in business. The program has helped organize its beneficiaries into twelve cooperatives, eight trade groups, and three market unions. Six of the cooperatives have opened their own bank accounts. More than 1,900 of the beneficiaries of the program have been trained in basic business skills, and about 500 have taken advanced training in marketing, record keeping, and business planning. More than 200 women are attending literacy classes. More than US$55,000 has been mobilized as savings, and US$150,000 has been disbursed as loans, with some beneficiaries now eligible for loans of more than US$300. In the marketplace, 60 portable market shelters have been provided on a cost-sharing basis to women who do not have rights to a permanent space. Hundreds of local bread-makers have been supplied with fuel-saving ovens, and 500 moneyboxes and 130 money-bags have been distributed to program beneficiaries. The program has also supported some environmental sanitation work, with 14 pit latrines built in market and residential areas. One savings and credit cooperative that was granted start-up capital for a public pit latrine and water line is now managing the project, with very little support from WISE.

Program Impact

An impact assessment study carried out in October 2000 found the program's training and credit facilities to be have been beneficial for most participants. Respondents to a survey indicated that the credit scheme successfully addressed their working capital needs; they also stated that they gained knowledge and skills that improved their marketing performance.

About 92 percent of respondents indicated that the profitability of their business had improved, and 86 percent of them indicated improvements in their standard of living. Some stated that they now can send their children to school, buy household items, save money, and pay for medication. Many revealed that their home life had changed with their newfound confidence in generating ideas and running the household. Some women who were beggars in the past reported that they can now feed their families.

Future Plans

WISE identified the following objectives in its 2001–03 plan: set up a micro health insurance plan that will be jointly funded by WISE and the beneficiaries; establish a micro-enterprise development center to continue the training of women; establish a federation of cooperatives to enable individual cooperative members to claim certain rights; engage in action research on micro-entrepreneurship to identify issues for advocacy work; and disseminate best practice findings to a wider audience.

AAE actively engages its partners throughout the duration of the relationship. and in particular is committed to building the capacity of its partners. Over the last seven years AAE has organized or sponsored training for local NGOs in savings and credit, management, ACCESS (Alternative Cost-Effective Centers within the School System), community-based health care, HIV/AIDS, and gender analysis. It has also sought to increase the exposure of development programs, both within Ethiopia and overseas.

Benefits

Partnership has benefited ActionAid in four main ways. It has:

- enhanced our capacity to work developmentally with NGOs and government organizations;
- enhanced our ability to work with different target groups, such as women, children, and people with HIV/AIDS;
- enhanced our understanding of the different dimensions of poverty, specifically through engagement in different geographical areas with people of diverse backgrounds, such as pastoralists, agro-pastoralists, highland farmers, and the urban poor; and
- increased our influence as an advocate for the poor and marginalized.

Challenges Experienced

The shift from independent operations to partnerships also has its challenges. From the outset, the sociopolitical context in Ethiopia defined the role of the INGO as resource provider rather than as stakeholder. The shift to partnership broke AAE's direct link with communities, obliging it to learn how to exert influence over its partners to ensure that their activities are consistent with its mission (for example, in terms of targeting and of the quality of engagement with the poor and marginalized).

Diversification into partnership also introduced new issues of accountability, confidentiality, and trust. For example, can AAE claim to speak for its autonomous partners, either individually or as a group? Can AAE bring its experiences of partnership into the public arena to inform the general debate in Ethiopia and beyond without betraying confidences? Can AAE reach through its partners to the target groups to understand the partner's experience without appearing to be checking on the partner's performance?

AAE's provision of funds may in some instances rule out the possibility of government funding. This could leave AAE in the role of resource provider to what is a de facto government program.

Differences in view between the government and AAE, as to the causes of poverty and how development should progress, make AAE's role as advocate both sensitive and difficult.

Another challenge is to balance demand and supply when providing organizational development support to partners.

The results of short-term partnerships can be too narrow to support conclusions for wider replicability.

The Way Forward for ActionAid Ethiopia

AAE's country strategy paper for 2000–04 specifies as a key strategy the promotion of partnerships against poverty. The group proposes using the expertise gained through its work in Ethiopia to bring together international NGOs, bilateral and multilateral donors, and government organizations to create a common ground for antipoverty work.

AAE is committed to strengthening its engagements with partner NGOs to achieve greater influence, particularly in joint advocacy; to improve the transparency of its operations; and to enhance its learning capabilities. It also is committed to developing new relationships with a wider range of partners and to increasing the flexibility of its operations in terms of physical reach, funding amounts, target populations, and sectoral and thematic mix.

ActionAid Ethiopia is also shifting from the conventional service delivery approach to a rights-based approach to development, both in its direct operational interventions and in operations that involve other stakeholders. To fully realize this change, AAE must increase its competence in the following areas:

- work undertaken directly with the poor and marginalized;
- leadership;
- gender analysis;
- action research and learning (to feed into advocacy work and to support program learning);
- partnership techniques;
- organizational development, capacity building, and institution building; and
- impact assessment and associated cost-effectiveness analysis.

Recommendations

Partnerships between government and civil society potentially can be highly beneficial, but it is essential to ask what each prospective partner can bring to a relationship, what it needs, and what it hopes to achieve.

For an aid agency in Ethiopia, the benefits of working in partnership with local institutions far outweigh the problems of partnership. Working with local institutions rather than alone is less expensive, has a higher likelihood of being sustainable, and is less threatening to local people and authorities. As seen in the AAE–WISE cooperation (see Box 15.1), the involvement of local groups can facilitate the growth of local civil society institutions that promote citizen participation and representation.

References

ActionAid Ethiopia. 2000a. *ActionAid Ethiopia Country Strategy 2000–2004.* Addis Ababa, Ethiopia: ActionAid Ethiopia.

———. 2000b. "Working Developmentally through Partnership: Workshop Report." Addis Ababa, Ethiopia: ActionAid Ethiopia.

———. 1999. *ActionAid Ethiopia Country Programme Review.* Addis Ababa, Ethiopia: ActionAid Ethiopia.

———. 1993. *A Review of the ActionAid Ethiopia Programme 1988–1993.* Addis Ababa, Ethiopia: ActionAid Ethiopia.

WISE (Women in Self-Employment). 2000a. *Organization for Women in Self Employment: Impact Assessment.* Addis Ababa, Ethiopia: Women in Self-Employment.

———. 2000b. *Plan and Budget 2000–2003.* Addis Ababa, Ethiopia: Women in Self-Employment.

16

Research Partnerships and Their Evaluation

Diane L. Stone

This chapter looks at the role played by partnerships in public policy research and at the difficulties in evaluating the work done by these partnerships. The discussion will focus on the Global Development Network (GDN) as an exemplar of a global policy research partnership (see Box 16.1).

The GDN is one of the programs through which the World Bank has sought to become a "knowledge bank" and to legitimize its claims of building partnerships with civil society organizations. It is inevitable that the Bank should seek to develop partnerships with organizations that share its values and norms, and the seven regional networks that form the basis of the GDN are devoted mainly to analyzing economic questions. They do not, however, reflect the diversity of the development research community. The privileging of development economics and the "choice" of existing Bank partners as the foundation of the GDN have alienated some other development actors. This is a perception that the GDN Secretariat and the regional networks have been working to overcome.

Policy Research and the Development Process

Demand for policy research comes mainly from government, but also from NGOs, corporations, the media, and international organizations. Each of these entities may have their own research capability, with its own advantages and constraints. Policy advisory units attached to government, for example, have direct bureaucratic and political access, while those outside or on the margins of the state typically find it more difficult to transmit new ideas into the corridors of power. Those on the outside, however, can be valuable social and

---

Diane L. Stone, reader in Politics and International Studies, University of Warwick.

Box 16.1
The Global Development Network

The GDN was launched by the World Bank in 1999 in cooperation with the United Nations; the governments of Japan, Germany, and Switzerland; and a group of regional research networks and some other private and public international development institutions. It is largely donor funded.

The GDN operates on the assumption that "the generation of local knowledge," when shared with local policymakers, "will ultimately lead to the solution of local problems" (GDN 2001). It aims to achieve this by enhancing the quality and availability of policy-oriented research by strengthening the local institutions—think tanks, research institutes, and development researchers—that undertake this work. It provides information about and access to resources, such as research funds, professional development programs, and networking opportunities, and helps to coordinate and disseminate research efforts and to build the capacity of institutes and individuals in developing countries.

The building blocks of the GDN are seven regional research networks, five of which (excepting the Latin American and Caribbean Economic Association [LACEA] and the Eastern European network) were established with assistance from the World Bank during the 1990s. The seven are the Africa Economic Research Consortium; the Center for Economic Research and Graduate Education (Eastern Europe); the East Asian Development Network; the Economic Education and Research Consortium (Russia); the Economic Research Forum (Middle East and North Africa); LACEA; and the South Asian Network of Economic Institutes. In the last two years, three OECD networks have been created to complement them.

In addition to building these regional networks, the World Bank Institute organized a series of capacity-building workshops to bring together a wide range of development research actors. These workshops helped to build interpersonal relations and cross-cutting networks, and began the process of generating awareness and support in the donor community. They also helped to construct a common perspective, impetus, and consensus for the creation of a global network of think tanks and research institutes (see Stone 2000).

Since its 1999 inaugural conference in Bonn, the GDN has consolidated rapidly. A governing body was appointed at the conference in 2000, and the network has already convened three large international conferences. It has established a Web site (*www.gdnet.org*) to help disseminate research, and it has launched several major projects, including the Global Research Project on Growth, the Data Initiative, Regional Research Competitions, and the Global Development Awards.

political critics, providing alternative perspectives to those propounded by a government.

A feature common to all researchers, government and nongovernment alike, is that none can cover all specialties. Addressing the inaugural GDN conference, former World Bank chief economist Joseph Stiglitz (2000) stated:

> If the developing countries are really to be "in the driver's seat," they have to have the capacity to analyze the often difficult economic issues which they face. Local researchers, combining the knowledge of local conditions—including knowledge of local political and social structures—with the learning derived from global experiences, provide the best prospects for deriving policies which are both effective and engender broad-based support. That is why locally based research institutions are so important.

It is fundamental to the GDN process that think tanks, government research units, university centers, and individual experts are viewed as partners in the sharing of global knowledge and the development of local research capacity. They are also seen as partners in encouraging home-grown policy reforms.

The evaluation of research partnerships therefore is not simply a matter of ascertaining the quality of research sponsored by the GDN; the effectiveness or influence of that research is critical. There are five main aspects to the question of effectiveness:

- *Effectiveness where?* While it may not influence national government, policy research may have considerable impact at a district or provincial level or in another country.
- *Effectiveness with whom?* Audiences for policy research exist apart from legislatures and political executives. While a government may reject policy research, it may be well received by the academic community. Similarly, international donors may give greater credit to policy research than do domestic audiences, and local NGOs may find greater use for research on, say, women's participation or water management than would a bureaucratic agency.
- *Effectiveness when?* Research findings may have a long-term and diffuse impact or, if picked up by the media or fed directly into policy design, an immediate impact. This can affect the culture of debate and the frameworks of understanding within which policymakers operate.
- *Effectiveness how?* Policy entrepreneurs use a range of strategies to make policy research effective, including advocacy, dissemination through Web sites and print, networking within policy communities, presentation to legislative committees, and expert appointments to government bodies.
- *Why is it effective?* Scholars have long had difficulty in accounting for the role of ideas in policy and politics (Braun and Busch 1999). The

causal nexus of knowledge, research, and ideas, and its implications for agenda-setting, political deliberations, and policy implementation, have never been clear. Furthermore, the use of information is a political process, and scientific findings are often regarded as disputable information rather than objective knowledge. It is therefore important in the evaluation of policy research partnerships to understand why ideas are selected, interpreted, applied, modified, or rejected by governments or international organizations.

Policy Research Partnerships

There is no universal template for the creation of a policy research partnership. Partnership arrangements vary according to their composition and character, their resources, and their objectives. All partnerships, however, share a common need to consider costs and benefits, and to address the issue of who chooses the partners. They also share the options of exit, voice, and loyalty, as described below.

Partnership Guidelines

The Swiss Commission for Research Partnerships with Developing Countries (KFPE) has developed guidelines for the internal management of research partnerships (KFPE 1998). Above all, the guidelines emphasize the establishment of strong working relationships. They are as follows:

- decide objectives together
- build up mutual trust
- share information and develop networks
- share responsibility
- create transparency
- monitor and evaluate the collaboration
- disseminate the results
- apply the results
- share profits and accolades equally
- increase research capacity

The KFPE guidelines instruct the actions of researchers and donors but do not address the question of how to involve external actors—for example, the subjects of the research—in designing the research or in managing the partnership. The GDN, however, has sought from the outset to incorporate internal and external opinions into the design of its objectives. The sheer scale of the project required the leadership to take a large degree of responsibility for launching the network, which was achieved with the input of researchers and donors, realized through surveys and consultations. The design of network governance, for example, was a transparent process that sought feedback through electronic discussion on the network Web site, *www.gdnet.org*.[1]

Despite these efforts toward inclusivity, the GDN has been criticized for its selection procedures—notably for appointments to its governing structure. Initially there was little transparency in its financial situation.

Benefits and Costs

A partnership must clearly define the costs and benefits to, and the responsibilities of, its partners. These need to be addressed at both the individual and the organizational levels.

On the benefits side, policy researchers are often willing to invest time and energy in developing regional or international links for the scholarly objective of advancing knowledge. For individual researchers and their organizations, involvement in partnerships such as the GDN potentially represents access to data, access to researchers in a similar field, and involvement in international conferences and workshops. For a university or research institute in a developing country, a partnership holds the prospect of improved access to resources, enhanced prestige, and capacity-building opportunities, such as training for students. There are also the sometimes significant sideline benefits of political visibility abroad, access to decision-making forums, policy experience, and even opportunities for personal advancement.

On the demand, or policy, side of the partnership, there are clear benefits for the many diverse groups, from diplomats to journalists to NGOs, which require high-quality research and analysis. Information apart, there are again benefits for the self-interested. For an international donor, for example, a partnership can also be a recruiting ground for staff or can serve as evidence that it is fulfilling its mandate to interact with civil society or stakeholder groups.

A research partnership may also produce unexpected benefits and externalities; for example, it may stimulate new ideas or develop a commitment among members that facilitates future joint enterprises. Not all outcomes are necessarily beneficial, however. In the case of GDN, the new European, Japanese, and North American hubs risk increasing the dominance of northern hemisphere research agendas. Furthermore, while GDN research may be relevant to improving the condition of the poor, individual network members are usually educated, middle-class professionals. There is a danger, given the technocratic and elite character of the network, that the GDN may actually aggravate social exclusion, inequality, and disarticulation in the global knowledge economy.

On the costs side of the balance sheet, partnering requires the investment of resources, time, and personnel. Hidden costs, such as the cost of networking, may prohibit some members from participating to the extent that they wish. In an open membership network such as the GDN, a structural bias may emerge whereby better-resourced, politically better-connected, or better-organized institutes are dominant. The costs, furthermore, need not be only financial. Institutes are all to some degree beholden to the funding priorities of donors, which potentially can close off valid avenues of local research.

Choice of Partners and Research Topics

Examination of the issue of choice exposes the unequal character of policy research partnerships. Who chooses?

Not surprisingly, it is the partner requiring the research data—the main supplier of financing—that usually holds sway over the choice both of partners and of the general parameters of the research agenda. The open nature of the GDN means that membership is largely self-selecting, but the original seven regional networks have played a central role in nominating and selecting GDN governing board members, and they also manage the regional research competitions. Given that the research themes tend to be economic questions, the "perception remains that this is a competition only for economists" (GDN Governing Body 2001). The institutes and researchers operating outside the regional networks are less club-like, but they have a lower profile in the GDN and fewer responsibilities. There is a clear danger of a class system becoming entrenched, which potentially could undermine trust within the wider research and donor communities.

Exit, Voice, and Loyalty

Notwithstanding the power differentials, all participants within policy research partnerships can exercise choice. The nature of that choice to participate was memorably characterized by Albert Hirschman (1970) as one of "exit, voice, and loyalty."

Loyalty—an expression of social capital—helps keep a partnership together. The mutual trust that engenders loyalty is valuable for its ability to ease the coordination of a partnership, but where loyalty is strong enough a partnership can even become an end in its own right, performing a social function where people interact, learn, develop friendships, and build histories, regardless of the success or failure of the endeavor.

Where loyalty is unable to hold a dissatisfied partner to the arrangement, the exit option awaits. The loss of a dissatisfied member can have a profound impact on a partnership, however, and should if possible be prevented.

One way to defuse dissatisfaction (and elevate transparency) is to enable the exercise of voice, for example through:

- annual meetings and regular committee meetings
- joint preparation by partners of annual reports, newsletters, and Web sites
- accessible lines of communication to partnership leaders (in the case of the GDN, to the secretariat, governing body members, and the GDNet advisory group)
- internal review procedures and evaluation mechanisms
- feedback mechanisms such as focus groups, electronic dialogues, and polls.

The balance of exit, voice, and loyalty is important to the sustainability of a partnership. The loss of too many partners can bring about the demise of the arrangement, but if no partner chooses to exit, the partnership may gradually run stale. Properly balanced, the voluntary movement of old partners out and new ones in can breath life—resources, intellectual capital, and ideas—into partnerships.

Evaluating the GDN Partnership

GDN Goals

Is the GDN meeting its goals? The GDN mission—to generate, share, and apply knowledge—is broad enough to invite numerous interpretations. Some partners emphasize the creation of knowledge as most important; some (as exemplified by the governing board of GDNet) stress the need to share knowledge; and others are interested primarily in the application of knowledge to policymaking and development.

The core problem to which the GDN is addressed is a lack of local knowledge in developing countries. Put simply, the solution to this problem is to build the capacity to create knowledge and to increase the supply of research (Squire 2000). The network is pursuing its capacity-building goals through the Global Research Project on Growth, regional research competitions, an annual conference, and coordination of information about scholarship schemes. It is too early to draw conclusions about the research being done, but mid-term, project steering committees and peer review processes are in place, conforming to the KFPE guideline to "monitor and evaluate collaboration."

To assess the value of policy-focused research work, conventional indicators of academic excellence (such as academic citations and scholarly peer reviews) will not suffice, since they do not reliably indicate policy relevance or impact. To judge the work performed by the GDN, other standards may thus need to be developed, such as:

- policymaker participation in research or the access of researchers to high-level interviewees or data

- timeliness
- the political standing of the researchers
- the weight and backing that sponsors give to propel the policy research into the public domain
- media interest
- utility of research reports to development agencies, NGOs, and local communities.

The network has demonstrated success in pursuit of its goal to share research. The Web site, notably, has proven valuable, with Growth Project workshops, annual conferences, and publications also assisting the dissemination of knowledge.

A focus on the third element of the network's goal—the application of knowledge—leads into the messy world of politics. Research is not apolitical. If it were, the GDN would inexorably affect the establishment of policy agendas, the shaping of the parameters of policy debate, and the pattern of policy reforms. The network does not have this level of influence, but does perform a lesser policy role, given the desire to encourage interaction between researchers and policymakers. In this sense, the GDN is a global public policy network (Reinicke and Deng 2000).

GDN Processes

Partnerships fail as often as they succeed. Rivalry, lack of common purpose, inefficiencies in delivering program services, squabbles over the distribution of resources, dissatisfaction with inclusion or access, and feuding over who controls resources are sources of division that can fracture policy research ventures. Process-based evaluations such as the KFPE checklist, geared to understanding how a program is carried out, are also useful for portraying to outside parties how a program truly operates.

Effective network coordination requires a clear idea of the basis of mutuality on which a research partnership is founded. According to Edella Schlager, as quoted in Braun and Busch (2000):

> Coalitions are more likely to persist if (1) the major beneficiaries that a coalition produces are clearly identified and are members of the coalition; (2) the benefits received by coalition members are related to the costs that such members bear in maintaining the coalition; and (3) coalition members monitor each other's actions to ensure compliance with agreed-upon strategies, resource contributions, and cooperative and supportive activities.

If the basis of mutuality in the GDN is taken as knowledge creation and knowledge sharing, the network can be seen to meet Schlager's conditions. All members of the GDN coalition, from the secretariat and governing body to donors and developing country researchers, are involved in creating knowledge. The main beneficiaries—the developing country researchers and institutes—are members of the coalition. And the benefits to the researchers mostly outweigh the costs, which are mostly borne by the donor agencies.

If the basis of mutuality is taken as the application of research, however, the major beneficiaries are a more diverse group of stakeholders, and include the consumers and subjects of research as well as the researchers. Achieving consensus on strategies and resource allocation potentially is more difficult, and the cost of monitoring behavior is higher.

This would suggest that limiting the basis of mutuality can help realize a common identity among partners and make management easier.

The need to find a common identity is most pronounced within the global networks. Within smaller partnerships or regional research networks, participants already often share a set of problems, a common language, or a shared history. Global research networks are still relatively rare, however, and face unprecedented coordination problems. The GDN is addressing this problem by in part circumventing it, working through pre-established regional networks to reach its goals.

A strong sense of common purpose is the source of coherence for a research partnership, but trust is the essential bonding agent (Jackson and Stainsby 2000). Lack of trust can undermine any relationship. It is difficult, however, to evaluate the relationship of trust that bonds a partnership based on "common identification, a sense of belonging or common purpose, and shared behavioral norms" (Serageldin and Grootaert 2000). In the absence of scientific methodology, anecdotal evidence and the stories told by key participants must establish the myths and moods of a partnership.

The creation and maintenance of trust depends in turn on transparency. According to Englehard and Box (1999), the key to the long-term success of any research network is the use of a formal governance structure with transparent decision-making procedures. In the early days of GND establishment, one of the greatest sources of dissension was the composition of the governing body. The first two conferences saw heated discussions about the lack of representation on the board in terms of gender, younger researchers, and disciplines other than economics. The GDN secretariat and governing body responded with a second call for nominations to the board to correct these imbalances.

GDN Outputs and Outcomes

Program outputs should not be confused with outcomes. The GDN is founded on the assumption that local policymakers need better information and better access to research. GDN program outputs include publications and policy reports, conferences and workshops, Web site and email interactivity, staff exchanges, training programs, and scholarship schemes. The purpose of these outputs is to help realize the desired outcomes, which generally are conceived in terms of enhanced learning (knowledge, perceptions and attitudes, or skills) or conditions, such as increased research capacity, policy improvement, or the alleviation of societal or economic problems.

Program outputs tend to be measurable, but evaluating outcomes is problematic. Even where increases in research capacity or improvements in the quality of research and analysis are evident, they may be the result of activities other than the work of the GDN. Conversely, policy research made available to policymakers may simply be ignored. Sharing does not necessarily mean that policy learning will take place.

It is thus necessary to make clear, when creating a policy research partnership, whether the intent is just to create policy-relevant research—that is, simply to deliver an output—or if there is a desire to see that the research is applied to policy. In the case of the latter, it must be understood that the causal relationship of ideas, knowledge, or research and decision making is unclear.

Evaluating the application of knowledge can range from assessing whether or not research is policy-relevant to judging the extent to which that research has helped alleviate problems of poverty. Some presumed indicators of success include the ability to acquire funds and political patronage, the ability to attract preeminent scholars and policymakers to conferences, and the number of column inches given to research results by the print media. However, these are surrogate indicators that may or may not correlate with policy influence; they do not demonstrate policy impact, learning among decision makers, or political influence.

Lessons

Mutual understanding is central to a policy research partnership. However, in a global research network with many participants, building trust is a long-term, slow, and intensive activity. Where network participants have different understandings of program goals and different interests, disagreements and dissatisfaction are to be expected. Effective leadership in the monitoring of the needs and interests of member institutes, donors, and other stakeholders is the key to managing expectations.

Network coordination requires the effective exchange of information, open channels of communication, and a sense of the future that guides network-participant behavior toward joint benefits.

Process is as important as outcomes. Subsidizing or containing the costs of partner interaction through Web sites or e-mail allows networks to be global in focus and participation. Weak capacity to subsidize participation could, however, open a global network to rent-seeking by better organized elements.

Providing opportunities for partners to make voluntary commitments to network goals sets up a dynamic for innovation, network learning, the development of new programs, and the formation of trust. It also increases the perception that ownership of the process can be claimed from the bottom up rather than endowed from the top down.

Consequently, in terms of evaluation, it is necessary to consider what is intangible and not amenable to measurement. In other words, partners need to be "ready to accept other scales of values" (KFPE 2000). GDN secretariat evaluation of programs, member institute priorities, and donor expectations differ. Accordingly, the different dynamics behind managerial, independent, and participatory sources of evaluation may well result in conflicting interpretations of policy research partnership goals, processes, and outcomes.

In the last instance, a *research* network must maintain the quality of output and the transparency of process or it is likely to flounder (Englehard and Box 1999). The epistemic credibility of policy research partnerships rests upon research excellence and rigorous standards of scholarly inquiry. This is the route to intellectual authority and legitimacy in policy debates.

Note

1. These discussions are archived at: *http://www.worldbank.org/devforum/forum_gdn.html*

References

Braun, D., and A. Busch, (eds.). 1999. *Public Policy and Political Ideas*. Cheltenham, U.K.: Edward Elgar.

Englehard, R. J., and L. Box. 1999. "Making North–South Research Networks Work." United Nations (UN) Conference on Trade and Development (UNCTAD).

GDN (Global Development Network). 2001. *The Global Development Network: A Snapshot*. Washington, D.C.: GDN.

GDN Governing Body. 2001. *Promotion of Research in All Social Sciences*. Washington, D.C.: GDN.

Hirschman, A. O. 1970. *Exit, Voice and Loyalty: Responses to Decline in Firms, Organizations and States*. Cambridge, Mass.: Harvard University Press.

Jackson, P. M., and L. Stainsby. 2000. "Managing Public Sector Networked Organizations." *Public Money and Management* 20(1): 11-16.

KFPE (Swiss Commission for Research Partnerships with Developing Countries). 1998. *Guidelines for Research in Partnership with Developing Countries*. Bern: KFPE.

Reinicke, Wolfgang, and Francis Deng. 2000. "Critical Choices: The United Nations, Networks and the Future of Global Governance." Executive summary available at *www.globalpublicpolicy.net/*

Serageldin, Ismail and Christiaan Grootaert. 2000. "Defining Social Capital: An Integrating View." In P. Dasgupta and I. Serageldin, eds., *Social Capital: A Multifaceted Perspective*. Washington, D.C.: The World Bank.

Squire, Lyn. 2000. "Why the World Bank Should Be Involved in Development Research." In Christopher L. Gilbert and David Vines, eds., *The World Bank: Structure and Policies*. Cambridge, U.K.: Cambridge University Press.

Stiglitz, Joseph. 2000. "Scan Globally, Reinvent Locally: Knowledge Infrastructure and the Localization of Knowledge." In Diane Stone, ed., *Banking on Knowledge: The Genesis of the Global Development Network*. London: Routledge.

Stone, Diane (ed.). 2000. Banking on Knowledge: The Genesis of the Global Development Network. London: Routledge.

17

Tactical Partnerships—A Philippine Case Study

Sandra M. Libunao[1]

In both the corporate and NGO worlds, strategic alliances of two or more organizations working toward a common goal are increasingly termed partnerships. But for collaboration between business and NGOs, "partnership" is a misnomer. Businesses pursue profit, NGOs the public good. Cooperation between the two should recognize both the different realities of the two parties and the different obstacles they face.

This chapter looks at how private sector companies and NGOs in developing countries can come together for mutual benefit, despite their innate differences. I shall anchor the discussion in an analysis of a successful tactical partnership in the Philippines that brought together a multinational textile manufacturer and local NGOs to undertake an evaluation with benefits for both.

Tactical Engagements between Business and NGOs

Most definitions of partnership between business and civil society actors suggest that these are collaborative, equitable relationships. This notion has little currency in developing countries, for several reasons:

- Socioeconomic, political, and cultural inequalities permeate all such relationships in the developing world. In practice, given differences in power; expertise; and human, material, and financial resources a company and an NGO do not share the responsibilities, costs, and risks of a partnership equally.

Sandra M. Libunao was formerly a director with Philippine Business for Social Progress (PBSP).

- The traditional partners of developing-country NGOs have been donor agencies from industrialized countries. Within such partnerships, the NGO typically depends on the donor for operating funds, while the donor typically relies on the NGO for knowledge about the host country.
- NGOs and business in developing countries have historically been suspicious of one another. Before the modern era of corporate social responsibility, this antagonism was often rooted in seriously conflicting political and social interests.

These features mean that businesses and NGOs should seek to engage each other tactically rather than strategically.

When a corporation and NGO join forces to achieve a specific, common objective through a short-term, tactical engagement there is enormous potential for success, provided that three essential conditions are met:

- Transparency of purpose. Both the business and the NGO must understand that the other has a genuine reason to cooperate, and that their reasons are not in opposition. Both must appreciate that they share a common value.
- Clarity about strengths and weaknesses. Each actor must be clearly aware of what it brings to the table and what its counterpart brings. For an NGO worker to acknowledge that there is something to be learned from a corporation is an important step; likewise, it is important that corporate executives appreciate the concept of voluntarism. Both must also be aware of the other's weaknesses and must ensure that they know the real limitations they face when working together.
- Openness to negotiation to resolve dissimilar or conflicting interests.

Case Study: An Engagement between Unequal Entities with Conflicting Interests

The story of a fruitful tactical engagement between a global manufacturer and local NGOs gives insights into the many potential benefits of working together.

In 1998, a global company invited NGO leaders in the Philippines to assess the workplaces of ten Philippine garment manufacturers the company had contracted with to handle various stages of its production. The multinational company had a code of conduct for its subcontractors, stipulating that they not hire children; that they maintain health and safety standards within the workplace; that they protect the right of workers to organize; that they uphold women's rights; and that they take steps to improve life in the communities where their manufacturing plants are located.

The multinational company believed that a critical review of its operations by Philippine NGOs could strengthen its reputation as a responsible company. It also knew that it was taking a risk, and that transgressions would be found. If the outside reviewers did not handle the project professionally and ethically, the company knew that it could suffer severe damage to its public image.

The NGO reviewers, too, would be taking a risk. The responses of the NGOs that were invited to be reviewers reflected the ambivalence in the Philippines toward multinational companies. The NGOs were aware that cooperating with a powerful foreign business firm could compromise their reputations, particularly if their involvement were to be used as a marketing ploy.

Nonetheless, five NGOs decided that the company's invitation gave them a tactical opportunity to pursue their own agendas, which included elimination of toxic industrial waste, improvements in factory working conditions, and protection of women's rights. The leaders of these five NGOs formed the evaluation team; they designed the evaluation framework and then carried out the evaluation through personal visits to the contractors' manufacturing plants over a period of several months.

The engagement was a success, for three reasons: (1) the company chose to operate with the NGOs through an intermediary, and found a good one; (2) the company and the NGOs had a clear objective, aligned around a common interest; and (3) the terms of engagement were established at the beginning through negotiations.

An Effective Intermediary

To bridge its political and cultural distance from the NGOs, the company pursued the engagement through an intermediary—a local organization that had been established and was supported by Philippine businesses, but which was run by NGO workers. The intermediary performed a vital role during the initial formation of the NGO team and then took on the role of secretariat for the project.

The intermediary had clear criteria for selecting the NGOs: expertise in labor conditions, community empowerment, women's rights, prevention of child labor, and environmental protection. Such issues were naturally troubling for the global company, but the intermediary insisted that the assessment team should be seen as uncompromised if the results were to have credibility.

Clear-cut Objective and Common Interest

The engagement was anchored in full agreement on the need to assess workplace conditions in the ten manufacturing plants. The NGOs expected the review to lead to improvements for the workers, their communities, and the environment. The company, for its part, expected the assessment to show that it was a socially responsible employer and thus enhance its public image.

Hard Bargaining on the Terms of Engagement

Without effective negotiation, which is based on the ability to facilitate, summarize, listen, and set an agenda, an engagement will fail. The case study highlights the importance of negotiation in determining the terms and scope of the engagement, designing the processes used, and seeing the project through.

The company began the engagement with the specific objectives of evaluating the process of implementing its code of conduct, the compliance of the contractors with the code of conduct, and the impact of the code of conduct on workers and on the community. The company wanted the evaluation to be within limits it could control—for example, it expected that the contractors' procedures for the treatment of wastewater would be reviewed, but not to the extent of determining where the sludge was deposited.

Knowing the commitment of the company to the project, the NGO leaders were able to bargain hard to push the evaluation beyond the company's objectives. They wanted the code of conduct itself evaluated, not just its implementation and impact. They also wanted to evaluate the company's own manufacturing plant. To retain their leverage during negotiations, the NGO leaders refused payment from the company for their work. They negotiated for greater independence to design and implement the evaluation; a commitment of immediate action by the company to address any blatant violations of the code; evaluation of the code itself; evaluation of the company's own plant; low-key public disclosure of the review findings, with no media coverage; and full, unedited publication of their reports.

The company responded positively: it agreed to take immediate action against blatant code violations, agreed to circulate the results only to selected stakeholders without media coverage, and promised not to amend the assessors' reports. Both parties agreed that the NGO report and the company's response would be two separate documents. The company also agreed to give the assessment team full independence, requiring only regular updates. The evaluation of the code itself was to be done outside the formal memorandum of agreement, with any report on the code made informally. The company executives agreed, however, to review and discuss the assessors' findings. On the final point of negotiation, that of reviewing the company's own plant, the NGO leaders accepted that the company held this plant to a separate and higher code of conduct than the contractors' plants and agreed to the compromise of a simple visual inspection.

Outcome of the Review

The review took six months to complete. The NGO leaders concluded that the code of conduct made contractors more aware and more protective of workers' rights, and that the contractors in general were more diligent than other firms in abiding by environmental and labor laws, and employment, health, and safety standards. The code also was found to have a positive impact on workers by preventing sexual harassment and gender discrimination. In unionized factories, the evaluation found that the contractors genuinely negotiated collective bargaining agreements.

The assessors also uncovered several weaknesses, including the following:

- Some facilities needed to reduce their use of temporary workers by hiring experienced and skilled temporary employees as regular, fulltime employees.
- A few contractors operated without the necessary permits and had poor waste storage and flawed wastewater treatment facilities.
- Some contractors had only superficial knowledge of labor and environmental laws and standards.
- Many workers were not informed about sexual harassment policy, occupational health risks, or company rules and regulations.
- The global company's internal monitoring mechanisms were faulty. Specifically, it failed to identify noncompliance with Philippine laws regarding permits and waste storage and waste treatment facilities.

The company acted on the permits and waste treatment problems of its contractors and planned a series of training sessions. It began to require its contractors to conduct awareness training for their workers. Internally, it tightened its monitoring of its own compliance with the laws.

Lessons

Real Stakes Are Necessary

Collaboration between companies and NGOs has the best chance of success when the interests of business and civil society converge. In this case study, both the NGO and the company had a clear stake in completing the assessment and bringing the plants up to standard; it was the large potential benefits of the project that ensured that both parties committed time and resources to seeing it through. The tension between the environmentalist NGO leader and the global company and its contractors was high, but while the relationship was at times confrontational, the engagement flourished.

Prejudices Can Change

Exposure to the internal operations of firms can provide valuable lessons for civil society organizations. Through their contact with the multinational company, the NGO leaders gained an appreciation of the difficulties faced by a corporation that seeks to balance its social responsibilities with the business imperative to be profitable. They also learned that the more businesses engage with NGOs, the better corporate citizens those businesses will become.

For their part, corporate executives found that by engaging with NGOs they could better understand what motivates NGOs; in some cases, an extreme bias against NGOs gave way to an understanding of the problems of workers as articulated by the NGOs. Many of the executives of the contractor companies also changed their views about NGOs.

Success Does Not Require Consensus

In our case study, the company and the NGOs found that so long as the agreed objectives and outputs were being met, and so long as the processes employed were acceptable to everyone, reaching full agreement on all decisions was of secondary concern.

Balancing the Engagement

A global corporation and a group of NGO leaders cannot share power equally but they can balance it. For example, by refusing payment for their work, the NGO leaders acquired a moral advantage to counterbalance the corporation's financial advantage. At the outset, a successful tactical engagement between civil society and the private sector depends on both actors having a significant interest in the outcome sought. But the process itself must balance consensus and effectiveness, and power and responsibility, and it is on these balancing acts that the quality of the outcome depends.

Implications for Evaluation

Evaluating engagements between business and NGOs is difficult, and has rarely been done. Based on the case cited here and comparable cases, and on emerging trends in the evaluation of NGO impact,[2] the following dimensions and questions commend themselves as tools for developing evaluation criteria and indicators:

Effectiveness

The effectiveness of an engagement should be evaluated in three dimensions.

Progress toward the engagement's stated goals. Key questions include the following:

- What were the vested interests of each actor in the engagement?
- Were these interests transparent to all parties?
- Were these interests clearly reflected in the objectives set for the engagement?
- What were the immediate outcomes?
- What changes were brought about by the engagement?
- To what extent was each party satisfied with the results?

Success of the negotiation process. Some key evaluation questions are:

- How consistently during the engagement was negotiation used, as opposed to unilateral decision making?
- What issues were negotiated? How were they resolved? How were problems addressed?
- How skilled were the negotiators?
- To what extent did the parties consider that the agreements reached were a result of genuine deliberation by both sides? Were non-negotiable issues such as values or mission compromised?
- How well facilitated were these negotiations?

Accountability of the parties to their respective stakeholders. NGOs do not represent communities, and global companies do not represent their contractors, but because both parties are linked to these stakeholders, consultations are an important dimension. Engagements are effective to the extent that the different actors consult and discuss results with their stakeholders. Some key evaluation questions include the following:

- Were stakeholders consulted? How? How often?
- What involvement did secondary actors (such as the indirect beneficiaries of the engagement) have in the process?
- To what degree were the views of secondary actors about the engagement and its expected outcome taken into consideration?
- To what extent were these views consistent with the design of the engagement? Was the engagement reconfigured as a result of the views of third-party stakeholders?

Efficiency

The efficiency of the financial, time, and human resource investments in the engagement should be assessed. Specifically, could the same results have been achieved at less cost or better results achieved for the same cost? Crucial dimensions of efficiency are the roles of primary and secondary actors, performance and outputs, the mechanisms for technical and logistical support, and the quality of the support structures. The following questions can shed light on the roles of actors and on performance and outputs:

- Were the roles of secondary actors, such as an intermediary organization and the secretariat, clearly spelled out and clear to all involved?
- What were the strengths and weaknesses in the performance of the secondary actors?
- To what extent did these strengths and weaknesses facilitate or hinder the attainment of objectives?

The following questions can be used to judge the efficiency of technical and logistical support:

- Were appropriate mechanisms in place to provide logistical support?
- To what extent did these mechanisms facilitate or hinder the attainment of objectives?
- What problems were encountered? How were they solved?

Impact

The significant and lasting changes brought about by the engagement should be evaluated. For short-term engagements between businesses and NGOs, the best time to conduct an impact evaluation depends on when the impact can reasonably be expected to show itself. Once this judgment has been made, it can be used to schedule the impact evaluation.

The dimensions of impact that can be used to evaluate partnership include policy, programs, systems, and people's attitudes and perspectives. In the case study examined here, the impact of the engagement should be assessed from the perspective of changes in the operations of the NGOs, the global company, and the contractors. For the NGOs, those changes are likely to be in policy toward business collaboration and in programmatic thrusts; for example, have they engaged with other businesses as a result of the initial engagement? For the global company and its contractors, one should look for policy changes in hiring; for example, in collective bargaining agreements, or in the terms offered to employees. Evaluators should also look for changes in the wording and implementation of codes of conduct and in the monitoring of code implementation. Changes in the lives of the workers and of the community as a whole—for example, in terms of quality of life and working conditions—can also provide evidence of impact.

Conclusion

Business–NGO tactical engagements are not for the faint-hearted, as evidenced by their rarity, but they can be a powerful means to effect beneficial changes at the core of an NGO mission or a company's business strategy. They could be encouraged by raising public expectations for responsible business practices, thus impelling corporations to be more proactive in their efforts to fulfill their civic obligations. Greater awareness among NGOs that corporations are prepared to respond to social issues also could push NGOs toward collaboration with the private sector. Finally, the development of methodologies to evaluate the effectiveness, efficiency, and impact of such engagements is essential.

Notes

1. The author would like to thank her editors Ricardo Wilson-Grau and Marissa Johnston for their assistance.
2. For an overview of impact assessment of NGOs, see *Impact Assessment for Development Agencies* (1999) by Chris Roche, Oxfam U.K.

18

Local Governments and Community-Based Partnerships

Nicoletta Stame

Italy is a *locus classicus* for the study of social capital. According to the literature, it simultaneously lacks capital—as held by the theory of "amoral familism" (Banfield 1958)—and has an abundant endowment of it (Putnam 1993). Whatever the truth may be, Italy is a place where various policies aimed at the creation or enhancement of social capital are undeniably being tested. Evaluations of these policies may provide pointers for how to evaluate the value added by community-based partnerships.

As many authors hold (for example, Evans 1996), local development can be seen as a mix of social capital and government institutions. Accordingly, local development policies may be distinguished by the way in which institutional arrangements seek to enhance or create social capital, and by the way they use social capital for development.

Evaluation of Local Development Policies: Where Are We?

The problem Italy faces with the evaluation of local development policies stems from the following paradox: The tradition of evaluation understands development projects to be projects based on infrastructural investments, but the reality of much local development is that it is based on the enhancement of *social* capital, and development founded on social capital is regarded as spontaneous growth that is not subject to evaluation.

Standard investment projects did in fact lead the state's "extraordinary intervention" in southern Italy. This program, which ran from the mid-1950s to the early 1990s, poured capital into heavy industry and infrastructure, but when evaluated for its return on investment—jobs created, impact on gross

---

Nicoletta Stame is president, Italian Evaluation Association, and University of Rome.

national product—was found not to have created the expected links with local industry. On top of this, the program was heavily criticized for alleged patronage and misuse of resources that undermined the relationship between the state and local communities.

In the 1970s, a strategy of decentralization and flexible production in central and northeastern Italy gave birth to new light-industrial districts that promoted the "Made in Italy" label for home and consumer goods. The impact of political intervention on the creation of industrial districts has never been evaluated, but as I shall explain below, in this instance the new manufacturers clearly benefited from existing political conditions.

It was not until the 1990s that development policies were targeted at specific areas, such as a territory to be upgraded or a particular cultural patrimony to be saved. The new policies sought to create partnerships between local and supra-local social and institutional actors, in which the local actors are active and creative members. National and EU funds often support these policies, and there is a new awareness about the lessons that can potentially be learned from their evaluation.

It is difficult, however, to know where to begin evaluating the partnership element of local development. In evaluating community-based partnerships, we clearly cannot use the historical evaluation model that disregarded social capital.[1] Neither can we depend on a tradition that focuses on the spontaneous working of social capital and ignores institutional development, and which therefore is insensitive to evaluation problems.

What we need is an evaluation of local development policies that is founded in an understanding of the working of community-based partnerships. Addressing a similar problem, Robert Picciotto (2000) said that in actual development projects for poverty reduction, one should add the criterion of institutional development and sustainability to the usual evaluation criteria of relevance, efficiency, and efficacy.

We now look at three models of local development policy, all centered on community-based partnerships and institutions, to see what role evaluation could play in each case.

Industrial Districts and Social Capital

Putnam worked out his famous thesis on social capital in a comparative study of the performance of regional administrations in Italy in the 1980s (Putnam 1993). He found that the better-faring administrations were those in central and northeastern Italy, where there was a greater endowment of social capital; that is, of norms of reciprocity, civic networks, and trust. These were the legacy of a tradition of democratic municipal governments, cooperatives, and other horizontal links. In contrast, southern Italy had known autocratic government in which trust and civic networks were replaced by individualism and "amoral familism." The southern regional administrations showed worse performance on many indicators. The natural conclusion was that the working of institutions depends on social context and history—a theory of path dependence that would seem to leave little hope to those who do not have the right ancestors!

As history bears out, Putnam's "happy regions" of the center and northeast are those in which the first industrial districts flourished. The socioeconomic systems of these regions have their roots in a centuries-old sharecropping relationship. When sharecropping ended in the 1950s, it released a workforce for industry. Industry grew through the 1960s and 1970s, at which point many big firms decentralized and workers, supported by their families, became their own bosses. The new firms collaborated with other small firms, and a local industrial network emerged.

Industrial districts are local systems; they have always been the alternative to the Fordist big factory of northwest Italy, the first region to industrialize. The small factory network was able to defy what at the time seemed the infallible superiority of big firms, because of its social institutions of trust and collaborative industrial relations, use of tacit and codified knowledge, and the intelligence provided by some local institutions.

The regions where these light industrial districts emerged also received political support, but from totally different quarters. The Veneto was run by a strong majority of Christian Democrats who thought of small firms as a shield of private property against proletarianization and communism. Tuscany and Emilia-Romagna, in contrast, were run by left-wing coalitions looking for autonomy from central state policies. Their supporters were the champions of small firms which they believed would be able to create an enormous mobilization of capacity to produce wealth and well being.

Studies on industrial districts by Giacomo Becattini and his colleagues emphasize how districts grow and change in terms of production and quality of products, type of work done, services offered, and so forth (Becattini et al. 2001). They also stress the importance of the social and institutional context and of local knowledge and its ability to combine with codified knowledge and technological innovation—in other words, of a territorial specificity and the contextual basis for its development.

This first wave of local development studies had two opposite effects: the literature on industrial districts had the positive effect of stressing the importance of context as a basis for different paths to development, and the literature on social capital inspired by Putnam's work had a discouraging effect on people, especially in the south, who lived in regions that did not follow the same historical path as the center and northeast.

Although a law was passed in 1991 to favor the establishment of industrial districts in other areas of Italy, especially where small and medium enterprises (SMEs) have been created through subcontracting, districts are in practice spontaneous social and economic phenomena that public policies may support, but not create. Those evaluations that find the implementation of the new law to have succeeded base their judgment on increases in jobs created, or in per capita GNP, not on evidence of an increase in social capital (Viesti 2000).

Territorial Pacts

In southern Italy, the policy of the "extraordinary intervention" came to an end in the early 1990s, in combination with a national political crisis. The system of national parties that had run the country during the Cold War was gradually giving way to an alternation of two main political coalitions and a decentralized federal system.

After an interregnum, in which it seemed that only "ordinary expenditure" could take place in the south, a new national policy was launched that borrowed some ideas of commonality and partnership to be fulfilled by state intervention. This policy was termed "negotiated programming," and used territorial pacts as its main tool.

With territorial pacts, the state in the first phase provides funding for local actors, such as municipalities, representatives of firms, trade unions, or banks, to organize around a new institution (the pact corporation) and decide what is best for their area. The state then cofinances the initiatives that they have selected for funding.

The rationale of the tool is that financial resources, in the forms of assistance to management and of funding of local productive initiatives, can elicit social capital if local actors are put in a situation in which they can identify their own needs. As Bonomi and De Rita (1998) say, this is a way in which public policies can indeed create relational goods.

Territorial pacts were invented in Italy. Their story is one of conflict between the first organizers of pacts at the decentralized level—the National Council of Economy and Labor (CNEL), a consultative body—and the Ministry of Budget, which selects the projects and allocates money. Nowadays, CNEL frequently criticizes the central level for its slowness and bureaucratic attitude in drafting rules to regulate the management of partnerships, while the Ministry of Budget criticizes the local organizers as lacking the capacity to design good projects.

The EU, undeterred, has launched territorial pacts for employment in various countries, even in Italy. As of spring 2001, 170 national pacts and ten European pacts had been approved and funded, with a further fifty-one awaiting approval.

Territorial pacts are an object of fierce debate, but they continue to be considered a leading tool for local development. However, almost no one has tried to answer the question: Why should territorial pacts work?

According to De Rita, who considers himself "the man who invented the pacts," development takes place when "artificial" communities[2] are created that link the local to the global by long networks. In this construction, social capital is not a necessary prerequisite of local development, and collaborative behavior can spring out of new rules and institutions. What is needed is a strong catalyzing idea around which many forces, from near and far, can be mobilized.

This hypothesis runs contrary to what its supporters term the "culturalistic" approach to social capital held by Putnam, which would doom the south to stagnation.[3] Contrasting with the culturalistic approach are also the views of yet another group of authors who maintain that social capital is not the cause of local development but can be the effect of public policies. These authors consider territorial pacts to exemplify this claim. As Cersosimo and Wolleb (2001) put it, "when the taboo of nontransferability of the experience of districts, due to their embeddedness in local history and culture, is broken . . . the contextual conditions . . . can be modified through public intervention." They believe that public policies can create social capital through rules, mechanisms of interaction, and communication.

Followers of a systemic (Cersosimo and Wolleb 2001) or a structural (Trigilia 1999) approach see the local community as an experimental context in which norms are defined that impose a specific behavior. In particular, Trigilia states that interventions aimed at promoting social capital as a tool for local development should support—on a financial as well as an organizational level—integrated development projects that provide incentives for cooperative networking and that steer external interventions toward that goal. Public institutions on an upper level could help local actors to mobilize from below.

It is recognized that the provision of financial support to local networks cannot avoid the creation of collusive coalitions that are more eager to share money than to create development; but it is also maintained that local actors can learn to design development projects and select better projects in a transparent way if consistent support is offered. In other words, good national institutions, like universalistic tenders, may create good collaborative behavior, such as transparency in selection criteria.

This is the program theory that Cersosimo and Wolleb want to test. They rightly reject any idea of evaluating territorial pacts through the simple indicator of return on investment, and maintain that evaluation should concentrate on the hypothesis that a new and collaborative behavior can originate from the pact. Evaluation should therefore answer two main questions:

- In the cognitive sphere: Do pacts create changes in behavior? Are new rules created? Are public goods created? Is there virtuous exchange between banks and firms and between entrepreneurs and trade unions? Does trust increase?

- In the practical sphere: Are new productive initiatives created as a consequence of these changes?

Changes in the cognitive sphere have been found where people think of collaboration as a positive feature and the territorial pact as a durable institution able to attract new investments. Evidence of practical initiatives is considered the creation of consortia or other institutions, new credit regulations, or new forms of industrial relationships. The authors suggest that some pacts have succeeded in both the cognitive and the practical sphere and show the potential for new forms of development, but that many have simply gotten access to public money in the old way. In the latter case, new ideas of collaboration have been at odds with the old behavior of individualism and self-interest.

Cersosimo and Wolleb (2001) find that the successful cases are correlated with the following factors:

- The external context. Pacts have worked better where the old party system was replaced by a new generation of mayors who often proved to be the soul of pacts. The national context has not provided clear rules, however, and this has created difficulties.
- The experimental context. Pacts have succeeded where there have been credible, reliable institutional leaders. This obvious point actually conflicts with the authors' standpoint. They admit that pacts work better where trust exists, but they previously had said: "if pacts fail for a weakness in social capital . . . it is the philosophy of the pact that fails; it is the bet to change context through a public intervention that is lost."[4]
- The normative system. European pacts have fared better because their norms are clearer. Especially lacking from the territorial pacts are suitable criteria for the selection of projects. There are criteria for business plans and increases in occupation, but incentives to SMEs are not consistent with the ideas of partnership and local development. Nothing has yet been worked out to reward successful collaborative processes, nor to sanction those who do not stick to engagement.
- The process of institution building. This hints at the passage from the negotiation phase, which is collaborative and consensual, to that of management, which is riddled by conflict. The better-faring pacts are those for which continuity in the composition of the institutional tool is ensured from one phase to the next.

The evaluation design that the authors have used is a typical goal-based evaluation: (1) clarify objectives (collaboration, creation of social goods); (2) identify results that correspond to those objectives (a model of collaborative thinking and behavior); and (3) check the findings against that model. Unsatisfactory results can be attributed either to the inadequacy of the theory or to inadequacy of implementation.

Other evaluation designs could, however, have been followed. One approach would be to look at what happened in these situations regardless of their stated objectives. Such a "goal-free evaluation" would permit the evaluator to be more open to indirect effects. Studying a few cases in depth—chosen perhaps from those that have the most and those that have the least endowment of social capital, or from where the political system was more or less in crisis—it would be possible to see what happens when a large sum of money is thrown at a given territory with no other obligation than to decide how to spend it. This analysis would have helped to detect those cases of internal fights for resources that have been reported in many accounts, and that cannot simply be considered as cases that had "no effect."

Another approach would be to test the theory that public policies can create social capital. This could be done by analyzing different programs inspired by public policy. Territorial pacts, for example, could be compared to other instruments. The evaluation would require a quasi-experimental design of comparison between two or more types of intervention.

Local Development through the Surfacing of Hidden Resources

A different strategy of local development is now being put forward as an alternative to the theory of spontaneous development of districts and to the "mobilization from above" of the territorial pacts. The new strategy is proposed by groups of researchers—economists, sociologists, architects, and urban planners—who in the last decade or more have inquired into the socioeconomic reality of their students. The students, mostly at southern universities, have been asked to simultaneously become participant observers, detached analysts, and local development agents.[5]

These researchers have found that there are hidden resources of social capital that aim at development but are trapped in particularistic behavior. These include, for example, subcontracting firms that have grown and could become independent but which choose instead to maintain the status quo for fear of losing subsidies, distrust of the local authorities, and so forth. Similarly, local areas that could thrive by exploiting their natural resources for tourism or industrial development continue to be degraded by shortsightedness and self-interest.

Situations such as these tend to occur when the law is severe but not implemented, and when people blame the state for aloofness but at the same time cheat it. In fact, what is observed is a dissonance between aspirations to development and behavior, in which social capital is more frequently used in a negative than in a positive way.

Brought to the surface, the underground economy could become a lever of local development (Meldolesi 2001). It is a vast reservoir of jobs, a space in which people are trained and capacities are formed. These underground forces, however, cannot expand because of irregularities that prevent them from taking advantage of industrial support policies for production, export, and technological research.

Such irregularities differ from one area to the next in terms of type (fiscal, wage, work security), the behavior of different actors, and the performance of public administration. Programs are needed that are specifically targeted to various locations, and that are able to identify the leading local forces—small firms, entrepreneurial associations, trade unions, regional administrations, and local municipalities—that could be grouped together to enable the underground economy to begin to realize its potential.

To this end, a National Committee for the Surfacing of Irregular Work (*Commissione nazionale per l'emersione del lavoro non regolare*) has been established in Italy, with responsibility for creating regional and provincial commissions to mobilize the underground economy. The committee is expected to do this by providing tools that can elicit virtuous behavior on the part of these underground actors. This is not simply a matter of giving voice to the voiceless, but is also one of opening, by trial and error, new collaborations that have in the past seemed infeasible because of distrust in public institutions. This process has been called "institutional mobilization."

Numerous practical examples show that the state and its citizens can work together. A few include service centers that help SMEs with individual regularization projects,[6] work done in industry to regularize working conditions,[7] and microcredit or aid-to-enterprise-creation that has regularized traditional activities.[8] These and other interventions suggest how to create an alliance between government and individuals: the agents of the former must act as part of the community it serves, and the latter must invest their social capital in a relationship of trust, not deception.

This policy of local development by "surfacing" differs from that of territorial pacts in many ways, including the following:

- It is based not on the offer of new financial support, but on showing the contrast between what is desired (a good job, a democratic country, a clean environment) and what actually exists. Once a proposal is approved, help is provided in acquiring funding through other local, state, and EU programs. In other words, funding comes second, not first.
- It is based on enhancement of local resources and support for actors who clearly warrant its help. The territorial pacts, in contrast, pursue negotiations on almost any social or institutional initiative.
- It is based on specific projects; it does not advance a single, one-size-fits-all model. In this respect, it depends on universities or research groups to furnish socioeconomic and cultural studies to support its proposed actions.

Territorial pacts seek to overcome bureaucratic rigidities by negotiation, but project funding still comes from the center, creating the possibility that funds will be diverted away from their target, local level. Development by surfacing recognizes this danger, and acknowledges that the state, local institutions, and citizens must have a relationship based on trust.

Because conditions are unique to each location, no single model can be used for the evaluation of this development approach. Instead we must identify individual interventions that successfully coordinate different actors in exploiting underused resources. This problem is in fact at the center of a debate between the national and European authorities who are looking for "indicators of surfacing" and the national committee, which is looking for ways to capture the value added of integrated local policies.

The method suggested by Saraceno (1999) for the evaluation of the LEADER projects (EU-funded projects for integrated rural development) may point to a solution. Saraceno argues that to evaluate policies that take local forces to be a strategic factor in development one should look for evidence of the greater efficacy and sustainability of development projects. Such evidence could include the use of tacit knowledge, the integration of various actions, or the participation of beneficiaries, for example. Identification of these signs can be done easily at the individual project level, and it can also provide the basis for fruitful comparisons. Given that different projects cannot usefully be graded according to universal performance indicators, categories such as type of innovation and type of actions implemented should be used. This method would allow distinctions to be made between alternative paths, and would support evaluation of their comparative advantage.

A method like this would also engage beneficiaries, local institutions, and the commission's experts in a participatory exercise. The goal would be to identify, put simply, "what mechanisms work better in what context" (Pawson and Tilley 1997).

Conclusion

This chapter reviewed three local development strategies. I have tried to investigate their different theories of social capital and the different institutional arrangements that they propose, in order to see how their effects can be evaluated.

The proposition that industrial districts develop naturally because of their favorable socioeconomic context holds that institutions merely need to fit the context. There is little space for policy evaluation. Territorial pacts are based on the idea that although social capital can be scarce, social policies can create it, and that a process of negotiated planning financed by the state provides a tool to achieve this. Development by surfacing considers social capital to be a resource buried by a dissonant sociopolitical environment, and holds that policies of development should act to remove this dissonance and allow the potential of hidden social capital to become visible.

Evaluation of these policies might answer the problem of how to evaluate the value added by partnerships. Possible solutions range from building models of collaborative behavior, as has been done with territorial pacts, to looking for mechanisms of change that remove dissonance, as is proposed in strategies for local development through surfacing.

Notes

1. That said, this approach continues to be championed by some economists who are looking only for the best single indicator for development, regardless of program specifics, and who propose per capita GNP as the best proxy (see, for example, Florio 2001).
2. Artificial communities are the opposite of natural communities, where values are created in face-to-face relationships.
3. Authors who criticize the "amoral familism" thesis, and have long investigated social relationships in the south, have shown that strong family and social networks, if studied with a dynamic and situational model, have kept society together and have allowed various forms of economic and social development (Piselli 1999).
4. The same inconsistency cannot be attributed to Bonomi, who, assuming De Rita's theory of "artificial communities," considers a failure due to excessive fighting among partners to be an external factor (Bonomi and De Rita 1998).
5. For a presentation of these points of view, see the "*forum sulle Università meridionali e l'emersione*," organized by the *Comitato nazionale per l'emersione del lavoro non regolare* in February 2000 at the following Web site: *www.governo.it/Presidenza/Comitati/Comitato_nazionale_per_l'emersione_del_lavoro_non_regolare*.
6. I refer to the pilot project of the CUORE centers (*Centri Urbani Operativi per la Riqualificazione Economica*) in Naples that have been successful in investigating underground small firms and providing regularization projects and services for expansion of their activities.
7. *Contratti di riallineamento* (realignment contracts) that have been more successful in conditions of lower wages and regular security payments than when the opposite was true.
8. Programs for enterprise creation, such as that run by Imprenditorialità Giovanile (law 44/1986), and programs of microcredit (law 608/1996, the "*prestito d'onore*") have had the positive indirect effect of regularizing a large number of irregular jobs and of offering opportunities for the surfacing of underutilized capacities.

References

Note: The word *processed* describes informally reproduced works that may not be commonly available through libraries.

Banfield, E. 1958. *The Moral Basis of a Backward Society*. Glencoe, Ill.: The Free Press.

Becattini, G., M. Bellandi, G. Dei Ottati, and F. Sforzi. 2001. *Il Caleidoscopio dello Sviluppo Locale*. Turin, Italy: Rosenberg e Sellier.

Bonomi, A., and G. De Rita. 1998. *Manifesto per lo Sviluppo Locale*. Turin, Italy: Bollati Boringhieri.

Cersosimo, D., and G. Wolleb. 2001. *Politiche Pubbliche e Contesti Istituzionali*. Una ricerca sui Patti territoriali. Processed.

Evans, P. 1996. "Government Action, Social Capital, and Development: Reviewing the Evidence on Synergy." *World Development*, no. 6.

Florio, M. 2001. "La Valutazione dello Sviluppo Locale." In R. Brancati, ed., *La Valutazione delle Politiche Industriali*. Milan: Angeli.

Meldolesi, L. 2001. *Sud. Liberare lo Sviluppo*. Rome: Carocci.

Pawson, R., and N. Tilley. 1997. *Realist Evaluation*. London: Sage.

Picciotto, R. 2000. "Concluding Remarks." In O. Feinstein and R. Picciotto, eds., *Evaluation and Poverty Reduction*. Washington, D.C.: World Bank.

Piselli, F. 1999. "Capitale Sociale: Un Concetto Situazionale e Dinamico." *Stato e Mercato*, no. 3.

Putnam, R. 1993. *Making Democracy Work: Civic Traditions in Modern Italy*. Princeton, N.J.: Princeton University Press.

Saraceno, E. 1999. "The Evaluation of Local Policy Making in Europe: Learning from the LEADER Community Initiative." *Evaluation* 5(4).

Trigilia, C. 1999. "Capitale Sociale e Sviluppo Locale." *Stato e Mercato*, no. 3.

Viesti, G. 2000. *Come Nascono i Distretti*. Bari, Italy: Laterza.

19

Partnerships for Integrated Community Development in Southern Africa

Vuyo Mahlati and Mandivamba Rukuni

The literature is rich with discussion and research around issues of participation by community members in development activities. But literature that focuses on the processes of creating and maintaining partnerships at the community level is virtually absent. We present here the findings of a specially commissioned survey of three community partnership programs in southern Africa supported by the W. K. Kellogg Foundation, and draw some practical lessons of experience.

According to Chambers (1974), various biases impede outsiders' contact with the rural poor. And the economic and political crises of the 1970s and 1980s have discredited service delivery systems based on centralized bureaucracy, forcing theorists of development to shift their focus from hierarchy and control to participation and empowerment (Brett 1996). When people have an influence on the decisions that affect them, it is argued, they will have greater interest in the outcome and will therefore work harder to ensure success (Narayan 1995).

Today the use of indigenous knowledge and bottom-up approaches is seen as the solution to many development needs. However, methods such as rural cooperatives and community development have their own limitations, such as possible hijacking by government activists—leaving local people with little control over the outcomes—or pressure to produce results—leading to a reliance on the local elite (Gow and Van Sant 1981).

Such problems have led to the realization that partnerships are of critical importance for developers and the community. Community partnerships are usually coordinated by NGOs, which work in close collaboration with donor

---

Vuyo Mahlati and Mandivamba Rukuni are members of W. K. Kellogg Foundation, South Africa.

agencies, whether public or private. Partnerships give community members, especially the traditionally voiceless, the opportunity to take ownership of their lives. In addition, developers can now deal directly with community members who are willing and able to be part of the process and have the knowledge about local conditions that is lacking in many development efforts (Shepherd 1998; Abraham and Plateau 2001).

The Community Partnerships Surveyed

Conducted in May–June 2001, the surveys undertaken for this study looked at the Community Partnerships Primary Health Program, the Initiative for Development and Equity in African Agriculture (IDEAA), and the Integrated Rural Development Program (IRDP) (see Box 19.1).

The surveys were qualitative, using interviews to assess the experience of key players involved in the three partnerships. Purposive sampling was used to select a diverse range of interviewees. The information presented here is a collation of their opinions, with a deliberate bias toward reporting the views of community representatives.

Findings of the Surveys

The Meaning of Partnership

The interviewees in all five surveys showed a common understanding of partnership, despite being engaged in significantly different arrangements. Their collective understanding is that partnership involves working together toward a common goal, and that it should be equitable, collaborative, and voluntary. It should be characterized by mutual trust, respect, participation, commitment, learning, reciprocity, transparency, and negotiated decision making.

The reasons given by the communities for engaging in partnership included their need for training and resources, their desire to share information, and their wish to build friendships. From the experience of the surveys, it is clear that community partnerships should be viewed as dynamic relationships that can change over time.

Founding the Partnership Programs

The intermediary organizations in each of the five study areas were chosen by the Kellogg Foundation, which had also established the criteria for site selection and set up the strategic framework for the programs. The goals,

Box 19.1
Community Partnership Programs Surveyed

The Community Partnerships Primary Health Program. Established ten years ago, this program employs partnerships between universities, public health departments, and poor and disadvantaged communities as a strategy for bringing community-based primary health care to neglected areas. The goal of the program is to both improve the access to health care of poor communities and to enhance the relevance of university training and research. The Mangaung University partnership in Bloemfontein, Free State of South Africa, was selected for the survey. This is one of seven community health partnerships established with assistance from the Kellogg Foundation. Inaugurated in 1991, it is a partnership between the Mangaung community in Bloemfontein, South Africa; the University of the Free State, also in Bloemfontein; and the Department of Health of Free State Province.

Initiative for Development and Equity in African Agriculture (IDEAA). Started in 1997, IDEAA is a regional program that seeks to improve and commercialize smallholder agriculture in southern Africa by bringing together coalitions of service delivery organizations at the community level. Eight community sites participate in the program; the survey covered the Tikhuba IDEAA in Swaziland. The Tikhuba program is coordinated by the University of Swaziland in partnership with the Ministry of Agriculture and Cooperatives and NAMBOARD, the public body responsible for agricultural marketing in Swaziland. Farm products from the Tikhuba program include bananas, fish, honey, and poultry.

Integrated Rural Development Program (IRDP). Also active since 1997, this program focuses on the social mobilization of community structures, human and rural economic capacity building, and the building of community-based comprehensive health care. It is operational at three pilot sites: Chimanimani in Zimbabwe, Mohlanatsi in South Africa's Northern Province, and Nyandeni in the Eastern Cape of South Africa. All three sites were included in the survey. Nyandeni, along with the other two IRDP sites, met the site criteria of relative poverty, high population density, economic potential, and community motivation for the Integrated Rural Development Program. The Nyandeni IRDP is coordinated by the Africa Cooperative Action Trust (ACAT), an NGO formally appointed by Kellogg as District Facilitating Agency (DFA) after a competitive selection process. Funded by Kellogg, the partnership comprises ACAT, other NGOs operating as service providers, and some private sector groups. The Mohlanatsi IRDP combines the Greater Letsitele/Gravellote and Giyani Tribal Trust lands of South Africa's Northern Province. It is coordinated by the Development Resources Center (DRC) as the DFA for Mohlanatsi. Chimanimani in eastern Zimbabwe was the third site. The Intermediate Technology Development Group (ITDG) serves as DFA.

objectives, and activities of the programs were established mostly through workshops with the different interest groups. No memoranda of agreement or definitions of operational parameters were signed—the partnership operations were based on trust alone.

In the Mangaung University Community Partnership Program, respondents said that though they had not been permitted to select their partners, the goal-setting and visioning process of the partnership was driven largely by the results of a consultative needs analysis. Monthly meetings offer all partners an opportunity to voice their opinions and to share information on progress. A representative from the Department of Health observed:

> It took years to agree on a plan by getting consensus from all partners. Next, we needed to create a space for the training, and the health department needed to find the funds. This program was done quite differently to anything I've been involved in. The process unfolded as the program was created. It was done the right way, with a constitution and executive and everything. The community involvement took a long time. There was an open channel of communication and many community meetings. This facilitated the fast movement of the system once it got off the ground.

Tikhuba was selected for an IDEAA program on the basis of its high level of community interest, including farmer commitment; presence and likely participation of women and young farmers; and its organized farmer groups. The program began with meetings among the traditional community leadership, the local member of parliament, and extension workers. This dialogue progressed through a series of workshops designed to help the community identify needs and establish the constraints, possibilities, and gaps that the program would need to address. The biggest gap identified was described by one respondent as one in which service providers waited for the producers (farmers) to come for service, while the producers waited for the service providers to bring the service.

The Nyandeni program began with community meetings to define the goals of the program, followed by a development conference. The process was generally considered to be fairly consultative, but one service provider suggested that service providers are more accountable to Kellogg than to the community.

In the Mohlanatsi program, meetings were held with traditional leadership, key opinion leaders, other NGOs, and government departments operating in the eight tribal authority communities that form Mohlanatsi. The holding of meetings on a national day under a *marula* tree (an important cultural symbol in the area) helped to create a good impression.

The Chimanimani community-based partnership selection process was initiated through discussions with local councilors, key opinion leaders, church-based organizations, women and youth groups, the district administrator, extension service workers, and traditional leaders. Subsequent workshops were held at a grassroots level to familiarize a wider constituency with the initiative.

Governance Structures and Processes

The five sites developed different governance structures, reflecting the different circumstances of each.

The Mangaung University Community Partnership Program is a registered organization with a full-time staff of nine. It is overseen by a board of governors and a management committee on which each of the partners is represented. The program has its own constitution, which was drawn up by the board in consultation with the management committee and other partner representatives. The board comprises the head of nursing at the university of the Free State, a representative of the nursing college, the original organizer, women prominent in the Mangaung community, the Bloemfontein local council and the YMCA chairperson. It also has a legal advisor. Within the MUCCP, decisions are made at different levels, depending on the matter at hand. The full-time staff is involved in the everyday running of the partnership, but decisions affecting the partnership are made at the board or committee level. In each case, all partners are consulted, and, if necessary, each returns to his or her organization for consultation.

The Tikhuba initiative has representatives from the Ministry of Agriculture, the University of Swaziland, the Enterprise Fund, and the farmer community. The implementing body comprises three fellows from the university, one from NAMBOARD, and one from the Enterprise Fund. Each receives a stipend from IDEAA.

The Nyandeni IRDP governance structure was set up jointly by the Kellogg Foundation and the IRDP. While Nyandeni has a governance structure loosely involving community representatives, traditional leaders, and local councilors, there is no clear structure of representatives from the three partners.

The Mohlanatsi community comprises a group of neighboring villages. A governing board called the *lekgotla* was put in place after several workshops and consultations with community representatives. The effort to make it representative of all sectors of the community apparently is much appreciated, but at twenty-five members it may be too large. One interviewee commented: "Because of the huge number, Mohlanatsi business becomes everyone's business and at the end of the day it becomes nobody's business." Board members have received no training and are unclear as to their roles. Workshops have shaped the creation of other special interest groups. Women, for instance, were given the opportunity to meet with local activists and subsequently created new partnerships with regional women's organizations.

The Chimanimani IRDP relies on the existing local government structure of the Rural District Council (RDC)—an arrangement that has entangled the program in the political dynamics of the local authority. Officers are elected, and all villages of the district are represented in the different associations. It was observed, however, that men still dominate the youth and the business development association committees, and that the RDC council lacks any female representation, with the result that articulation of women's issues has not been actively pursued.

Implementation and Maintenance of Community Partnerships

In Mangaung, the program's Board chairman commented that "Significant community leadership [was] involved in the development of the program. Getting the community involved in that way has strengthened the relationship between the partners. . . . The partnership has resulted in the development of leadership within the community, and some members of the community have moved to take on roles within local government. The development of the program has created a process of identifying and screening potential leaders."

The Tikhuba partnerships are coordinated by a program coordinator based at the University of Swaziland. The five IDEAA fellows work directly with their partner communities and farmers, meeting every two weeks. But within the partnership, the university may wield too much power, and there is also a danger of the farmers becoming overdependent on the IDEAA. One cited example is of farmers with chickens ready for marketing, waiting for the fellows to organize the marketing for them. But the farmers have now formed their own association which has representation from the various projects in the area; with more support, the association should be able to continue independently of the IDEAA.

The Nyandeni Development Program appears to have overcome initial suspicion from the community, but continues to suffer from poor communications and a lack of transparency. Two comments are illustrative: "Communication is not that good. Some meetings fail. Communication with the DFA is not good; it is very last-minute." "We [service providers] do not have a formal relationship with the governing body of Nyandeni. We are not accountable to the people. We signed an agreement with [Kellogg]; we are only accountable to them and not to the community. This should not be the case."

Communication is also a problem in the Mohlanatsi program, in part because of poor transport in this large district. Community leaders expressed concern that the organization of the program distances community groups from their external partners, and that the DFA did not initially appreciate the remoteness and technological backwardness of Mohlanatsi. Feedback to the broader Mohlanatsi community was reported to be random and unsystematic. Follow-up by the DFA has been poor, with its failure to implement projects raising concerns about its management of funds. There is a general feeling of frustration with the IRDP in the community.

The Chimanimani DFA used workshops as the main tool for building and maintaining relationships between the different partners, but lack of follow-up—notably a failure to deliver promised funding—has caused disaffection among the community groups. Communication also has been inadequate, resulting in a gap between community expectations and action by the partner organizations, which have tried to pursue a rigorous development process before releasing funds. One youth group submitted a proposal for project funding but instead received an invitation to go to another country in the region and learn from it, prompting the following reaction: "Why don't they give us the money instead so that we work on our project? It's nice to fly, stay in a hotel, eat nice food, but when you come back home in Chimanimani you are still faced with the same level of poverty and unemployment."

Summary of Findings

Key success factors:

- Selection of a project community that has a capacity for self-organization and action.
- Selection of partners with similar development goals and orientation values.
- Selection of partners already involved with the community.
- Involvement within the partnership of community (tribal) leaders, local government, and local political leaders.
- Participation of the community in planning, to build community ownership of the program.
- Transparency and openness, underlined by constant communication among all partners.
- Equality of commitment from all partners. Contributions from each partner should be afforded equal respect.
- Use of a program approach that emphasizes stakeholder participation.

Key factors contributing to failure:

- Lack of transparency on the part of the intermediary organizations.
- Lack of accountability to the community and exclusion of community groups from decision making.
- Failure to fulfill promises, especially in relation to project activity and funding.
- Gaps between the expectations of communities and the actions of the partnership.
- Poor coordination among partners, impacting the delivery of services.
- Differences in priorities: "We don't eat planning and workshops; we need to get assistance to implement projects that will provide us with sustainable livelihood systems."

- Absence of return agreements, leading to misunderstanding of governance, reporting, and accountability structures.
- Use of intermediary organizations as gatekeepers rather than facilitators, denying community groups access to external partners.
- Lack of conflict resolution mechanisms.
- Abuse of gender and power relations, leading to exclusion especially of women and youth groups.

Lessons

- The process of selecting community sites and working partners needs to be as objective and rigorous as possible.
- Engaging traditional leadership, local NGOs, and key opinion leaders almost always enhances the community's acceptance of the partnership.
- Working with the community to define program goals and objectives is crucial to building trust, ensuring congruence of goals and mission, and establishing mutual agreement.
- Signing a memorandum of agreement with the community can clarify roles, responsibilities, governance, accountability, conflict resolutions, work plans, and timelines.
- All dialogue relating to a specific community should involve a representative of that community, to cultivate a feeling of empowerment and a spirit of commitment and responsibility toward the partner organization.
- If partner selection and partnership building is poor, there is a danger of a single partner taking a gate-keeping role, to the detriment of balanced development.
- The partnership selection process must be transparent, and transparency must extend throughout all partnership decision making and activities.
- The overriding principle of community partnership development should be that of shared or congruent principles, mission, goals, objectives, and approach.
- Good communication is essential to prevent misunderstandings and failure of trust. Effectively managed workshops and meetings can be invaluable in keeping the partnership together.
- Knowledge and appreciation of the community's culture and practices are important in maintaining the partnership.
- When community partnerships are young, there is a greater likelihood of tension and conflict. Effective conflict resolution practices can turn these tensions around and use them to accelerate the maturation of the partnership.
- Building effective partnerships is a slow process. Partners should be prepared to commit themselves over the long term.

- Governance structures should make visible the usually voiceless majority within the community, such as women and youth. As far as possible, all sectors should be given leadership positions to ensure that they have a voice in the decision-making process. Allowing traditional community leadership to control partnership boards can result in the board becoming a gatekeeper for development.

References

Abraham, A., and J. Plateau. 2001. *Participatory Development in the Presence of Endogenous Community Imperfections*. Namur, Belgium: Department of Economics, University of Namur.

Botha, C. A. J. (ed.). 1999. *Human Aspects of Development: Towards Inclusive Participatory Development*. Pretoria, South Africa: Department of Agricultural Economics, Extension and Rural Development, University of Pretoria.

Brett, E. A.1996. "The Participatory Principle in Development Projects: The Costs and Benefits of Cooperation." *Public Administration and Development* 16: 5–19.

Chambers, Robert. 1974. *Managing Rural Development*. Uppsala, Sweden: Scandinavian Institute of African Studies.

Gow, D. D., and J. Van Sant. 1981. "Beyond the Rhetoric of Rural Development Participation: How Can It Be Done?" IRD Working Paper. Washington, D.C.: Development Alternatives, Inc.

Jeppe, W. J. O. 1985. *Community Development: An African Approach*. Pretoria: Africa Institute of South Africa.

Narayan, D. 1995. "The Contribution of People's Participation: Evidence from 121 Rural Water Supply Projects." Environmentally Sustainable Development Occasional Paper No.1. Washington, D.C.: World Bank.

Shepherd, A. 1998. *Sustainable Rural Development*. New York: Macmillan.

20

Partnerships for Community Development—World Vision

Frank G. Cookingham

World Vision is a Christian humanitarian organization that works in eighty-nine countries. This chapter concentrates on our experience in community development, and particularly on the processes by which we assess what works and what does not work in partnerships for community development.

The primary aim of our community development work is to facilitate community ownership and management of community development processes. While it is obviously important for their quality of life that communities achieve their development goals, we believe it is also important that communities improve their ability to manage their own development processes. The overarching goal of community participation is to put in place representative groups that can organize and monitor development planning, implementation, and evaluation. As our projects mature, World Vision staff become advisors rather than initiators of development activities.

We believe that a primary outcome of a partnership for development should be sustainable processes of change. Such processes meet the physical needs of people without destroying the environment, and enable faith-based organizations to deal with those aspects of spirituality that undergird the causes of poverty. People should be encouraged and empowered to confront attitudes and beliefs that devalue persons, and should participate in reconciling those who are estranged.

Before 1990, most of our community development projects were undertaken in individual villages: we typically partnered with a church or organization of churches to help communities achieve their development goals, and in many cases we also provided funds to help churches recruit the development workers needed to complete their projects within five years. We have

---

Frank G. Cookingham, director of evaluation, World Vision International.

since phased out this approach in many countries. Instead, we now employ development workers ourselves to work with villages in a single province or district, usually for ten to fifteen years. Our focus is now on helping villages work together, in collaboration with government and nongovernmental agencies, to alleviate common needs. World Vision staff stimulates community participation in planning, implementing, and monitoring development activities. In some cases, they work with community members to perform project evaluations.

World Vision uses evaluation, monitoring, and operations audits as processes that can identify what works and what does not work in partnerships for community development. The results are used to shape our goals and approaches. For example, a series of workshops about ten years ago examined what was working and what was not working in World Vision's partnership with child sponsors and community residents in project communities, and led to major changes in our approach to support for community development.

Working Definitions

The term "evaluation" typically refers to a written document of conclusions and recommendations drawn from evidence accumulated during an investigation of the value of a program. But participation in the work that produces the document may affect program quality more than the document itself.

By teaming representatives from the different stakeholder groups in the data collection and analysis process, evaluation can increase awareness of the different perceptions that are held, and show how these perceptions can contribute to a more meaningful interpretation of evidence. People who participate in the evaluation work, including reporting, are more likely to put into practice the evaluation findings. In this manner evaluation can infuse new energy into a partnership, enhancing its mission.

Based on these considerations, my definition of program evaluation is the facilitation of informed judgments by stakeholders about the merit and worth of a program, based on verifiable evidence. The core concepts in this definition have the following meanings.

Facilitation

Many people think of an evaluator as an expert who can judge the merit or worth of the program that is being evaluated. They expect an evaluator of a community development program, for example, to be able to tell them in what ways the program is good or bad in terms of achieving its goals or of empowering people to manage sustainable development in their community.

I view the development program evaluator more as a facilitator than an expert. While an effective evaluator must have an understanding of the principles of development work, evaluation is most likely to have a positive influence if the evaluator succeeds in facilitating expression of the opinions of community members and project staff on the quality of the work.

Why is this true? Evaluation of my situation by someone else is threatening. If I am told that my situation is not up to standard, my natural response is to defend myself—or at the least to resist changing my attitudes or behavior. But if I reach my own conclusions about the quality of my situation, and if quality matters to me, I am more apt to make adjustments to improve that situation.

An important aspect of the evaluation of community development programs is clarification of the community reality in relation to the shared vision for that community. A major task for the development evaluator is thus to encourage and guide deeper thinking about the reality and its relationship to the vision for empowerment in that community. A second task is to enable stakeholders to acquire and strengthen the skills to evaluate development work.

In sum, I believe the purpose of facilitation in community development evaluation is to encourage and guide deeper understanding of whatever is being evaluated, and to enhance development and evaluation knowledge and skills.

Judgments by Stakeholders about Merit and Worth

A *judgment* is a conclusion based on comparison of an indicator reading, or results from a group of indicators, against a standard or group of standards. For the comparison to be useful, the standard must be described clearly and the information provided by the indicator must be described clearly.

Merit is the intrinsic value of the program without reference to its context. *Worth* is the value that the program adds to its context or situation. For example, a development program that is designed well according to the principles for effective empowerment has merit, and it has worth for the community to the degree that program aims, goals, and objectives are actually accomplished.

I believe that judgments of merit and worth should be made by the people who have a strong claim on the resources or outputs of the program or evaluation, or who are affected by either in a substantial way. My responsibility as an evaluator is to facilitate the process that leads to sound judgments.

Informed Judgments

The more perspectives on a situation that are considered, the better informed will be any conclusions drawn about that situation. The role of the development program evaluator is in part to help stakeholders consider the perspectives of other stakeholders.

I strongly recommend that stakeholders be encouraged to participate in the evaluation process to the extent that their responsibilities allow. Data collection in the community, for example, should be done by a diverse team of outside evaluators, stakeholders, and people that are directly involved in program implementation, rather than by a group of outsiders.

Evidence

Evidence is documented observations or experiences or events that can be examined and reexamined to ascertain truth about some aspects of a situation. Evidence is used to support conclusions regarding the merit or worth of a program. An evaluation team should seek to assemble strong evidence that is credible to the people affected in the program. The evidence should include a full description of the program and the contexts within which outcomes (outputs, results, impacts) occurred.

Verifiable Information

Information is verifiable if it can be checked by someone else. Evidence that is verifiable provides a much stronger base for making judgments. To be verifiable, evidence must include documentation of how the evaluation procedures themselves influenced the evidence. It also should be organized in a way that allows a third party to determine whether the information and interpretations are based solidly on events and experiences.

Tasks for Evaluation

Assess Achievement of Goals

A common objective in our partnership evaluations is to determine the extent to which the partnership is achieving the purpose for which it was formed. Another typical objective is to measure the synergy generated within the partnership, which allows members to do more than they could do if there were no partnership. Given that partnership means different things in different settings, a third objective of evaluation is to help stakeholders understand the different perspectives on partnership that may exist among the partners.

Assess Underlying Beliefs

The quality of partnership for community development is clearly affected by the different beliefs that the partners hold about development. Evaluation can help partners to explore their views of development and can strengthen their commitment to support each other in moving toward a shared vision.

Beliefs about development are rarely expressed in partnership agreements. To be fully comprehensive, partnership evaluation should seek to establish both the nature of these beliefs and the ways in which they change as the partnership evolves.

Ensure Accountability

Accountability within a partnership is difficult to define, and exploring the relationships that exist between accountability, quality assurance, and stewardship may stimulate new thoughts about the role of monitoring and evaluation in community development.

In the usual sense "accountability" refers to a relationship between two parties, in which one of the parties has authority to impose fair negative sanctions on the other if the latter fails to fulfill an agreement or meet an obligation, or violates a trust. Two parties are mutually accountable if each has such authority over the other, although the sanctions that each can impose may be quite different.

When World Vision accepts money from a donor to accomplish specific objectives, World Vision is accountable to that donor. If World Vision does not accomplish the specified objectives, the donor may impose negative sanctions by, for example, refusing to donate additional funds, requesting repayment, or trying to prevent others from supporting World Vision.

Audit work and evaluation work provide two types of information pertinent to this definition of accountability, enabling the responsible exercise of sanctions. Project auditing is designed to detect misuse of funds and verify reported expenditures. Evaluation identifies problems in facilitating development and verifies that project practices are consistent with agreed upon development strategies and principles.

Ensure Quality

Quality assurance describes another form of accountability that applies in particular to project managers. The work of quality assurance is to protect those distinctive features of a program that determine excellence. Managers ensure quality in large part by protecting key program features from risk.

The manager must have the technical expertise to know what to protect and how to deal with program features that are in danger. Technical advice may thus be needed to ensure that resources are allocated and activities implemented consistent with the objectives of the program.

Monitoring and evaluation for quality assurance clearly must go beyond simple documentation of project outcomes and the relationships between project activities and outcomes.

Encourage Stewardship

Stewardship involves taking care of something that has been entrusted to us. This has two implications for evaluation work. First, our evaluation processes and procedures should provide information that helps all stakeholders be good stewards. Second, those processes and procedures should encourage and build up people, not demean or diminish them.

Monitoring

Monitoring can be defined as a limited form of evaluation that is focused on program implementation. Typically, it involves collecting evidence sys-

Table 20.1
Features of Monitoring and Evaluation

Feature	Monitoring	Evaluation
Function	Guide project implementation	Guided policy formulation and strategic planning
Time orientation	Examine what is happeneing now	Examine what happened over a long period of time
Evidence	Inputs, activities, and outputs related to project work targets	Results or impact related to project aims, goals, or objectives
Use of Information	Detect variations from plan so that adjustments can be made	Document results to affirm or challenge project strategies
Information produced	Problems in implementation to be solved for this project	Lessons learned that can be applied to similar projects
Primary actor	Project staff or supervisor	Persons external to the project, or a team that may include project staff
Project design	Assuming the design is valid; use information to change activites so that the design becomes reality	Challenge the design; use information to change the design for future projects

tematically about project implementation, with the goal of identifying problems so that adjustments can be made to ensure that program goals and objectives are achieved on schedule and within budget (see Table 20.1).

Operations Audits

Every three years, a World Vision financial auditor and operations evaluator simultaneously perform a financial audit and an operations audit of World Vision work in the thirty-five countries where we have community development projects supported by child sponsorship. A financial audit alone is undertaken in the further thirty-five countries in which our community development and relief projects are funded by other means. The purpose of the operations audit is to assess the likelihood that our commitments to project communities and child sponsors or other donors will be met.

An operations audit typically is completed in eighteen workdays. Managers are interviewed, documentation is examined, and two development projects are visited for four days each. In the development projects, monitoring and evaluation reports are examined, audit reports are examined, and interviews are done with managers and development workers, community committees, and a small sample of beneficiary families. Major development accomplishments are verified through observation wherever possible.

Twenty-seven areas of work are examined in the operations audit. Areas related to partnership, monitoring, and evaluation include the following:

- the involvement of community members in identifying development needs and planning long-term development goals;
- the extent to which community members participate in planning, implementing, monitoring, and evaluating development activities;
- the extent to which communities work together to meet development needs that cannot be met by communities working alone;
- the extent to which management uses information from project monitoring and evaluation;
- the extent to which recommendations in audit and evaluation reports are implemented;
- the scope of evaluation work planned and completed;
- the relevance to community development of monitoring information; and
- other areas of examination: compliance with standards for child sponsor relations, and staffing.

For each of these areas, evidence is compared against descriptions of conditions that represent six levels of risk.The description of risk levels for community participation are as follows:

- Lowest risk. Community members representing the full range of community groups participate substantially in all aspects of planning, implementation, and evaluation. They contribute money as well as other material resources and labor.
- Minimized risk. The project committee informs the community regularly about program status, and actively seeks input and feedback. There is age and gender balance among committee members.
- Limited risk. The project committee participates substantially in planning and implementation.
- Acceptable risk. The project committee meets regularly, and provides some input for planning and organizing development activities.
- Significant risk. Community members contribute labor for project activities, but there is no project committee. There is minimal community involvement in planning or evaluation activities.
- Unacceptable risk. Project activities are planned, implemented, and evaluated by World Vision staff without community participation.

To identify where our projects are not working, findings are compiled annually across operations audits. For example, in fifteen of twenty-four operations audits completed between October 1998 and September 2000, evidence showed that there was a need for improvement in the capacity of community committees to carry out their own planning processes. Specific areas of need included resource acquisition, budgeting, and monitoring.

By policy, each World Vision office at the country level is required to complete a financial audit of every project every two years. Offices are encouraged to expand the scope of the financial audit to include operations areas. As this is achieved, the World Vision International Audit and Evaluation Department will carry out tests to determine if the local audit findings can be relied upon. Where the conclusion is that the local findings can be relied on, the findings can be compiled to give a more comprehensive picture of what is not working.

References

Huxham, C. 1996. "Collaboration and Collaborative Advantage." In C. Huxham, ed., *Creating Collaborative Advantage.* Thousand Oaks, Calif.: Sage.

Myers, B. L. 1999. *Walking with the Poor: Principles and Practices of Transformational Development.* Maryknoll, New York: Orbis.

21

Partnerships between International Organizations and Private Foundations[1]

Melinda Kimble

The role of philanthropy today is shaped by a growing need for public goods. The poorest one-third of the world's population is malnourished and typically has no access to health care or clean water. The next third of the world's population is only slightly better off. The United Nations and the Bretton Woods institutions have evidently failed in their promise to deliver the "economic and social advancement" of all peoples.[2] Individuals, nations, and institutions must all think differently about partnerships.

Partnerships for Development, Post-1945

The structure of partnerships post–World War II was initially defined by collaboration among nation states, notably in the forum of the United Nations. But while the UN and its specialized agencies hosted the conversation on development, much of the resources and power remained apart from that debate. The UN's specialized agencies were designed to collect, analyze, and disseminate information and to advocate best practices in fields as diverse as education, health, agriculture, and labor policy (Righter 1995), but as their majority constituency became a coalition of the developing countries, they evolved into providers of technical assistance for them. Tensions grew between the developing countries that demanded assistance and the industrialized countries that funded it.

Frustration with the UN system, particularly in the United States, strengthened the role of the World Bank and the regional development banks as channels of development assistance. The banks can move significantly more development resources than the UN system because of their capital structure;

Melinda Kimble, senior vice president for programs, UN Foundation.

as a network, they also enjoy greater donor confidence because of their use of weighted donor voting. Furthermore, their greater resource base affords these institutions an expertise that often exceeds that of the UN operational and technical agencies.

The pressure for more equitable development in the face of globalization, however, continues to heighten tensions between and within societies—and even within multilateral organizations. This pressure has forced the multilateral banks to become more client-sensitive and has lifted poverty alleviation above the profit motive in the assessment of individual loans—a point that has become increasingly debated by shareholders (Blustein 2001). With the decline of bilateral development assistance and the rising criticism of developing-country debt, multilateral banks are seeking greater flexibility in lending and have become increasingly interested in raising more grant funds to support technical assistance and capacity building. In particular, their interest in mobilizing private support to supplement limited grant funding has grown.

Early Charitable Foundations

The recent surge in international grant-making by U.S. foundations has given prominence to these partnerships, but cooperation between foundations and international agencies is not new: the Ford, Rockefeller, and MacArthur foundations were cooperating with multilateral institutions as long ago as the 1960s and 1970s. The Ford Foundation's investments in education, institution building, and the rule of law were a factor in promoting liberal democratic values globally, and the Rockefeller Foundation's commitment to food security and reproductive health was instrumental in building international awareness of population growth (Dowie 2001). The MacArthur Foundation invested in universities in Africa and Asia, and is now engaged in a foundation partnership to strengthen four universities in Nigeria.

The work of these foundations drew others to the international arena, and their advocacy occasionally led to an intergovernmental response. The establishment of the UN Fund for Population Activities (UNFPA) as an arm of the UN Development Program at the beginning of the 1970s, for example, was a direct outgrowth of private interest in promoting family planning globally.

These partnerships created new opportunities for foundations and the UN to work together. The Rockefeller Foundation's investment in modern agricultural practices and hybrid food crops was a driving force behind the "Green Revolution" in developing countries, for example. Rockefeller's research operations are now institutionalized within the Consultative Group on International Agricultural Research (CGIAR), a global network of research units that is jointly supported by the World Bank, the UN Food and Agriculture Organization, and the U.S. Agency for International Development (USAID) (Dowie 2001).

These cooperative arrangements were not without frictions, and have been criticized as efforts to dictate to developing countries, based on Western assumptions. The independent work of foundations has nonetheless influenced both the United Nations and the World Bank as development institutions. In addition to their contributions to the development of institutional structures such as UNFPA and CGIAR, their research work was instrumental in instigating the quest for truly sustainable development.

Impact of the New Philanthropists

The United Nations and the World Bank have made poverty alleviation their highest priority (World Bank 2000b), and with the AIDS/HIV epidemic wreaking devastation in Africa, they are calling repeatedly for the international community to devote more resources to development assistance.[3] Multilateral institution, consequently, are increasingly rethinking their relationships with private corporations and foundations. For the United Nations, with its past efforts to regulate the behavior of transnational corporations, this represents a sharp reversal of direction. Today, both the UN and the Bank are rebuilding their relationships with the major U.S. private foundations and are establishing new relationships with the foundations established by "new economy" entrepreneurs. This new support may help build momentum for solving some major problems, but whether it can restore the promise of truly global cooperation and redress the imbalances of economic and social equity remains to be seen.

Among the more visible and dominant new philanthropists are George Soros, Ted Turner, and Bill Gates. Each of these individuals has a different target. Soros, through his Open Society Institute, has been actively promoting democratic governance, public accountability, and public health in Eastern Europe and the former Soviet Union and in the United States (Foundation Center 2000a). Soros recognized early the threat of antibiotic-resistant tuberculosis in Russia and has worked hard to mobilize resources to fight the spread of these new forms of the disease.

Turner, the founder of Cable News Network (CNN), made a personal commitment of US$1 billion to UN causes as a result of the United States' failure to meet its assessed peacekeeping obligations—a failure that threatened the very survival of the United Nations. Turner's gesture led to the establishment of the UN Foundation (UNF), an organization that has an advocacy and information agenda in addition to a grant-making role (Foundation Center 2000b). The UNF's grant making emphasizes reproductive and children's health, environmental issues, and conflict prevention.

Finally, the Bill and Melinda Gates Foundation has made a major commitment to international public health, providing support to vaccine research and reproductive health agendas. Support from the Gates Foundation has dramatically expanded both the Global Alliance for Vaccines and Immunizations (GAVI), which supports immunization efforts throughout the developing world, and the International AIDS Vaccine Initiative, a fund that supports vaccine research and testing for an HIV vaccine. The foundation also joined the UNF in an early, major grant to eradicate poliomyelitis. In 1999, the Gates Foundation provided $1.2 billion to the international public health agenda, a sum roughly equal to the annual investment of the United States in international public health.[4]

Two other large foundations, the William and Florence Hewlett Foundation and the David and Lucille Packard Foundation, have also raised their international profile and are likely to provide significantly more resources, particularly to reproductive health issues in the future, since reducing fertility rates was a major interest of the founders of those foundations.

Managing the Funding Shortfall

The Council on Foundations' Review of International Grant Making reports that international grant making jumped 47 percent between 1994 and 1998, from US$289 million to US$424 million (Foundation Center 2000c). Information from the top ten foundations in this area for 1999 and 2000 suggests that this trend will continue.[5] Yet, given the demand for US$7–10 billion in new resources annually to fight HIV/AIDS alone, private foundation funding is unlikely to close the gap in either development assistance resources or public goods.

In the past, some private philanthropies worked in concert with government objectives, but direct philanthropic contribution to public institutions, especially in the multilateral arena, has not been common. As long as the agenda of multilateral institutions is set by member states, pursuing a single objective or adopting new approaches often will be difficult, and the impact of discretionary monies therefore muted. Reflecting this skepticism, some funders are actively seeking nongovernmental organizations in the developing world as both beneficiaries and partners.

Paradoxically, this shift in focus is occurring just as established institutions such as the World Bank and the United Nations are exploring ways to partner directly with foundations and the private sector. This raises some important questions:

- Does cooperation among multilateral institutions, foundations, and the private sector really make sense?
- How would such partnerships serve societal goals, the institutional goals of the foundations, or the goals of individual philanthropists?
- How do we balance similar, but sometimes differing, objectives?

Contributions from the Commercial Sector

The commercial private sector is another potential contributor to the social goals advanced by international organizations and/or civil society. The potential in this area is significant and unexplored. In the United States, corporate contributions to the arts, civic and community activities, education, and public health are a part of the landscape. Since most U.S., European, and Japanese firms sell to the global marketplace, there should be scope for building more cooperation between corporations and the developing world.

The World Health Organization (WHO), for instance, has effectively structured programs that permit targeted drug donations or low-cost procurement of pharmaceuticals. The Tropical Disease Research (TDR) program also has brought together UN agencies (WHO, UNDP, and UNICEF), bilateral donors, private foundations, and pharmaceutical companies to work on diseases, including onchocerciasis (river blindness) and leprosy. These programs assess a country's ability to diagnose illness, distribute drugs, administer follow-up care, and reduce prevalence of disease through better public health practices. Drugs are provided, along with technical assistance to strengthen local clinical practice. Since WHO also sets pharmaceutical standards, proposals for collaboration are handled on a case-by-case basis to ensure there is no conflict of interest. UNICEF additionally has been able to work out some donations or volume-discounted procurement arrangements for micronutrient supplements and vaccines.

The Global Alliance for Vaccines and Immunizations was established in response to increasing concern about vaccine availability and the need to ensure that developing countries maintain their immunization rates. GAVI received an initial grant of US$750 million from the Gates Foundation.[6] Its small secretariat tracks vaccine needs and responds to country requests for help with immunizations. It has been particularly important in ensuring the supply of less well-known vaccines, including hepatitis-B. Recent decisions by pharmaceutical companies to reduce the cost of anti-retrovirals—a response in large part to criticism of the pricing of HIV/AIDS drugs—are likely to lead to new opportunities for public–private cooperation. GAVI and the TDR both potentially are models for the new Global Fund for HIV/AIDS and Health.

Altruism or Self-Interest?

Other commercial support in the health area includes Coca-Cola's offer of its delivery trucks to transport vaccines in Africa. The company is also exploring how it can mobilize its networks in an HIV/AIDS prevention campaign. British Petroleum has directly funded UNDP in Angola to improve conditions in villages that are near its oil production facilities, and Shell in Nigeria and Indonesia has run its own community development efforts. Each of these efforts has been ad hoc and targeted to specific problems rather than to big solutions.

Relatively new firms, such as Microsoft and Cisco Systems, also have made specific contributions to UN efforts to improve information systems. During the Kosovo crisis, Microsoft established a system to track refugees and manage family reunification. More recently, it has applied that experience to the development of a UNHCR program to systematize refugee registration and tracking in other emergency situations. Cisco is working with the United Nations and UNDP to develop "networking academies" in developing countries. These initiatives, while undeniably valuable, are not only altruistic: Microsoft's work has helped it extend the capacity of its software, and Cisco, by improving the skills of workers abroad, is expanding both its worker and its market base.

Representatives of civil society continue to debate whether or not such partnerships will diminish their own advocacy for the poor. A greater fear is that commercial sector actors could effectively co-opt public institutions to their own agendas of liberal markets and global trade, and that the social impact of such policies could be overlooked. As public–private partnerships grow in importance, addressing these concerns is an increasingly important challenge.

Community-Based Partnerships

Foundations and public charities[7] in the United States have learned that working with governments or established public institutions is not always the best way to reach people. The response of many, including the MacArthur Foundation and the Ashoka Foundation, has been to increase their award of grants and fellowships to individuals. Others have sought to bring their interventions to the community level by employing development mechanisms, such as microcredit, to move communities out of poverty or by investing in local schools in poor areas. These interventions have been pursued both globally and in the United States.

Many of these new initiatives have arisen from a growing understanding of how individuals work within societies, and how decisions that affect families and the community as a whole are related to individual initiatives and capacities. For example, microcredit works best when it is embedded in a thorough understanding of markets and marketplace mechanisms. Small-scale pilot experiments with these ideas—including the promotion of water users groups—were often promoted by foundations in partnership with NGOs and adopted later by established development agencies. These community-based techniques, however, are labor-intensive for donors and can be sustained only within institutional structures that support social change.[8]

The success of small-scale, community-based partnerships has transformed public health initiatives since the early 1980s (Dowie 2001). Although Americans were reluctant to accept the community-based partnership approach within WHO, Canada and the Europeans strongly supported it. Analysis of work done in Canada and Europe subsequently demonstrated that families and communities are critical in improving health outcomes, with the result that U.S. foundations increasingly have been looking for ways to support community-based initiatives.

Implementing community-based programs internationally is harder than setting them up at home, but the concept is receiving more and more support. The HIV/AIDS pandemic is transforming the debate about how to manage care, treatment, and prevention across the globe. Many advocates now are demanding that we make efforts to deal directly with the problems of communities, building on existing family and other social structures to mitigate the impact of the disease. Donors and private partners also are recognizing that global-level interventions are critical to manage the pandemic.

Collectively, the international community has recognized that national governments, simply because of the nature of their state apparatus, can prevent assistance getting to people. Furthermore, to philanthropists, and often also to corporations, the idea of supporting bureaucratic structures and processes is anathema. If we are to realize the potential of such engagements, however, we need to break down these barriers.

We also need to recognize that historically successful private networks, such as Rotary, the Kiwanis, the Lions, and United Way raise money for charitable causes globally and invest their funds locally. The model provided by these networks may help guide multilateral institutions that want to ensure that communities are connected to the effort to expand charitable giving.

New Partnering Efforts: Models for the New Century

This new stage of public–private partnerships is just beginning, but there are indications that these efforts can help to:

- integrate public and private sector development initiatives;
- expand public awareness of the importance of providing some level of public goods to the most vulnerable populations; and
- implement cost-effective, community-focused solutions, particularly in public health.

Box 21.1 outlines selected program activities, undertaken with public foundations, charities, private firms, and governments during the late 1990s, that illustrate where new partnering arrangements have produced innovative efforts to solve major problems.

Box 21.1
New Partnering Efforts to Solve Major Development Problems

Polio Eradication

In 1998, the new director general of WHO, Dr. Gro Brundtland, determined that an international campaign to eliminate poliomyelitis presented an opportunity for an early victory against the disease as well as an opportunity to reenergize international support for sound public health practices. The World Health Organization sought to generate public and private support for this effort, bringing old and new partners into an international task force. The Bill and Melinda Gates Foundation (US$50 million) and the UN Foundation (US$28 million) jump-started the initiative with a US$78 million grant to WHO. This laid the foundation for a campaign to raise US$500 million in support of the effort.

In addition, in 2000 the Gates Foundation contributed US$10 million to India directly for immunization efforts. And the UNF established a partnership with Rotary International in support of the effort. (Rotary has contributed in the past to both smallpox immunization and polio efforts.)

The Gates Foundation, Rotary, and the UNF have been exploring options with the World Bank to ensure that additional funds will be available for the project. One option would permit foundation contributions to be assigned against credits issued by the Bank's International Development Agency (IDA), turning these low-interest loans into grants. The grants would be made available to the remaining "reservoir" countries for immunization and surveillance campaigns. The leverage gained in such an arrangement would be roughly 2.6:1.

Democracy and Human Rights

George Soros, through The Open Society Institute, has led the way toward new investment in democratic institution building in Eastern Europe and the countries of the former Soviet Union. National governments and Western aid donors, including private foundations, have joined this effort.

The Ford and MacArthur Foundations, along with Mott, Carnegie, and The Open Society Institute, sharply increased their funding for human rights programs in the late 1990s and continue to make this a priority. These grants have focused on building local networks that can monitor human rights practices, and they have supported the strengthening of the UN Human Rights Commission and the relatively new Office of the High Commissioner for Human Rights.

Environment and Sustainable Development

The UNF is a new philanthropy with a specific goal of partnership with the United Nations. Beyond its signature polio eradication effort discussed above, the UNF is investing in projects and programs that are designed to develop broader partnering arrangements and improve the United Nations' ability to undertake effective collaborations with NGOs. These activities concentrate on adolescent reproductive health, children, biological diversity, and sustainable energy practices. The UNF's efforts toward institutional change have produced arrangements that link several foundations, UN agencies, and NGOs into a single program. These programs include the following:

Galapagos Program on Invasive Species

This program, funded by a US$4.2 million grant, links UNF funding, the UNESCO World Heritage Center, the Charles Darwin Society Research Institute, and the Government of Ecuador in an effort to eradicate or control invasive species (for example, cats, dogs, and rodents) in the Galapagos Islands. The results achieved during the first phase of the activity prompted the Global Environmental Facility (GEF) to commit another US$18 million to the program. This is the first ecosystem-wide effort to deal with invasive species.

New Nigeria Foundation

This is an innovative US$2.4 million program that links the UNDP, Citizens International, and the UNF in an effort to create local fundraising capacity in Nigeria and to bring other funding partners into critical social areas. Activities include community and reproductive health; a rural livelihoods program focused on adolescent girls that invests in cassava processing; computer skills training programs; and debt management. The program's health activities are now in twenty-two communities and, assisted by a joint UNF–Packard grant of US$600,000, will expand to Bauche State. Roughly US$3 million in parallel resources has been mobilized to date, including US$850,000 from the Gates Foundation.

International Coral Reef Action Network (ICRAN)

This recently approved activity has US$10 million of UNF core resources and US$5 million from other sources to support monitoring, assessment, and action to protect coral reefs. These funds are to be spent over the next five to seven years as other monies are raised. The program uses UNF funds to link the UNEP Regional Seas Programs with a multilateral umbrella organization of nineteen national governments and seven NGOs in a global effort to mitigate damage to coral reefs and to manage the reefs sustainably.

HIV/AIDS

The Bill and Melinda Gates Foundation has been a leader in this area, with a major contribution to the International Alliance for an AIDS Vaccine Initiative (IAVI). In 2000, Gates, Merck, and the Merck Foundation announced a US$38 million program in cooperation with the Government of Botswana to strengthen the public health system's clinical management of HIV/AIDS patients. This program is expected to guide the improvement of care, treatment, and prevention in other southern African countries.

Also in Botswana, UNF, UNDP, and Merck Foundation funding will link Botswana's public health system with Brazilian experts in HIV/AIDS education and awareness to create a national distance-learning program for adults and adolescents.

The UNF has directly supported preventive strategies that have been developed through national HIV/AIDS action plans through its southern Africa youth initiative. This partnership involves UNAIDS with cosponsors UNDP, UNICEF, UNFPA, and UNESCO, as well as governments.

Serving Global, National, and Foundation Objectives

Many partnerships offer worthwhile opportunities for foundations to meet both their own institutional objectives and those of the multilateral partner. Maintaining innovation and ensuring that cultural and social differences are taken into account nonetheless remains difficult. Rather than innovate, most institutions—foundations as well as the public sector—tend to replicate successful programs. That said, foundations are more likely than the United Nations or the World Bank to rethink and redirect their approaches, thanks mainly to their independent funding base and the guidance of their trustees.

The interest in international grant making is likely to continue among U.S. foundations and possibly among corporate partners, but new resource flows are unlikely to fill the demand for global public goods. Foundation resources in the United States are primarily a function of the U.S. equity market, however, and a prolonged slump in share prices would certainly decrease these resources. With some foundations already facing constraints in this area, short-term growth in total foundation giving is unlikely to expand as rapidly as it did in the late 1990s (Dowie 2001).

One virtually untapped resource is public charity. Roughly 1 percent of these resources, which are raised from individuals, support international efforts, and most of them go to humanitarian rather than development purposes. Achieving the full potential of charitable public contributions will take work, but even UN agencies are looking at this option. For example, working with the clothing company Benetton, the UN Food and Agriculture Organization (FAO) operates an EU-wide telethon on World Food Day. In the United States, UNICEF, UNHCR, and UNFPA have established private but related committees that help raise funds. Given that people and corporations tend to want their gifts to "do" something, international institutions might seem unlikely beneficiaries of charitable contributions, but UNICEF's focus on children and UNFPA's emphasis on reproductive health and family planning have yielded results. The Global Fund for HIV/AIDS and Health may also be a mechanism that can attract public support.

Conclusions

New and established philanthropies, mainly in the United States, are potential partners in the effort to achieve sustainable development and a more equitable distribution of resources, but there has not yet been a systematic effort to channel their resources to development objectives. It is critically important in the early establishment of partnering arrangements to identify activities that have a high probability of success. Individuals, foundations, corporations, or private charities are unlikely to give to "development," but they may give to "defeat HIV/AIDS," to save the Galapagos, or to other programs with clear objectives. One of the major challenges of the new foundations, including the UNF, is to find a formula that can capture public attention and resources, and thus achieve worthwhile results.

Notes

1. This chapter concentrates on the United States, where a long upward surge in stock prices and a tax system that encourages gift-giving have created a new generation of philanthropists. In Europe, social welfare policies that provide more public goods and different tax structures may have limited the growth of similar philanthropy.
2. As stated in the preamble to the UN Charter.
3. *UN Millennium Summit Declaration,* September 2000; Kofi Annan, "A Call to Action," Abuja, Nigeria, April 2001.
4. Data from the Gates Foundation Web site: *www.gatesfoundation.org*.
5. Since this chapter's presentation, the stock market decline has impacted negatively on many of these philanthropic endeavors. While the key foundations mentioned above will continue to be major players, the level of grant making is likely to be reduced in the near term.
6. The WHO Web site (*www.who.int*) explains in detail the GAVI partnership and the public–private context in which it was established.
7. In the United States, a foundation is a grant-making institution that is supported by an endowment. Under U.S. tax law, a foundation must disburse a certain percentage of its assets annually. Foundations also perform limited public advocacy, or set up an independent entity to do advocacy work. Public charities may receive a majority of support from a single benefactor (the UNF is an example). To maintain this status, however, they must raise additional funds amounting to a fixed percentage of their income from other sources. Such charities may do advocacy and public awareness work.
8. Grameen Bank of Bangladesh is an example of a microcredit scheme that expanded to a national level and now offers technical assistance internationally. Grameen provides strong institutional support and training to all its clients, an element that has made a difference in its ability to both sustain investments and expand.

References

Blustein, Paul. 2001. "O'Neill Again Criticizes World Bank." *The Washington Post*, June 8, 2001.

Chace, James. 1998. *Acheson*. New York: Simon and Schuster.

Dowie, Mark. 2001. *American Foundations: An Investigative History*. Cambridge, Mass.: MIT Press.

Foundation Center. 2000a. "Trends in International Grant Making." In *International Grant Making II*. New York: The Foundation Center.

———. 2000b. "International Grant Making in the Era of Globalization." In *International Grant Making II*. New York: The Foundation Center.

———. 2000c. "Where the Money Goes." In *International Grant Making II*. New York: The Foundation Center.

Rich, Bruce. 1994. *Mortgaging the Earth: The World Bank, Environmental Impoverishment, and the Crisis of Development*. Boston: Beacon Press.

Righter, Rosemary. 1995. *Utopia Lost: The United Nations and the New World Order*. New York: Twentieth Century Press.

World Bank. 2000a. *Annual Report 1999*. Washington, D.C.: World Bank.

———. 2000b. *World Development Report 2000*. Washington, D.C.: World Bank.

22

Partnerships among Business, Government, and NGOs: Lessons from the South African National Business Initiative

Theuns Eloff

This chapter discusses how an organization with a broad mandate, the National Business Initiative (NBI), is working to assist development in South Africa. It focuses on the principles the NBI uses to achieve effective partnerships with government, business, and other NGOs.

The NBI was formed in 1995 as a not-for-profit, public interest, business-based organization dedicated to helping "make the new South Africa work." It has three main goals:

- In partnership with government, to bring business and management skills to public tasks such as enterprise development, education, and local government.
- To help the business community make a collective contribution to the reconstruction of South Africa, focusing on socioeconomic development issues that are the foundation both for national stability and for the creation of an environment conducive for business.
- Through the above, to help government and business build constructive relationships based on mutual trust, for the good of the country as a whole.

These three objectives together support the NBI's larger goal, to help reduce poverty and inequality.

Background

For the first seven years after the 1994 abandonment of apartheid, South Africa focused on macroeconomic fundamentals. President Thabo Mbeki re-

---

Theuns Eloff, director, Membership and Communications, South Africa National Business Initiative, South Africa.

cently sent a strong signal that, having established a sound macroeconomic foundation, the country is ready to shift emphasis to the microeconomic aspects of development, including socioeconomic development. In this regard, the key challenges include the following:

- The HIV/AIDS pandemic. This is South Africa's greatest challenge. Two-thirds of the world's infected people are in Africa, and South Africa has the highest reported rate of infection.[1]
- Economic growth. The immediate objective is to increase the rate of growth from less than 3 percent to at least 6 percent, and to increase foreign and domestic investment.
- Poverty and inequality. A recent University of Cape Town/World Bank survey shows that 30–50 percent of households in South Africa are poor. In 2000, South Africa's Office of Statistics reported that the country's Gini coefficient was 0.73.
- Unemployment. Using a narrow definition, unemployment in South Africa is 23 percent.
- Skills shortages. South Africa has skills shortages in the managerial and professional category, and a surplus of unskilled people.
- Education. The education system still suffers from the effects of apartheid. Results generally are poor. In 2000, only 59 percent of pupils passed grade 12, and the performance of pupils in mathematics and science is especially bad. South Africa is training only 10 percent of the mathematics and science teachers it needs.
- Local government issues. Although the local elections held in December 2000 were peaceful, free, and fair, the new demarcation from 842 to 284 local authorities and the consequent transformation of local government have raised concerns about capacity, governance, infrastructure, service provision, and financial sustainability.
- Infrastructure and service backlogs. The government has achieved impressive targets in the delivery of water and electricity, but huge backlogs remain.
- Crime. While South Africa's overall crime rate is in keeping with international trends and is stabilizing, it is still too high. Of particular concern is the increase in violent crime.

South Africa clearly needs a breakthrough on issues of a microeconomic nature and in socioeconomic service delivery. The government has said that it cannot achieve this on its own, and needs the help of the rest of South African society. The NBI was formed to address this problem.

Strategic Approach and Methodology of NBI

The National Business Initiative is funded by its 185 member companies and through cost recovery for its projects. Its core budget for 2001 was 24 million rand (US$3 million). In addition, it manages projects worth more than 70 million rand (US$9 million). The staff complement of the NBI is sevety-eight.

As a business-based organization working in development, the NBI does not work directly with its ultimate beneficiaries—South Africa's 12 million learners, its millions of unemployed, and the country's rate- and taxpayers. Instead, it identifies target groups, mainly in the public sector, and delivers specific products and services to them in the expectation that they will then render better services (at scale). Specifically, NBI does the following:

- gives policy input on socioeconomic issues to government;
- designs and facilitates frameworks for socioeconomic delivery, and tests these frameworks as models for replication;
- provides training, mentoring, and assistance to public sector officials and entrepreneurs; and
- builds trust and cooperative relationships between business and government.

NBI's programs are business-driven and seek to instill business principles, such as efficiency, effectiveness, and entrepreneurship, within the development community. To achieve its goals, the National Business Initiative must use partnerships.[2]

The Concept of Partnership in South Africa

The term "partnership," like the term "community," is often misused. In general, a partnership comprises two or more different interests willingly brought together, formally or informally, to achieve common objectives while sharing risks and rewards. The partners need not be equal in skills, funds, or resources, but they must trust each other's commitment to the common goal. Depending on the specific circumstances, a partnership lies somewhere on the continuum between cooperation and union.[3]

In the experience of the NBI and its predecessors, the Urban Foundation and the Consultative Business Movement,[4] partnerships have taken the following forms:

- Commercial partnerships between the public and the private sectors (or public–private partnerships) for the provision of basic services, such as water and sewerage, or for infrastructure, such as toll roads.
- Noncommercial (non-profit-making) partnerships between the government and NGOs, in which the latter provide a specific service at cost.
- Other noncommercial partnerships including arrangements between companies and NGOs for the implementation of corporate social investment programs. For example, the NBI partners with companies to provide mentors for entrepreneurs in a business plan competition.

An interesting South African example of partnership is the "macro sociopolitical" partnership between stakeholders. The NBI itself was formed by business in response to the government's call for help in addressing the development needs of the country. Other examples include the Business Trust, a partnership between business and government to address unemployment and skills development; Business Against Crime, a partnership to assist the government in crime prevention; and the recently formed Millennium Labor Council, a partnership between organized business and labor to address critical issues and agree on a common strategic vision.

Why Partnerships?

Corporate business and civil society have real and important roles in development. For example, they can:

- leverage valuable resources (financial, technical, and managerial) for delivery and implementation;
- offset and help to remedy a lack of capacity in the public sector;
- assist in skills development and shared learning;
- help develop an integrated and comprehensive approach to socioeconomic service delivery;
- build strong institutional capabilities, supporting sustainable delivery; and
- build trust and shared values, preparing the foundation for future and more intensive cooperation.

NGOs can rarely contribute material resources to a partnership, but they have specific strengths. They can be implementers or service providers. More and more, companies outsource their corporate social investment programs to credible NGOs, while retaining their own branding. NGOs can act as barometers of attitudes and perceptions at the grassroots level. NGOs often work best on the ground, while government and business operate from the head office. NGOs offer an extensive network for lobbying, communication, and influence.[5]

A Practical Approach to Setting Up a Partnership, Based on the NBI Experience

Identify and Clarify Goals and Strategy

As with any endeavor, it is important to identify and clarify the objectives of a partnership. It may be that one partner is clear on its objectives, but the other equivocal. For example, when business leaders in South Africa approached government in 1998 to discuss ways of ensuring closer cooperation, the two parties had different views of the possible process and it was only after numerous meetings that enough trust was built for the two sides to open up to each other's views. The eventual result was the establishment of the Business Trust, overseen by a board of both government and business leaders. The trust agreed to the investment over five years of more than US$100 million of business contributions in job creation and education. The lesson of this example is that it may be advisable to approach a partnership without preconceived ideas of what that partnership should be. In the case of the Business Trust, once the two partners found common ground it was relatively easy to forge a common strategy.

Estimate Needed Resources before Choosing Partners

It is important to determine what resources are needed to achieve the objectives of the partnership. In this regard, each member should ask whether a potential partner is able and ready to contribute to the pursuit of those objectives.[6] Ideally, a partner should be able to add value, including resources, that the initiating organization cannot deliver or can deliver only at great cost.

The resources provided by the partners need not be equal. In a number of cases in South Africa, businesses have provided monetary resources and expertise, and government legitimacy and human resources. This is the case with the NBI's Education Quality Improvement Program (EQUIP). The NBI, on behalf of a sponsoring company, partners with provincial education authorities to improve governance, planning, and teaching in selected schools. The business community provides funding (a CSI sponsorship) and expertise (the NBI's education personnel), and the government assists by supporting the training of district officials as program facilitators. Various education NGOs additionally operate as service providers at the school level, under NBI coordination.

What is most important is that all partners should be committed to the goals and to realizing the mutual benefit of the partnership. In the case of EQUIP, the common purpose is improvement in the quality of education; the mutual benefit rests on the fact that none of the partners could do alone what the joint effort can achieve.

Use Care in Partnering with Government

Partnering with government can be productive only if government officials (as opposed to the political leadership) accept and welcome the involvement of business and NGOs. If officials fear that their role is being usurped by the partnership, the arrangement is doomed to failure. On the other side of the arrangement, the nongovernmental partners must be willing to assist government to implement its policies—if they do not agree with the government's policy objectives, the partnership will fail.

The exceptions to these conditions depend on the legitimacy and standing of the nongovernmental partner. It may be possible to engage the government and to try to convince it to change its policy. This was the case when the NBI was contracted by the northwest provincial government in South Africa to manage a US$2 million fund to assist small enterprises and microenterprises. Originally, the funds were to be dispersed only to individual entrepreneurs, but the NBI succeeded in persuading the government that it would be better for long-term results to fund support structures for small business instead.

Approach and Negotiate Honestly and Transparently

Once the preliminary work has been done, the potential partner should be approached in an honest and transparent manner. Sometimes it may be necessary to use an intermediary—especially where there are negative perceptions from the past or where political baggage exists. Once the approach has been made, the process becomes one of negotiation, whose key steps are as follows:

- The potential partners must agree that the partnership is both necessary and mutually beneficial. Each partner must be convinced that the other can add value to its objectives, and the different objectives should be aligned. (This does not mean that the mutual benefits need to be the same. In government–business partnerships, for example, in which government may be seeking to meet its political responsibilities, the business partner may want most of all to see political stability maintained.)
- It is important to agree early on to joint decision making and conflict resolution procedures and structures. These may even apply to the negotiation itself. If this work is left too late, the first difference of opinion may also prove the last. The South African constitutional negotiation process is renowned for its creative mechanisms in this area, such as its use of joint and/or rotating chairmanship, technical expert committees, breakaway weekends in the bush, and the principle of "sufficient consensus."
- The next step is to align the contributions of the separate partners. As stated earlier, these need not be equal, but if they are not, this must be agreed to and noted up front, to prevent perceptions of inequality emerging.
- It is vitally important to agree on specific roles and responsibilities. Desired outcomes and timeframes should be recorded, and evaluation and impact measurement processes established. These are the only ways to determine the success of the partnership.
- Shared risks and rewards must be negotiated. This can be particularly sensitive when the resource input into the partnership is unequal.

- Attention should be given to the sustainability of the project, during both negotiation and implementation. In the socioeconomic field, project sustainability often depends on the government's willingness and ability to make the project part of its policy and implementation.
- Special attention should also be given to financial procedures and management. Mismanagement or corruption can destroy both a partnership and the reputation of all parties involved.
- Finally, it is imperative to agree to and sign a memorandum of understanding or a formal contract. This is not always easy to achieve when working with government, especially when business and NGOs are providing the financial and human resources and government is essentially a recipient. This should not deter nongovernmental partners from pursuing such a document, however. The NBI, for example, when promoting the concept of public–private partnerships as a mechanism to deliver basic services and infrastructure, signed a memorandum of understanding with the National Treasury defining the specific and measurable roles and responsibilities of all partners concerned.

Managing the Partnership

Governance and management arrangements should be shaped entirely by the nature of the partnership. When a joint body is formed to carry out the objectives of the partnership, joint governance is necessary. This is the case with the Business Trust, in which eight of the twenty trustees are senior government ministers or officials and twelve are senior business leaders. Management of the projects is in the hands of not-for-profit service providers, working in close cooperation with government officials at the different levels.

Other key components of management include the following:

- It is important to build relationships and trust in the partnership. In the South African context, this is critical, as the country's democracy is young and prejudices are not yet forgotten. Time and patience are needed.
- Where applicable, one should consult regularly with stakeholders and give them feedback. Bad communication with stakeholders has in the past ruined good partnerships.
- Regular, honest, and clear communication with the other partners is essential. Concerns and problems should be aired quickly and honestly. If these are allowed to fester and cause mistrust, the partnership is doomed.
- Finally, partners should celebrate the successes of their work—publicly, if possible. This reinforces the partnership and its benefits, and can support a further ongoing role for the partnership. Public celebration should be made with extreme sensitivity, of course. The government will not wish to be portrayed as the junior partner; nor will a business sponsor want its efforts to be a good corporate citizen underplayed.

A difficult issue is that of personality clashes. On paper, partnerships may be about organizations, but one should not underestimate the damage that can be done by leaders with bruised egos. If the project leaders cannot get along, it may be appropriate to make a change of personnel for the good of the partnership.

Conclusion

South Africa's experience has shown the necessity of partnerships for development, and has returned some notable successes. These have largely followed the principles described in this chapter. The one challenge remaining for the NBI—which is being addressed—is that of going to scale and making a real impact. This must be achieved, in the interests of all of the country's citizens.

Notes

1. The word "reported" is used advisedly, as there is a strong suspicion that many African countries do not have accurate statistics and/or do not report them.
2. More information is available on the NBI's Web site: *www.nbi.org.za*.
3. The NBI's Public–Private Partnership Resource Center describes a partnership as "more than a contract, but less than a marriage."
4. The Urban Foundation and the Consultative Business Movement worked during the apartheid era for the abolition of influx control; they were also involved in the peace process and in the constitutional negotiations.
5. South Africa's numerous NGOs are used extensively in socioeconomic service delivery by both government and business. It should also be noted, however, that while some NGOs are multinational organizations with track records stretching back decades, the country's local NGOs generally have struggled in the last seven years to acquire funding. This is largely because many of the international aid organizations that funded NGOs during the apartheid era have rechanneled their funds to the post-apartheid government's Reconstruction and Development Program (RDP). Many NGOs have had to struggle to stay relevant in the new South Africa. In a sense, the NGO sector was the bridge between funding and delivery during apartheid; this function has now moved to partnerships.
6. In certain situations, however, such as political negotiations of a multiparty nature, there may actually be no option other than to seek negotiation partners. The political parties in pre-1994 South Africa were forced to negotiate if they did not want to inherit an economic wasteland.

Index

For Product Safety Concerns and Information please contact our EU
representative GPSR@taylorandfrancis.com
Taylor & Francis Verlag GmbH, Kaufingerstraße 24, 80331 München, Germany

www.ingramcontent.com/pod-product-compliance
Ingram Content Group UK Ltd.
Pitfield, Milton Keynes, MK11 3LW, UK
UKHW022203190926
475702UK00003B/185

* 9 7 8 0 7 6 5 8 0 1 7 1 5 *